WINNING THE WHITE HOUSE, 2004

WINNING THE WHITE HOUSE, 2004

Region by Region, Vote by Vote

*Kevin J. McMahon, David M. Rankin,
Donald W. Beachler, and John Kenneth White*

WINNING THE WHITE HOUSE, 2004
© Kevin J. McMahon, David M. Rankin, Donald W. Beachler, and
John Kenneth White, 2005.

First published in 2005 by
PALGRAVE MACMILLAN™
175 Fifth Avenue, New York, N.Y. 10010 and
Houndmills, Basingstoke, Hampshire, England RG21 6XS
Companies and representatives throughout the world.

PALGRAVE MACMILLAN is the global academic imprint of the Palgrave
Macmillan division of St. Martin's Press, LLC and of Palgrave Macmillan Ltd.
Macmillan® is a registered trademark in the United States, United Kingdom
and other countries. Palgrave is a registered trademark in the European
Union and other countries.

ISBN 1–4039–6880–2 hardback
ISBN 1–4039–6881–0 paperback

Library of Congress Cataloging-in-Publication Data

McMahon, Kevin J.
    Winning the White House, 2004: region by region, vote by vote / Kevin J.
McMahon . . . [et al.].
      p. cm.
    ISBN 1–4039–6880–2—ISBN 1–4039–6881–0 (pbk.)
      1. Presidents—United States—Election—2004—Statistics.
    2. Presidents—United States—Election—2004. I. Title.

JK5262000.M33 2005
324.973'0931—dc22   2005043045

A catalogue record for this book is available from the British Library.

Design by Newgen Imaging Systems (P) Ltd., Chennai, India.

First edition: July 2005

10 9 8 7 6 5 4 3 2 1

Printed in the United States of America.

For Stephanie
—K. J. M.

For Helena, Noah, & Liam
—D. M. R.

For Brigid
—D. W. B.

For Professor Norman L. Zucker
—J. K. W.

Figure P.1. The 2004 Presidential Election Results by State

Table P.1. The 2004 Presidential Election Results

Northeast	Bush #	%	EV	Kerry #	%	EV	Midwest	Bush #	%	EV	Kerry #	%	EV
Connecticut	693,826	44.0		857,548	54.3	7	Illinois	2,346,608	44.5		2,891,899	54.8	21
Delaware	171,531	45.8		199,887	53.4	2	Indiana	1,479,438	59.9	11	969,011	39.3	
DC	21,256	9.3		202,970	89.1	3	Iowa	751,957	49.9	7	741,898	49.2	
Maine	330,201	44.6		396,842	53.6	4	Kansas	736,456	62.0	6	434,933	36.6	
Maryland	957,892	42.9		1,223,813	55.9	10	Michigan	2,313,746	47.8		2,479,183	51.2	17
Massachusetts	1,071,109	36.8		1,803,800	61.9	12	Minnesota	1,346,695	47.6		1,445,014	51.1	10
N. Hampshire	331,237	48.9		340,511	50.3	4	Missouri	1,455,713	53.3	11	1,259,171	46.1	
New Jersey	1,670,003	46.2		1,911,430	52.9	15	Nebraska	512,814	65.9	5	254,328	32.7	
New York	2,962,567	40.1		4,314,280	58.4	31	N. Dakota	196,651	62.9	3	111,052	35.5	
Pennsylvania	2,793,847	48.4		2,938,095	50.9	21	Ohio	2,858,727	50.8	20	2,739,952	48.7	
Rhode Island	169,046	38.7		259,760	59.4	4	S. Dakota	232,584	59.9	3	149,244	38.4	
Vermont	121,180	38.8		184,057	58.9	3	Wisconsin	1,478,120	49.3		1,489,504	49.7	10
West Virginia	423,550	56.1	5	326,541	43.2								
Total	**11,717,245**	**43.8**	**5**	**14,959,544**	**55.5**	**117**	**Total**	**15,709,509**	**51.1**	**66**	**14,965,189**	**48.3**	**58**

continued

Table P.1. continued

South	Bush #	%	EV	Kerry #	%	EV
Alabama	1,176,394	62.4	9	693,933	36.8	
Arkansas	573,182	54.3	6	470,230	44.6	
Florida	3,964,522	52.1	27	3,583,544	47.1	
Georgia	1,191,254	58.0	15	1,366,149	41.4	
Kentucky	1,069,439	59.6	8	712,733	39.7	
Louisiana	1,102,169	56.7	9	820,299	42.2	
Mississippi	684,931	59.4	6	457,766	39.7	
N. Carolina	1,961,166	56.0	15	1,525,489	43.6	
Oklahoma	959,792	65.6	7	503,966	34.4	
S. Carolina	937,974	58.0	8	661,699	40.9	
Tennessee	1,384,375	56.8	11	1,036,437	42.6	
Texas	4,526,917	61.1	34	2,832,704	38.2	
Virginia	1,716,959	53.7	13	1,454,742	45.5	
Total	**21,249,074**	**56.5**	**168**	**16,119,691**	**42.9**	**0**
Bush National	*62,040,237*	*50.7*	*286 Electoral Votes*			

West	Bush #	%	EV	Kerry #	%	EV
Alaska	190,889	61.1	3	111,025	35.2	
Arizona	1,104,294	54.8	10	893,524	44.3	
California	5,509,826	44.4		6,745,485	54.3	55
Colorado	1,101,255	51.7	9	1,001,732	47.0	
Hawaii	194,191	45.3		231,708	54.0	4
Idaho	409,235	68.4	4	181,098	30.3	
Montana	266,063	59.1	3	173,710	38.7	
Nevada	418,690	50.5	5	397,190	47.9	
N. Mexico	376,930	49.8	5	370,942	49.1	
Oregon	866,831	47.2		943,166	51.3	7
Utah	663,742	71.5	5	241,199	26.0	
Washington	1,304,894	45.6		1,510,201	52.8	11
Wyoming	167,629	68.9	3	70,776	29.0	
Total	**12,574,469**	**48.9**	**47**	**12,871,756**	**50.0**	**77**
Kerry National				*59,027,612*	*48.3*	*252 Electoral Votes*

CONTENTS

FIGURES AND TABLES

FIGURES

TABLES

PREFACE

During the final weeks of the campaign, Democratic candidate John F. Kerry repeatedly noted that this was the most significant election of his lifetime. He may have, in fact, been correct. When President George W. Bush captured 50.7 percent of the popular vote, he became the first presidential candidate since his father in 1988 to win a majority of the votes. Moreover, no Democrat has reached that percentage level since Lyndon B. Johnson trounced Barry Goldwater four decades ago. Indeed, led by chief Bush political strategist Karl Rove, Republicans have already begun comparing the 2004 election to the critical election of 1896. Then, William McKinley reinvigorated the GOP's alliance by sweeping past William Jennings Bryan to usher in an era of Republican dominance that lasted until 1932. Not surprisingly, Democrats dispute the significance of Bush's victory, noting that he won by a mere 2.4 percentage points and just 34 electoral votes. And if 60,000 Ohioans had voted for Kerry instead of Bush, the Massachusetts Democrat would have won the presidency.

In the chapters that follow, we consider the election through an analysis of critical issues and electoral groupings across America's four main geographic regions. Each of us has contributed two chapters, and they stand as individual contributions. As a result, we don't always offer a unified interpretation of the election. Rather, it might be said that we each participate—from the vantage point of the process, issue, or region in focus—in a discussion of the meaning of the election. In many ways, we are at the beginning of what will most likely be a long national conversation about the historical and enduring significance of this election.

John Kenneth White begins the book by exploring the 2004 primary season and nomination process, arguing that Democrats were most focused on "beating Bush" in their comparatively rapid selection of the Vietnam War veteran John Kerry. We then turn to an examination of three issue areas that attracted much of the electorate's attention. Kevin McMahon begins by analyzing social and cultural issues, with his focus less the importance of "moral values" on the 2004 election and more on how recent Supreme Court decisions influenced the candidates' positions on these "culture war" issues. Donald Beachler then examines the role of the economy and domestic issues, including tax policy and health care, in a campaign where voter concern over jobs was often secondary to the terrorist threat and war in Iraq. John White concludes the second section by explaining how the war on terrorism, tax cuts, and moral values appealed to a coalition that Ronald Reagan forged and George W. Bush relied upon to win reelection.

In the third section of the book, we turn our electoral analysis to each of the nation's four main regions. Beyond examining each region's electoral history and trends in the context of the 2004 presidential and congressional elections, we focus special attention on one battleground state. Kevin McMahon begins in the Northeast, home to Massachusetts Senator John Kerry and the source of nearly half of his electoral votes. We then travel through the South with Donald Beachler's analysis of the growing Republican dominance of the region, including President Bush's home state of Texas. From there, David Rankin takes us to the Midwest, a region divided into battleground states of the Great Lakes and firmly Republican states of the Great Plains. Finally, Rankin moves our regional focus to the West. From its red Republican central Plains and Mountain West states to its Democratic blue Pacific Coast states, it is a region increasingly viewed as the new electoral frontier in the competition for the presidency and the Congress.

In assisting us with the journey, we owe a special thanks to our editor, David Pervin. Heather VanDusen and Alan Bradshaw of Palgrave were very helpful in putting the book in proper shape in a short time span. Finally, we thank Ann Deakin for willingly giving her time and energy to construct the maps that appear within the pages of this book.

Kevin J. McMahon
Farmington, CT

David M. Rankin
Fredonia, NY

Donald W. Beachler
Ithaca, NY

John Kenneth White
Gaithersburg, MD

Part I

THE NOMINATION

1
_____

CHOOSING
THE CANDIDATES

John Kenneth White

Yogi Berra and Will Rogers are fondly remembered for their famous sayings. Managing the New York Mets back in 1973, Berra coined the phrase, "It ain't over 'till it's over." And Rogers liked to tell audiences: "I belong to no organized party. I'm a Democrat." These aphorisms have frequently been applied to commentary surrounding the often divisive and legendary battles among the Democratic presidential contenders. In 1972, Democrats did not choose their candidate until the party's convention, when South Dakota senator George McGovern beat former vice president Hubert H. Humphrey; in 1976, former Georgia governor Jimmy Carter clinched the nomination in June; in 1980, Carter and Massachusetts senator Edward M. Kennedy carried their rivalry into the convention hall; in 1984, former vice president Walter Mondale spent several months running against ex–Colorado senator Gary Hart; and in 1992, Arkansas governor Bill Clinton secured the nomination in the late spring after a long battle with former Massachusetts senator Paul Tsongas and former California governor Jerry Brown. Only in 1996 did Democrats have an easy time of it with Clinton, as president, running unopposed. That is, until now.

In 2004, the Democratic presidential race, though spirited, ended unusually early. After the Super Tuesday primaries were held on March 2, 2004, Massachusetts senator John F. Kerry stood atop the heap, having won the nomination without the usual recriminations that have often accompanied previous victories. Kerry's winning streak began with the all-important Iowa caucuses held on January 19, 2004.

The Vietnam veteran proved to be such a powerful candidate that he lost only five primaries out of the forty held: South Carolina and North Carolina (both to North Carolina senator John Edwards), Vermont and the District of Columbia (to Howard Dean), and Oklahoma (to retired general Wesley Clark). In short, Berra's and Rogers's famous quotations did not hold true.

In 2004, Democrats were more organized and energized than ever. This chapter describes *how and why* this happened. It is a fascinating story filled with interesting characters and surprising twists and turns. Yet the real meaning of this tale lies not in the personalities of the candidates, nor in the rising and falling fortunes of their respective campaigns, but in something more fundamental. The year 2004 was different, and what made it so was that Democratic voters were thinking like the old-time party bosses. These men—whose ranks once included the late John M. Bailey, the Connecticut Democratic chief, and Richard J. Daley, who built the infamous Chicago machine—were hard-headed thinkers who believed that winning mattered most. But we are getting ahead of our story.

At the beginning of 2003, Democrats were discouraged and disheartened. Chief Bush political strategist Karl Rove had engineered a surprising Republican victory in the 2002 midterm elections—a rout of the opposition party that was unprecedented for a first-term president since the early days of Franklin D. Roosevelt's New Deal.[1] Republicans took control of the U.S. Senate with a slim 51–48 majority; added ten more seats in the U.S. House of Representatives; and reduced their gubernatorial losses to one.[2] More impressively, the GOP gained 105 seats in the state houses and 36 seats in the state senates—marking the first time since 1952 that there were more Republican than Democratic state legislators.[3]

These GOP victories—coming in the aftermath of the divisive Supreme Court decision in *Bush v. Gore*—were a boon to George W. Bush. In essence, these Republican wins were "belated ballots" for the popular vote "loser" in 2000—that is, clear, unequivocal endorsements of Bush's leadership in the days following the September 11, 2001, terrorist attacks. But Democrats did not suffer their midterm losses gladly. In a memorable television moment, Democratic strategist and CNN political commentator James Carville put a waste basket over his head as the returns came pouring in over the news wires.

Of the many Democratic defeats, none rankled more than Max Cleland's loss of his Georgia U.S. Senate seat. Republicans ran television advertisements charging that Cleland had aided Osama bin Laden and Iraqi President Saddam Hussein by supporting labor protections in the Bush-proposed Department of Homeland Security. Cleland, a triple amputee and Vietnam War hero, was narrowly beaten by Republican Saxby Chambliss. John Kerry was appalled at the Republican-inspired hardball tactics: "That they could think of doing that to a guy who left three limbs on the ground in Vietnam." His wife, Teresa Heinz-Kerry, was even more pointed: "Whoever did that will rue the day."[4]

Ironically, the 2002 election left Democrats both *discouraged* and *emboldened*. *Discouraged*, because 56 percent of those surveyed by pollster John Zogby in March 2003 believed their nominee would be a sacrificial lamb in a contest with Bush.[5] And *emboldened*, because having lost control of all three branches of government Democrats had nothing left to lose. Thus, 57 percent said they would support a hypothetical "Candidate A" who "opposes the Bush tax cut because it favors the rich and says that under Bush this country is facing a class struggle between the super-rich who are favored by this administration and regular, hardworking Americans." Only 35 percent favored "Candidate B," who also disliked the Bush tax cuts "but rejected the talk of a class struggle."[6] Democrats wanted to draw clear distinctions with Bush because they so strongly disapproved of his performance. One year prior to Kerry's selection, 71 percent of Democrats gave Bush either a fair or poor job rating.[7] *This was long before support for the Iraq War began to wane and no weapons of mass destruction were found.*

The Iraq War only stoked the Democrats' anger. As the death toll mounted—the post-invasion numbers eventually exceeding the body count prior to the cessation of "major hostilities" on May 1, 2003—Democratic opposition to the war in particular and the Bush administration generally spiked upward. According to Zogby polls conducted in the first trifecta of Democratic contests during 2003, only 36 percent of Iowans thought their party should nominate a candidate who supported the Iraq War; in New Hampshire, 39 percent; in South Carolina, 48 percent.[8] Disapproval of the Bush administration's conduct of the war resulted in a general indictment. By year's end, 74 percent of Democrats said Bush was doing either a "fair" or "poor" job.[9]

The Iraq War became a lens that colored Democrats' collective opinions of Bush as a person. *Fifty percent* of likely voters in both Iowa and New Hampshire said they disliked Bush personally.[10] Undoubtedly, this feeling arose because many believed that Bush did not tell the truth about the presence of weapons of mass destruction in Iraq and used trumped-up evidence as a pretext to begin the war. According to an ABC News/*Washington Post* poll conducted in February 2004, 39 percent said the Bush administration had lied about its evidence concluding that Iraq had weapons of mass destruction; an additional 57 percent thought Bush had exaggerated his claims.[11] These results strongly suggested that few Democrats either admired George W. Bush or would cross over to support the Bush–Cheney ticket in November. That proved to be the case. Despite some prominent Democratic endorsements from Georgia senator Zell Miller and former New York City mayor Ed Koch, 89 percent of Democrats stuck with the Kerry–Edwards ticket; only 11 percent left their party to back Bush.[12] The relative Democratic unanimity stood in sharp contrast to the one-in-four Democrats who backed Ronald Reagan in 1980 and 1984, and the one-in-five Democrats who supported George H. W. Bush in 1988.[13]

In the days following the September 11, 2001, terrorist attacks, George W. Bush presented himself as a unifying leader. Standing before a joint session of Congress, Bush drew a bright line between the twisted thinking of the terrorists and those who loved freedom: "Every nation, in every region, now has a decision to make. Either you are with us, or you are with the terrorists."[14] Bush's appeal for unity won broad bipartisan support. After his speech, then-Democratic Senate majority leader Tom Daschle gave him a warm embrace. Even former vice president Al Gore told a partisan audience of Iowa Democrats that Bush was "my Commander-in-Chief," adding: "Regardless of party, regardless of ideology, there are no divisions in this country where our response to terrorism is concerned."[15]

In many ways, George W. Bush echoed two other wartime presidents, Franklin D. Roosevelt and Dwight D. Eisenhower. In 1940, after war clouds had fallen over Europe, Roosevelt installed two prominent Republicans into his cabinet: Henry Stimson, who became secretary of war, and Frank Knox, who became secretary of the navy. Now Dr. New Deal (a very partisan president who had denounced the Republicans as "economic royalists"[16]) had become Dr. Win the War (a nonpartisan commander-in-chief). Another Republican president, Dwight D. Eisenhower, also sought to distance himself from overt partisanship in the face of a foreign threat. Addressing the delegates at the 1956 Republican National Convention, Eisenhower sought to elevate the Republican Party above the usual give-and-take of American politics:

> The Republican Party is again the rallying point of Americans of all callings, races, and incomes. They see in its broad, forward-moving, straight-down-the road, fighting program the best promise for their own steady progress toward a bright future. Some opponents have tried to call this a "one-interest party." Indeed, it is a one-interest party; and that one interest is the interest of every man, woman, and child in America! And most surely, as long as the Republican party continues to be this kind of one-interest party—a one-universal interest party—it will continue to be the Party of the Future.[17]

But George W. Bush turned out to be a very different wartime president than his predecessors. Parting company with the bipartisan spirit created by Roosevelt, who fought World War II, and Eisenhower, who fought a global war against communism, Bush viewed bipartisanship as a needless waste of time and energy. In *The Price of Loyalty*, author Ron Suskind reports Bush telling then-treasury secretary

Paul O'Neill in 2001 that he would refuse any compromises, quoting him as saying: "I won't negotiate with myself. It's that simple. If someone comes to me with a plan for this, and they have a significant amount of political backing, I'll sit down with them—talk it out. But until then, it's a closed issue."[18] Bush applied this same "total victory" approach to his foreign and domestic initiatives—often winning, but at the expense of Democratic goodwill. Louisiana senator Mary Landrieu candidly expressed the private sentiments held by her fellow Democrats:

> For Democrats who were trying to work with the president on national secu-
> rity issues and support a more hawkish stand than might seem natural for a
> Democrat, this president discounts it, ignores it, and acts as if it's not rele-
> vant. Any time the country is poised for war and about to engage on behalf
> of the security of the country, it's very important that the president make that
> the priority and make everything else come in second. Unfortunately, the
> president has done exactly the opposite of that. . . . [Bush] has earned
> this polarization. It hasn't just happened. He pushed it to happen.[19]

HOWARD DEAN: RIGHT MESSAGE, WRONG YEAR

Enter Howard Dean. The former Vermont governor's opposition to the Iraq War became the lens by which prospective Democratic primary voters initially judged him. Dean's vociferous objections to the war were unmistakably clear, and they stood in stark contrast to the equivocations offered by Missouri congressman Richard Gephardt and Massachusetts senator John Kerry, both of whom supported a congressional resolution authorizing the use of force. Only later (and after much soul-searching) did each man express his misgivings about the war. Yet their criticisms—especially Kerry's—were not about Bush's decision to use force per se, but its timing and execution. Democrats were initially intolerant and dismissive of these positional nuances. Retired Army general Wesley Clark sought to capture the Democratic discontent with Bush and their own party leadership in Washington, D.C. But this rookie candidate "bobbled" (his adjective) a reporter's question on the war—making it unclear how he would have voted on the all-important congressional reso-lution.[20] That mistake—coupled with Clark's words of praise for Bush and members of his administration at a 2001 Arkansas GOP dinner, and his admission that he had previously supported Richard Nixon and Ronald Reagan—doomed his candidacy. Another candidate, Connecticut senator Joe Lieberman, was the strongest supporter of the war and was so out-of-step with the Democratic rank-and-file that he was often booed at the various intra-party presidential debates. The remaining candidates, Ohio congressman Dennis Kucinich and civil rights activist Al Sharpton, were never taken seriously. Consistent majorities said they could "never" support Sharpton, while Kucinich remained a niche candidate who was largely ignored. (Former senator and ambassador Carol Mosely Braun dropped out of the race just before the Iowa caucus.)

This left Howard Dean, whose opposition to the Iraq War became his rallying cry. But Dean was hardly a one-issue candidate. Initially, he entered the race to oppose Bush's overspending and tax cuts, promising to take steps that would eventually balance the federal budget. Dean was also a physician, and to him reforming health care was an important issue. As Vermont's governor, he initiated a "Dr. Dinosaur" program that gave health care coverage to the state's children. But with the passage of time, Dean sharpened his criticisms of Bush to include an attack on all special interests. In many ways, Dean saw his critique of the Bush administration as systemic, not partisan.

But what especially riled Dean was the support Bush received from the Democratic congressional leadership for going to war with Iraq. Dean interpreted this Democratic backing as the final abandonment of party principles in pursuit of tactical advantages and big campaign dollars. As the lone major candidate with an unequivocal position on the war, Dean and his Deaniac followers became the antidote for all that they saw was wrong with the Democratic Party.

By accusing Democrats of playing it safe and not standing firm, Howard Dean took a page out of the late Barry Goldwater's playbook. In 1964, Republican Goldwater ran a losing campaign against Democratic President Lyndon B. Johnson using the slogan, "In your heart, you know he's right."[21] Goldwater's heartfelt conservatism was seen by his supporters as indicative of his superior character, especially against an opponent the Goldwaterites likened to a "wheeler-dealer." Interviewing delegates at the 1964 Republican Convention, political scientist Aaron Wildavsky was struck by their passionate pursuit of ideological goals, even to the point where most were willing to sacrifice winning for the joy of being proved right. Among the comments about Goldwater were these: "He is frank." "He has courage." "He stands up for what he believes." "He's different from most politicians." "Goldwater speaks about things others avoid."[22]

Unlike other calculating politicians, the Goldwater "purists" cared more about the righteousness of their cause than victory. One supporter, asked if the primary qualification of a presidential candidate should be to choose a winner, replied: "No; principles are more important. I would rather be one against 20,000, and believe I was right. That's what I admire about Goldwater. He's like that."[23] Such praise aside, Goldwater endured a landslide defeat by capturing just six states and 39 percent of the popular vote.

By mid-2003, 66 percent of Democrats said that it was important to find someone who stood up for what he or she believed, even if those positions were unpopular. Only 30 percent said choosing someone who could beat Bush was more important.[24] Democrats may not have had Goldwater in mind, but they clearly believed that if their 2004 nominee followed orders and stood on principle, the result would be another loss (possibly even a landslide defeat). As early as January 2003, 60 percent of Iowa Democrats believed that no matter who was chosen at their party's convention in Boston, Bush would be reelected. In New Hampshire and South Carolina, the Democratic doomsayers totaled 63 percent and 61 percent, respectively.[25] Whenever Democrats thought about their general election prospects for November 2, 2004, it was often with a sense of dread. One could only imagine James Carville placing another trash can over his ears to stop hearing the bad news. (In fact, on the November 15, 2004, telecast of *Meet the Press*, Carville smashed an egg on his forehead.)

Like the Goldwaterites, the Deaniacs believed that their man's unyielding position on the Iraq War meant that he had passed an important character test—much in the same way Goldwater's unpopular conservatism reflected his integrity. The Deaniacs not only saw their man as the polar opposite of a poll-driven Bush, but a welcome balm from former president Bill Clinton, whose strategy of "triangulating" between New Deal–minded Democrats and conservative Republicans alienated members of his own party. In 1996, Clinton famously intoned during his State of the Union address that "the era of big government is over"—hardly the words most pro-government-minded Democrats wanted to hear.[26]

In making the case for what the late Minnesota senator Paul Wellstone once called "the Democratic wing of the Democratic party," Howard Dean implicitly rejected Bill Clinton's "third way" strategy of appealing to independents by opposing more big government bureaucracies. Clinton's lessons came the hard way after a health care plan drafted by his wife Hillary was doomed, and Republicans won a landslide victory in the 1994 midterm elections. In a speech outlining his governing philosophy, Dean declared: "While Bill Clinton said that the era of big government is over, I believe we must enter a new era for the Democratic Party—not one where we join the Republicans and aim simply to limit the damage they inflict on working families. . . . I call now for a new era, in which we rewrite our Social Contract. We need to provide certain basic guarantees to all those who are working hard to fulfill the promise of America."[27] William Saletan, chief political correspondent for *Slate*, declared in December 2003 that Howard Dean's rise meant that, for Democrats, "the era of Bill Clinton is over."[28]

In sum, the Deaniacs had much in common with Goldwater's backers. By out-maneuvering longtime Republican officials who were intent on winning elections,

Goldwater's followers represented something new in contemporary politics. Political scientist Wildavsky worried about the ruthless tactics and single-minded adherence to conservative principles that characterized the Goldwater followers: "Could it be that the United States is producing large numbers of half-educated people with college degrees who have learned that participation (passion and commitment) is good, but who do not understand (or cannot stand) the normal practices of democratic politics?"[29] Unlike Goldwater, Dean set about to capture the Democratic machinery not by secretly trying to take over state party organizations (as the Goldwater people did), but by openly using the Internet to empower disenfranchised Democrats.[30] Dean's favorite slogan was, "You have the power."[31] Still, Wildavsky's concerns about the Goldwaterites were echoed by inside-the-beltway Democratic strategists whenever they envisioned the passionate "Deaniacs" plotting their man's victory in front of their computer screens.

Howard Dean's blueprint of attracting web-savvy voters to his cause amplified his message of empowerment. Disillusioned Democrats could turn on their computers and check the daily "blog" (a shorthand for web blog) on the Dean website. They could go to Meetup sessions held across the country and share ideas and strategies. The results were remarkable. At the beginning of 2003, Dean had just 432 known supporters and $157,000 in the bank. By year's end, more than 600,000 people were registered online as Dean supporters. In addition, more than 200,000 gathered at Meetup sessions. And, thanks to his Internet-based fund-raising machine, Dean accumulated an astounding $45 million, exceeding records set by Bill Clinton in 1996.[32]

Pundits and party leaders took notice. In December 2003, Al Gore added to Dean's momentum by endorsing him. Gore admired Dean's use of the Internet-based technologies to rebuild the Democratic Party, and he agreed with his antiwar stance. With all these advantages, Dean's nomination seemed all but certain. After all, the one remaining political maxim that seemed to hold true in the Information Age was this: the candidate with the most money on December 31 in the year prior to the election became the party's nominee. Given Dean's millions, the man and the moment seemed to meet. Or, had they?

BACK FROM THE ABYSS: THE RISE OF JOHN KERRY

Following another lackluster performance in a Democratic presidential debate, John Kerry was overheard muttering to himself, "Dean, Dean, Dean, Dean."[33] If anyone in 2003 was on a road to nowhere, it was Kerry. His staff was in turmoil, and campaign manager Jim Jordan was abruptly dismissed. Fund-raising lagged, and at year's end the Massachusetts senator was forced to inject $6.4 million of his own money into his cause just to keep pace with the front-running Dean. Yet these blows were nothing compared to Kerry's decline from putative nominee at the beginning of 2003, to "has-been" status by year's end. In New Hampshire, Kerry went from a two-to-one lead over Dean in February 2003, to a 42 percent to 12 percent deficit the following December. In other states, the picture was the same: Dean was rising and Kerry was in a free-fall.[34]

But attitudes altered dramatically as the calendar page turned from December 31, 2003, to New Year's Day 2004. Increasing numbers of Democrats sensed that Dean was the candidate most likely to succumb to a Bush reelection rout. (And this was long before Dean made his infamous "I Have a Scream" speech after losing the Iowa caucuses.) Certainly, Republicans made no attempt to hide their glee at the prospect of facing Dean. At a July 4, 2003, parade in Washington, DC, Karl Rove saw a group of Dean supporters and reportedly chanted, "Go, Howard Dean!" Rove was over-heard chortling to a confidant, "Heh, heh, heh. That's the one we want."[35] Dean's entire campaign was premised on winning decisively in Iowa and New Hampshire. But with each attack from his Democratic rivals—especially from Dick Gephardt—Dean's temper rose. At one Iowa event, a Republican farmer asked Dean to "please tone down the garbage, the mean-mouthing, the tearing down of your neighbor and being so pompous," at which the former Vermont governor retorted, "George Bush is not my neighbor." Dean continued to admonish the disgruntled farmer, saying: "You sit down. You've had your say and now I'm going to have my say. Under the guise of 'support your neighbor' we're all expected not to criticize the president because it's unpatriotic. I think it's unpatriotic to do some of the things that this president has done to this country."[36]

Dean's rebuttal surely would have resonated with Democrats in 2003. But his answer strongly suggested that he did not have the right temperament to be presi-dent. Iowans, like so many other Americans, pride themselves on neighborliness. And as with Goldwater, something seemed not quite right with Dean.[37] His angry demeanor led Democrats to suddenly realize (1) that they had a chance to win and (2) that the presidency itself was at stake. Instead of searching for a messenger, Democrats began looking for a president. The first qualification—and their only one—was to find a winner.

The person they found was John F. Kerry. Kerry had always appealed to Democrats based on his service and heroism during the Vietnam War. But the Massachusetts Democrat lost his audience in 2003, thanks to his inability to explain his Iraq position and a series of poor debate performances. By concentrating all his resources on a good Iowa showing, Kerry was, as one advisor stated, following "a strategy born out of desperation."[38] It worked. Iowa Democrats wanted to send a messenger, not just a message, to the White House. And Kerry made a powerful argument. His reenergized campaign adopted the slogan "The Real Deal," as Kerry emphasized his military service and years of government experience. In so doing, Kerry crossed an important threshold: Iowans could picture him as their next president. (Much the same thing happened when Kerry debated Bush. In each of these encounters, especially after the first, Kerry came across to most Americans as more "presidential" than the president.)

At the same time, Kerry's military biography was underscored when a Republican and retired Los Angeles County sheriff named Jim Rassman came forward and described how Kerry rescued him from near-death in Vietnam. Rassman described how he had seen Kerry's "bravery and leadership under fire," and that he would be "a great commander-in-chief."[39] For his heroism, Kerry received the Bronze Star. The two men, who had not seen each other since 1969, had an emotional reunion on the Iowa circuit. And when Kerry connected his military service to public values (including patriotism, service, and community), his support rose. Starting with a mere 15 percent of the vote in an Iowa poll on January 10, Kerry's support increased to 25 percent eight days later and he was an easy first-place winner.[40] Kerry won 38 percent of the Iowa vote to John Edwards's 32 percent.

Following his Iowa win, Kerry replicated that strong closing performance in New Hampshire, rising from 23 percent on January 18 to 37 percent eight days later.[41] On primary day, Kerry finished first with 38 percent to Howard Dean's 26 percent and John Edwards's 12 percent.

FORGET GOLDWATER, REMEMBER BAILEY AND DALEY

But something more important than the rising fortunes of the Kerry campaign was occurring. Democratic voters were employing a calculus once used by the old-fashioned party bosses: find a winner. In a fascinating 1966 book titled *The Power Broker*, Joseph I. Lieberman noted that in his native Connecticut it was state Democratic boss John M. Bailey who anointed candidates based on their chances of winning. Bailey was instrumental in John F. Kennedy's rise to national prominence in 1956, when Bailey supported JFK's unsuccessful bid for his party's vice-presidential nomination. Bailey gravitated to Kennedy not because the two men shared a religious faith, but because he believed a Catholic could garner more votes. Four years later, the "Bailey Memorandum" was circulated to the other party bosses. In it, he maintained that a presidential ticket headed by Kennedy would bring more votes than it

would lose.[42] Fourteen battleground states were listed along with their percentages of
Catholic voters. Bailey's calculus proved correct: Kennedy won in 1960, and Bailey
was rewarded with the post of chairman of the Democratic National Committee.[43]

In Chicago another old-style Democratic boss, Richard J. Daley, was also backing Kennedy. Daley built a strong party machine whose operating principles were
twofold: (1) unshakable loyalty to the boss and (2) beating Republicans at the polls.
One Democratic Central Committee member described how prospective candidates
were selected during Boss Dailey's rule:

> The candidate would come forward and make a speech, and answer some
> very perfunctory questions. Usually, there are two questions. One, "If you
> were not to be slated for the office you seek, would you accept slating for
> any other office?" And the right kind of guy would be expected to say, "I'm a
> loyal Democrat, and if, in the wisdom of this committee, I'm chosen for
> some other post, I can assure you that every bit of energy and talent that
> I have will be devoted," and so on. Another question is, "If you are not
> slated, will you support the guy that is slated?" And you are supposed to say,
> "I will be disappointed if I were not chosen, but I am a loyal Democrat and
> I will support whomever you choose." And another question is, "Will you
> support the candidate of the party after the primary against the Republican
> opponent?" And you say, "Of course I will."[44]

Strikingly, it is this same Daley-like calculus that Democrats applied when it
came to selecting their party's 2004 presidential nominee. For the first time since
the rank-and-file began choosing their presidential candidates in 1972, it was the
Democratic voters who believed that winning was *the* crucial variable when choosing
their nominee. It is that sole criterion that doomed Howard Dean's candidacy and
contributed mightily to John Kerry's rise (see table 1.1). But among voters who chose
"he stands up for what he believes" as the most important candidate quality, Kerry
fared quite poorly (see table 1.2). As Dean recalled after his defeat: "The most
effective argument [the Kerry campaign] made [was] that I was unelectable. And
there was nothing the Democrats wanted more than to win."[45] But when voters were
asked either if their party's nominee is either "very likely" or "somewhat likely" to beat
Bush (or, specifically, if John Kerry could beat Bush), more than seven out of ten
Democrats saw victory within reach. This is a remarkable turnaround from 2003,
when 56 percent of Democrats did *not* think their candidate had much of a chance
to win.[46] And like the prospective Chicago machine Daley candidates, the losers were
expected to loyally support the Democratic ticket. Thus, Richard Gephardt, Joseph
Lieberman, Howard Dean, and John Edwards gracefully bowed out and endorsed

Table 1.1. The Head Rules: John Kerry and the "Beat Bush" Factor

State	% Can Defeat Bush	Quality Importance	Kerry % of Those Voters
Arizona	28	#1	65
California	37	#1	80
Connecticut	36	#1	82
Delaware	28	#1	71
Georgia	27	#1	66
Iowa	26	#2	37
Massachusetts	34	#1	89
Maryland	38	#1	80
Missouri	23	#1	78
New Hampshire	20	#2	62
New York	37	#1	82
Ohio	31	#1	70
Oklahoma	19	#2	55
Rhode Island	42	#1	89
South Carolina	18	#2	58
Tennessee	25	#1	64
Vermont	26	#2	60
Virginia	27	#1	76
Wisconsin	23	#2	69

Source: Edison/Mitofsky, exit polls. Text of question: "Which one candidate quality mattered most in deciding how you voted today? He cares about people like me, he has the right temperament, he stands up for what he believes, he has the right experience, he has a positive message, he can defeat George W. Bush, he understands (name of state)."

Kerry. This was done not only out of deference to the putative nominee, but to preserve whatever future they might have within this new, strategically minded Democratic Party. Edwards proved to be so adept at doing this that he received the second slot on the Democratic ticket.

THE END OF AN ERA:
OLD DEMOCRATS vs. NEW DEMOCRATS

It is hard to overstate the importance of this newfound, boss-minded, hard-headed thinking within the 2004 Democratic electorate. When Democratic voters replaced the party bosses and began choosing their party's nominees in 1972, their participation followed the disastrous convention four years before when riots in the Chicago streets marred Hubert H. Humphrey's coronation. Presidential chronicler Theodore H. White described Humphrey as "being nominated in a sea of blood."[47]

Table 1.2. The Heart: John Kerry and Democratic Believers

State	% "Stands Up for What He Believes"	Importance of Quality	Kerry % of Those Voters
Arizona	23	#2	25
California	18	#2	53
Connecticut	17	#2	34
Delaware	23	#2	32
Georgia	15	#3	40
Iowa*	29	#1	26
Massachusetts	21	#2	53
Maryland	16	#2	45
Missouri	22	#2	40
New Hampshire	29	#1	21
New York	19	#2	45
Ohio	20	#2	45
Oklahoma	22	#1**	19
Rhode Island	16	#2	47
South Carolina	19	#1	18
Tennessee	20	#2	34
Vermont	39	#1	9
Virginia	20	#2	36
Wisconsin	25	#1	24

Source: Edison/Mitofsky, exit polls. Text of question: "Which one candidate quality mattered most in deciding how you voted today? He cares about people like me, he has the right temperament, he stands up for what he believes, he has the right experience, he has a positive message, he can defeat George W. Bush, he understands (name of state)."
* Iowa question is phrased somewhat differently: "Takes strong stands on issues."
** Tied with "he cares about people like me."

The McGovern-Fraser Commission, created by the 1968 convention to examine the party's nominating procedures, bluntly told the power brokers to surrender. As George McGovern later recalled: "I drove home the contention that the Democratic party had two choices: reform or death."[48]

The Democratic Party changed, but not necessarily for the better. Chicago mayor and symbol of the political bosses, Richard J. Daley, was ejected from the 1972 convention hall. Establishment figures, who gave paramount importance to winning elections, were astounded. The Democratic ticket headed by George McGovern and Sargent Shriver lost forty-nine of the fifty states against Richard Nixon.[49] In effect, the Democratic Party did die—just as McGovern had forecast. In its death throes, Old Democrats—who adhered to the New Deal philosophy—squared off against New Democrats—outsiders who were not enamored of big government, and were more culturally attuned to the social revolutions of the 1960s and 1970s. In 1972, George McGovern (New Democrat) was challenged by Hubert H. Humphrey and

Edmund S. Muskie (Old Democrats). Four years later, Jimmy Carter (New Democrat) was challenged by Henry "Scoop" Jackson and George Wallace (Old Democrats). Carter temporarily glued these two wings together by choosing Walter F. Mondale (Old Democrat) to be his running mate, and obscuring his platform positions rather than sharpening them.

Carter's 1976 victory provided a temporary truce. But in 1980, the acrimonious party battles began anew when Edward M. Kennedy (Old Democrat) challenged Carter. Carter was significantly weakened by the Kennedy insurgency, and he decisively lost to Ronald Reagan. In the ashes of defeat, the intra-party battles resumed with a vengeance. Walter F. Mondale (Old Democrat) narrowly beat Gary Hart (New Democrat). Michael S. Dukakis (New Democrat) vanquished Paul Simon and Jesse Jackson (Old Democrats). Yet, Mondale and Dukakis each lost to Reagan and George H. W. Bush, respectively. Former *New York Times* columnist Tom Wicker wrote that the internal party warfare meant that the Democrats had become a *"party of access* in which the voiceless find a voice," while the Republicans "maintain enough coherence and unity to become a *party of government.*"[50]

By 1992, Democrats seemed ready to resume their familiar struggles despite the golden opportunity history presented with the end of the Cold War. Arkansas governor Bill Clinton and former Massachusetts senator Paul Tsongas (New Democrats) were ready to face off against New York governor Mario Cuomo (Old Democrat). But at the last minute Cuomo dropped out, and Clinton and Tsongas squared off, with guest appearances by former California governor Jerry Brown (New Democrat) and Iowa senator Tom Harkin (Old Democrat). The typical Old Democrat vs. New Democrat struggle never really materialized. With Clinton's dual victories in 1992 and 1996, the New Democratic philosophy and the organization created to spearhead it, the Democratic Leadership Council, triumphed. Its supremacy came not because Clinton was a masterful strategist (he was), but because the Old Democrats ceded power.

With the passage of time, Old Democrats—with the notable exception of Edward M. Kennedy—have either left office, died, or both. Bill Clinton, Al Gore, and the Democratic Leadership Council transformed the Democratic Party into one dominated by so-called third way thinkers who believed in balanced budgets (not deficits). They also wanted government to act as a strategic partner with individuals and private organizations, rather than create more big government bureaucracies. These, they thought, were the keys to more economic prosperity and desired social changes.

But what gave the post-Clinton Democrats their passion and commitment was not their new ideas, but the intense partisan divisions as represented by the Red (Bush) and Blue (Gore/Kerry) states.[51] The Democratic anger directed at George W. Bush is

Table 1.3. Attitudes of Democratic Primary Voters toward the Bush Administration

State	% Angry	% Dissatisfied	% Satisfied	% Enthusiastic
Arizona	46	37	13	3
California	49	35	11	4
Connecticut	58	32	8	1
Delaware	51	37	10	1
Florida	49	38	9	2
Georgia	32	43	13	8
Louisiana	33	41	16	8
Massachusetts	51	35	9	3
Maryland	45	40	9	4
Missouri	39	42	13	4
New Hampshire	46	37	14	2
New York	57	31	8	2
Ohio	44	39	12	2
Oklahoma	33	43	17	5
Rhode Island	57	32	7	2
South Carolina	35	49	11	2
Tennessee	39	45	11	3
Texas	42	38	14	8
Vermont	65	26	6	2
Virginia	44	42	8	4
Wisconsin	44	30	12	5

Source: Edison Media Research and Mitofsky International, exit polls.

readily apparent in the exit polls from the primary states. In each, overwhelming majorities said they were either "angry" or "dissatisfied" with the Bush administration (see table 1.3).

Anger at George W. Bush concentrated the minds of Democratic voters in 2004. Instead of letting their passions rule, Democrats began to think strategically. The result was the creation of the voter-as-pundit, where buyers mulled over which presidential prospect had the best chance of beating Bush. As Internet blogger Matt Stoler wrote, "The web has allowed punditry to scale dramatically, cracking open the social structure of the political establishment and force feeding the real storyline to every political junkie with a computer and phone line."[52] Instead of being addicted to old turf battles between Old Democrats and New Democrats—full of sound and fury but signifying little—Democrats became single-mindedly focused on beating Bush. Though that did not happen and Democrats suffered another bitter defeat, the importance of this fact should not be lost. The profound silence within the Democratic establishment following Bush's reelection signifies that the party remains hell-bent on winning and is unlikely to engage in the kinds of recriminations that followed the defeats of Jimmy Carter, Walter Mondale, Michael Dukakis, and Al Gore. For Democrats in the Bush era, initial cooperation (especially in the days following the September 11, 2001, terrorist attacks) has given way to the hard-headed reality that they are out of power and that their politics must focus single-mindedly on regaining it.

NOTES

1. In 1933, Democrats had 313 House seats while the Republicans had 117. Two years later, Democrats increased their majority, holding 322 House seats to 103 for the Republicans. In the Senate, Democrats held 69 seats in 1933 and 76 seats two years later. Republicans held onto just 25 seats and 16 seats, respectively. In 1998, Democrats added to their congressional majorities, but that was in the sixth year of the Clinton administration and thanks to a backlash against heavy-handed Republican tactics during the impeachment scandal. The 2002 Republican victories suggested that Rove's wish of a partisan realignment was more than a glimmer of wishful thinking.
2. Vermont Republican senator Jim Jeffords switched his party affiliation from Republican to Independent in May 2001, and often votes with the Democrats. The current makeup of the U.S. House is 232 Republicans, 202 Democrats, and 1 independent. Democrats added one seat in February 2004 when Kentucky's Ben Chandler defeated Republican Alice Fogy Kerr. This marked the first time since 1991 that Democrats picked up a Republican-held seat in a special election.
3. See Michael Barone, "Life, Liberty and Property," in Michael Barone and Richard E. Cohen, *The Almanac of American Politics, 2004* (Washington, DC: National Journal, 2003), 21.
4. Quoted in Melinda Henneberger, "John Kerry's Secret Ingredient," *Newsweek*, http://www.msnbc.msn.com/id/3761423. Heinz-Kerry, widow of the late Republican Senator John Heinz, changed her party registration from Republican to Democratic after Cleland's defeat.
5. Zogby International, survey, March 5–7, 2003. Democratic despair was even higher in the early voting states. In Iowa, 60 percent of those polled in January believed Bush would be reelected; in New Hampshire, 63 percent; in South Carolina, 61 percent.
6. Ibid.
7. Ibid.
8. Zogby International, surveys of likely caucus or primary participants in Iowa, September 8–9, 2003; New Hampshire, August 23–26, 2003; and South Carolina, September 2–3, 2003.
9. Zogby International, survey, December 4–6, 2003.
10. Zogby International, Iowa survey, September 8–9, 2003. Fifty percent said they disliked George W. Bush; only 35 percent liked him. Zogby International, New Hampshire survey, September 24–25, 2003. Fifty percent disliked George W. Bush; only 38 percent liked him.
11. ABC News/*Washington Post*, survey, February 10–11, 2004.
12. Edison Media Research and Mitofsky International, exit poll, November 2, 2004.

13. ABC News, exit poll, 1980 and ABC News, exit poll, 1988. Eighteen percent of self-described Democrats backed George H. W. Bush.

14. George W. Bush, Address to a Joint Session of Congress, September 20, 2001.

15. Quoted in Dan Balz, "Gore Pledges to Back Bush, Calls for Unity," *Washington Post*, September 30, 2001, A3.

16. See especially James MacGregor Burns, *Roosevelt: The Lion and the Fox* (New York: Harcourt, Brace and World, 1956), 274.

17. Dwight D. Eisenhower, Acceptance Speech, Republican National Convention, August 23, 1956.

18. Ron Suskind, *The Price of Loyalty: George W. Bush, the White House, and the Education of Paul O'Neill* (New York: Simon and Schuster, 2004), 117.

19. Quoted in E. J. Dionne, Jr., *Stand Up and Fight Back: Republican Toughs, Democratic Wimps, and the Politics of Revenge* (New York: Simon and Schuster, 2004), 64.

20. See Associated Press, "Gaining in the Polls, Clark Brushes Off Critics," MSNBC, January 12, 2004. Clark later made it clear that he would have opposed the congressional resolution, but by that time it was too late.

21. Johnson loyalists countered, saying, "In your heart, you know he's nuts!"

22. See Aaron Wildavsky, "The Goldwater Phenomenon: Purists, Politicians, and the Two-Party System," in Norman L. Zucker, ed., *The American Party Process: Readings and Comments* (New York: Dodd, Mead and Company, 1968), 445.

23. Ibid., 446.

24. Zogby International, survey, July 16–17, 2003. Text of question: "Which is more important, nominating a candidate who stands up for what he or she believes, or nominating someone who can defeat George W. Bush in November 2004?" Stands up for beliefs, 66 percent; defeat Bush, 30 percent; not sure, 4 percent.

25. Zogby International, surveys of likely Democratic voters in Iowa, New Hampshire, and South Carolina, January 27, 2003, February 25, 2003, and March 11, 2003, respectively.

26. Bill Clinton, State of the Union Address, Washington, DC, January 23, 1996.

27. Quoted in William Saletan, "The Era of Bill Clinton is Over," *Slate*, December 18, 2003.

28. Ibid.

29. Wildavsky, "The Goldwater Phenomenon: Purists, Politicians, and the Two-Party System," 447, 460.

30. For more on this see Rick Perlstein, *Before the Storm: Barry Goldwater and the Unmaking of the American Consensus* (New York: Hill and Wang, 2001), *passim*.

31. See Howard Dean, *Winning Back America* (New York: Simon and Schuster, 2003).

32. For more on this see Joe Trippi, "Down from the Mountain," speech, February 9, 2004.

33. John Kerry overheard talking to himself after a press conference following a Democratic presidential debate, September 9, 2003. See Politicsus.com, September 12, 2003.

34. Zogby International, poll of likely New Hampshire Democratic primary voters, February and December 2003. In February, Kerry led Dean 26 percent to 13 percent.

35. Quoted in Juliet Eipern, "Rove Spends the Fourth Rousing Support for Dean," *Washington Post,* July 5, 2003, A10.

36. Associated Press, "Voter Blasts Dean for Knocking Bush," January 11, 2004.

37. Johnson emphasized the perception that Goldwater was unstable by creating a group labeled Psychiatrists for Johnson.

38. Quoted in James Kuhnhenn, "How Kerry Bet on Iowa—and Won," *Philadelphia Inquirer*, February 16, 2004.

39. See http://www.cbsnews.com/elements/2004/07/23/in_depth_politics/whoswho631596

40. Zogby International, Iowa tracking polls, January 8–10, 2004, and January 16–18, 2004.

41. Zogby International, New Hampshire tracking polls, January 18–20, 2004, and January 24–26, 2004.

42. Democrat Al Smith, the first Catholic to be nominated by a major political party, lost in a landslide to Republican Herbert Hoover in 1928.

43. See Robert Caro, *The Power Broker* (Boston: Houghton-Mifflin Company, 1966), especially 196–197.

44. Quoted in Adam Cohen and Elizabeth Taylor, *American Pharaoh: Mayor Richard J. Daley: His Battle for Chicago* (Boston: Little Brown and Company, 2000), 105.

45. Quoted in E. J. Dionne, Jr., "What Dean Did," *Washington Post*, July 20, 2004, A17.

46. Zogby International, poll, March 5–7, 2003.

47. Theodore H. White, *The Making of the President, 1968* (New York: Atheneum, 1969), 376.

48. George McGovern, *Grassroots: The Autobiography of George McGovern* (New York: Random House, 1977), 137.

49. The lone holdout was Massachusetts.

50. Tom Wicker, "A Party of Access?," *New York Times*, November 25, 1984, E17.

51. For more on this topic see John Kenneth White, "E Pluribus Duo," an analysis of the O'Leary Report/Zogby International Values poll, December 24, 2003.

52. Matt Stoler, "Reacting to Gore: A Speedy Media Cycle," posted on The Blogging of the President, 2004, December 9, 2003. Available at www.bopnews.com

Part II

THE ISSUES

2

A "MORAL VALUES" ELECTION?

The Culture War, the Supreme Court, and a Divided America

Kevin J. McMahon

DEFINING "MORAL VALUES"

In the immediate wake of the 2004 presidential election, exit poll results propelled commentators to focus on "moral values" as the deciding factor in President George W. Bush's popular and electoral vote victories over Democratic challenger John F. Kerry.[1] But what do we mean by "moral values"? And why did more voters—22 percent in all—choose "moral values" from a list of seven issues as the most important of the election? In searching for an explanation to so much voter concern about the nation's values, conservative *New York Times* columnist William Safire thought of Janet Jackson, whose bare right breast was exposed—allegedly due to a "wardrobe mal-function"—to millions of Americans watching the Super Bowl halftime show in early 2004. Others might have pointed to another provocative television event, the kiss between Britney Spears and Madonna at the MTV Video Music Awards a few months earlier. Before a nation considering the moral legitimacy of same-sex marriage, the once prim and proper Spears—donned in a risqué wedding gown— locked lips with the legendary envelope-pushing Madonna, who—dressed in groom's black and a top hat—entered the stage from a wedding cake singing "Hollywood."

Still others would have set their sights on shock jock Howard Stern, who waged an open war against the Michael Powell–run Federal Communications Commission and the Bush administration, urging his listeners throughout the election season to vote for John Kerry. All these examples were likely significant to voters concerned that television, radio, and film—often referred to more generally as "Hollywood"—have gone "too far" in loosening the standards of yesteryear. And in this sense, Stern's constant bashing of the Bush administration may have had the opposite effect than he intended; seemingly clarifying to those voters anxious about the nation's moral direction which candidate best represented the values of a simpler time.

Beyond these recent cultural provocations, however, most "values voters" likely concentrated on other issues when they entered the voting booth; most importantly: abortion, school prayer, and gay marriage. Some of these voters would add affirmative action to this list. This chapter considers these issues from the standpoint of the Supreme Court, particularly its role in shaping policy on these matters and the effect its recent decisions had on the contest between Bush and Kerry. Before doing so, however, it considers the roots and worthiness of the moral values explanation of the 2004 election.

A MORALS MYTH? DISPUTES ABOUT THE IMPORTANCE OF VALUES IN THE 2004 ELECTION

Three Election Day results primarily drove the conclusion that the 2004 presidential race hinged on the significance of moral values. First, of the 22 percent of voters who considered "moral values" as the most important issue of the election, 80 percent supported President Bush. Just 18 percent of values voters backed Senator Kerry. Second, religiously conservative voters reportedly turned out in unprecedented numbers to support the president's reelection. This turnout was a significant change from four years earlier. Then, according to chief Bush political strategist Karl Rove, approximately 15 million evangelical Christians came out to support his candidate, instead of the expected 19 million.[2] The exit polls of 2004 suggest that approximately 22 million evangelical Christians turned out for the president.[3] Specifically, of the 23 percent of voters who described themselves as born-again or evangelical Christians, 78 percent voted for Bush. These numbers virtually mirror those of the values voters. Of the 77 percent who did not define themselves as evangelical Christians, only 43 percent supported the president. Moreover, "the percentage of voters who said they attend church more than once a week grew from 14 to 16 percent, a significant difference in an election decided by [2.4] percentage points." Of that group, Bush actually increased his 2000 numbers by 1 percent, from 63 percent to 64 percent.

"Without question," Alan Cooperman and Thomas Edsall write, "Bush's conservative Christian base was essential to his victory."[4] Bush's conservative appeal, however, was not limited to evangelical Christians. With the aid of some staunchly conservative church leaders, he also won among Catholics, who made up 27 percent of voters. Although Kerry is Catholic, Bush bested him 52 percent to 47 percent with this group of voters; and of those Catholics who attend mass at least once a week—typically a more conservative lot—he won 56 percent to 43 percent. Finally, according to Leonard Leo, a Catholic adviser to the Bush campaign, in the two battleground states of Ohio and Florida, "the Catholic vote helped carry the president across the finish line."[5]

The third values factor centered on the eleven state referenda banning same-sex marriage that passed by wide margins on Election Day (see table 2.1). According to those advancing the moral values story of the election, these eleven referenda inspired religious conservative voters to go to the polls, feeding the huge evangelical turnout. Indeed, John Kerry won just two of these eleven states, both by narrow margins.[6] In Ohio, where a constitutional amendment banning same-sex marriages and civil unions passed by a 24-point margin, Kerry lost by approximately 118,000 votes. And as we know, if Kerry had won Ohio, he would have won the presidency.

While these three factors are no doubt telling indicators about the importance of "moral values," not all commentators agree on this explanation of the election. Conservative *New York Times* columnist David Brooks, for example, dismissed what he called the "official story" of the election: "that throngs of homophobic, Red America values-voters surged to the polls to put George Bush over the top." Instead, according to Brooks, "what we are seeing is a diverse but stable Republican coalition

Table 2.1. Same Sex Marriage Bans in the States

State	% Vote for Ban	% Vote against	% Vote for Bush	% Vote for Kerry
Arkansas	75	25	54	45
Georgia	76	24	58	41
Kentucky	75	25	60	40
Michigan	59	41	48	51
Mississippi	86	14	60	40
Montana	67	33	59	39
North Dakota	73	27	63	35
Ohio	62	38	51	49
Oklahoma	76	24	66	34
Oregon	57	43	48	51
Utah	66	34	71	26

Note: Based on the final election figures from the individual states.

gradually eclipsing a diverse and stable Democratic coalition. Social issues are important, but they don't come close to telling the whole story." Conservative columnist Charles Krauthammer also took exception with the values explanation of the election results, dismissing it after combining answers from the exit poll to create three main issues: war issues (combining the answers "terrorism" and "Iraq"), economic issues (combining "taxes," "health care," and "economy/jobs"), and moral values. After making this adjustment, he concluded: "If you pit group against group, moral values comes in dead last: war issues at 34 percent, economic issues at 33 percent and moral values at 22 percent. And we know that this is the real ranking."[7]

Brooks and Krauthammer both blamed "liberals" and "the media" for advancing this myth of the "redneck vote." In targeting liberals, each might have had Thomas Frank in mind. In his 2004 bestseller *What's the Matter with Kansas? How Conservatives Won the Heart of America*, Frank argued that Republicans have repeatedly won elections by convincing working-class Americans to vote against their economic interests by stressing cultural concerns such as abortion and Hollywood smut.[8] Others have suggested that the religious right has the most to gain by advancing this line of electoral analysis, noting that by doing so its leaders would have more influence in a second-term Bush administration. And indeed, many religious conservative leaders have emphasized the moral values story of the election. For example, Mary Ann Kreitzer of Les Femmes, an organization of conservative Catholic women, described the race in the following terms: "Voters rejected the party of gay activists, radical feminists, the Hollywood elite, pornographers, death-peddlers, anti-Christian bigots and apostate Catholics."[9]

With this in mind, Brooks and Krauthammer may be correct in cautioning against overemphasizing the importance of moral values in determining the winner of the presidential election. In a similar vein, political analyst Charlie Cook warned against making too much of Bush's victory. As he writes: "If the country has gone from being a 49–49 nation . . . to a 51–48 nation, that is an important shift but hardly a massive one."[10] Indeed, there was a remarkable amount of consistency between the 2000 and the 2004 presidential elections. In the end, only one red state went blue (New Hampshire) and only two blue states went red (Iowa and New Mexico). Moreover, each of these states was decided by narrow margins in both 2000 and 2004. President Bush did improve upon his 2000 two-party percentage in 32 states, but his popular vote total rose only 3 percent, from 47.8 percent to 50.7 percent.

Nevertheless, the values story of the election may—as journalists like to say—have some legs. By analyzing Krauthammer's breakdown of the exit poll numbers, for example, it is clear that the values issue pushed President Bush to victory (see table 2.2). If only voters who identified war and economic issues as the most important are counted, Kerry would have won the election in a landslide. If the "education"

Table 2.2. Issue Groups as Percentage of Bush and Kerry Totals

Issue Groups	Most Impt. (%)	Bush Vote (millions)	Kerry Vote (millions)	Bush Vote (%)	Kerry Vote (%)	% of Bush Total	% of Kerry Total
War	34	24.7	16.7	59.7	40.3	39.8	28.3
Economic	33	10.1	29.6	25.4	74.6	16.2	50.2
Moral	22	21.5	4.8	81.8	18.3	34.7	8.1
Education	4	1.3	3.6	26.5	73.5	2.0	6.1

Note: Based on percentages compiled from the National Election Pool exit poll and the total popular vote of approximately 122 million (actual total: 122,284,728). Numbers will not equal 122 million or actual totals for Bush and Kerry because 7 percent of respondents did not provide an answer to this question ("most important issue").

voters are added, Kerry would have extended his margin of victory. Only by incorporating values voters does Bush surpass Kerry in this hypothetical election. Of course, if the values issue had not been listed by poll takers—as in 2000—these same voters would likely have still voted, but would have identified another "pro-Bush" answer in response to the exit poll.[11] If this had occurred, the conventional wisdom of the election would likely have been different. Moreover, because it wasn't asked in 2000, it is difficult to compare whether values voters provided Bush with a greater share of their vote than they had four years earlier.[12] Nevertheless, to more than one out of every three Bush voters, the moral values issue was the issue that divided the two candidates and determined their vote. This fact is significant by itself.

REPUBLICANS, SOCIAL CONSERVATIVES, AND THE SUPREME COURT

The intent of this chapter, however, is not to resolve these controversies. It is instead to assess the role of the Supreme Court in shaping the issues that commonly sway values voters. To be sure, in 2004, the Supreme Court played a far less significant role than it had four years earlier. The Court did not need to resolve ballot controversies—a la its *Bush v. Gore* decision of 2000—to determine the winner of this election. George Bush scored clear—albeit narrow—victories in both the popular vote and the electoral college. However, the nation's highest tribunal did affect this election. It did so with its decisions on issues at the center of the culture divisions—sometimes known as the culture war—between Blue and Red America.[13]

The Rehnquist Court is a body of divided minds on these issues, and this reality has undermined the Republican-led effort to undermine "liberal" judicial rulings of the past. Indeed, many Republicans are profoundly displeased with their inability—despite their success at the ballot box—to produce a thoroughly conservative Supreme Court. Nevertheless, I suggest that this failure has aided the GOP because the Rehnquist Court's decisions have yet to unsettle the Republican electoral alliance as the Democratic-constructed Warren Court disrupted the Democratic coalition in the 1950s and 1960s. Instead, the Rehnquist Court's hesitancy toward a full endorsement of conservative doctrine has tended to rally social conservative voters to more action rather than silencing their political desires; desires that are decades old.

While Republican presidential candidates had publicly questioned the rulings of the Supreme Court before, the election of 1968 was a turning point in the effort to "conservatize" the Supreme Court. In that year, Republican Richard Nixon narrowly won the White House largely by highlighting the "social issue" to attract socially conservative disgruntled Democrats. With the segregationist George Wallace also drawing many social conservatives—mostly white southerners—to his third party candidacy, Vice President Hubert Humphrey garnered only 42.7 percent of the vote (to Nixon's 43.4 percent and Wallace's 13.5 percent). In other words, nearly 60 percent of voters did not support the Democratic Party's chosen candidate. Just four years earlier, Democratic President Lyndon Johnson had won in a massive landslide with 61.1 percent of the vote and all but six states. While defining the "social issue" of the late 1960s and 1970s is much like defining "moral values" today, Nixon's passiveness on civil rights, his promise to restore "law and order," and his defense of traditional values seemed to matter most in the end. In emphasizing the social issue, Nixon was most successful in attracting white southerners and Catholics in the North. While Wallace won five southern states, Nixon captured all the rest except Texas. It was the first time a Republican had captured a majority of the southern states since 1928 and only the third time in the party's history. With the Catholic vote, Nixon dramatically improved on his numbers from eight years earlier when he faced off against the Catholic John F. Kennedy. In 1960, Kennedy attracted 78 percent of the Catholic vote to Nixon's 22 percent. In 1968, the Democratic share of the Catholic vote dwindled to 59 percent as Nixon captured 33 percent and Wallace 8 percent. In 1972, Nixon won the Catholic vote with 54 percent.[14]

As suggested above, GOP positioning on the social issue was principally driven by a string of "liberal" Supreme Court rulings that surprised and outraged social conservatives who had traditionally voted for the Democratic presidential candidate. And with socially conservative white southerners and northern Catholics departing the party, Democrats had an exceedingly difficult time in capturing the White House. In the six presidential contests between 1968 and 1988, the five men who headed up the Democratic presidential ticket won a total of 54 states.[15] If the Watergate-affected election of 1976 is excluded, the figure falls to 31 states, an average of just over six states per race. While the GOP's appeal to both southern whites and northern Catholics is based on a broader set of issues today than it was in the days of Nixon, social issues are still central to these voters. And as it was in 1968, the Supreme Court is at the heart of the Republican "values" message. However, conservative Republican presidents have not had as much success as expected in turning back the liberal decisions of the Warren and early Burger Courts.

Indeed, one of Thomas Frank's complaints about the Republicans' use of culture war issues to attract voters is that its party leaders—despite attaining power—often fail to deliver on the promises they make during the election season. As he writes: "Abortion is never halted. Affirmative action is never abolished. The culture industry is never forced to clean up its act."[16] Frank does have a point. For example, on the issue of abortion, the central holding of the pro-choice *Roe v. Wade* decision—which gave women a right to terminate an unwanted pregnancy—remains in place even though Republican presidents have appointed eleven of the last thirteen Supreme Court justices and seven of the nine sitting justices. In fact, the progress made on the Court in repealing the essence of *Roe* might be summed up in a single phrase: one, perhaps none. In the thirty-two years since the U.S. Supreme Court decided *Roe*, the number of justices that Republican presidents have added to the high bench who have explicitly called for *Roe's* end amounts—at most—to one. More specifically, only three of seven sitting Republican-appointed justices have stated that they would vote to overturn *Roe*: William Rehnquist, a 1972 Nixon appointee who Ronald Reagan elevated to Chief Justice in 1986; Antonin Scalia, who filled Rehnquist's associate slot; and George H. W. Bush's 1991 appointee, Clarence Thomas. When the Court decided *Roe* in 1973, there were two dissenters (then Associate Justice Rehnquist, and 1962 Kennedy appointee Justice Byron White), Chief Justice Warren Burger, a 1969 Nixon appointee, was sympathetic to Texas's (Wade's) position, but strategically decided to join the majority at the end of the day. Along with Rehnquist, Scalia, and Thomas, there are four other Republican-appointed members of the current Court: John Paul Stevens (by Ford in 1975), Sandra Day O'Connor (by Reagan in 1981), Anthony Kennedy (by Reagan in 1988), and David Souter (by Bush I in 1990). Each of these four has declared in clear terms that the essence of *Roe* should stand as the law of the land. This does not mean that the Rehnquist Court has not reduced the extent of the "right to choose" outlined in *Roe*. It has. For example, the majority opinion in *Planned Parenthood v. Casey* did reject *Roe's* trimester system, replacing it with the vaguer "undue burden" test and allowing states to enact more restrictive legislation.[17] Nevertheless, abortion remains legal across the United States.[18]

THE DEMOCRATIC DEFENSE:
TEDDY KENNEDY'S TRIUMPH?

Despite the validity of Frank's point about Republican inability to "halt" abortion once in office, he fails to discuss the major reason underlying this difficulty. After all, abortion—like most cultural war issues—is a judicial issue; and therefore, elected officials cannot easily alter the governing policy through legislation or executive action. Frank, however, barely mentions the Supreme Court. And while Democrats have compromised on a range of issues that might have enhanced their appeal to all working-class Americans, on most matters involving the Supreme Court—especially on appointments—they have decided to fight it out with Republicans. In fact, Republicans could convincingly argue that the inability of their presidents to produce a thoroughly conservative Supreme Court does not primarily lie with the GOP. Rather, it is due to the presence of a Democratic majority in the Senate during most of those times when Republican presidents had an opportunity to fill vacancies on the Court. Indeed, one might even argue that it was under the leadership of another senator from Massachusetts—Edward M. Kennedy—that Democrats successfully secured a moderately conservative Court (at least on most social matters).

In fact, when the justices issued their two "liberal" decisions at the end of the 2003 term—on affirmative action and gay rights—it appeared as though the person who had the most influence on the product of the Rehnquist Court was not Ronald Reagan or George H. W. Bush, but Teddy Kennedy. After all, it was Senator Kennedy who famously rushed to the Senate floor in 1987 on hearing the news that President Reagan's choice to replace Lewis Powell was Robert Bork. Once there, he proclaimed:

> Robert Bork's America is a land in which women would be forced into back alley abortions, blacks would sit at segregated lunch counters, rogue police could break down citizens' doors in midnight raids, school children could not be taught evolution, writers and artists could be censored at the whim of government, and the doors of the federal courts would be shut on the fingers of millions of citizens for whom the judiciary is—and is often the only—protector of the individual rights that are the heart of our democracy.[19]

It was also Senator Kennedy who, six years earlier, eliminated any potential liberal opposition to Reagan's first choice for the Court—Sandra Day O'Connor—by providing his quick support (in contrast to conservative skepticism) to her nomination.[20] Indeed, given Justice O'Connor's essential role in the *Grutter* decision on affirmative action, and the expansive opinion of Justice Kennedy—Robert Bork's replacement—in *Lawrence* striking down Texas's ban on same-sex sodomy (both decisions are discussed below), liberals should rejoice in the current construction of the Court. After all, Lyndon B. Johnson was the last president to proudly display the liberal banner on judicial issues. And despite the string of Republican appointments, many conservatives remain distressed about the Court. In fact, none other than Robert Bork is one of its sharpest critics. For example, writing in 2002, Bork noted: "The Court as a whole lists heavily to the cultural left." To him, "no matter how many Justices are appointed by Republican presidents, the works of the Warren Court and the victories of the ACLU are not reversed." Instead, the Court is the most "elite institution in America," in that it is most often "ahead of the general public in approving, and to a degree enforcing, the vulgarization or proletarianization of our culture."[21]

THE REPUBLICAN RESPONSE

While the Democrats' defense of judicial rulings like *Roe* has produced a Supreme Court that is clearly not as conservative as Republican presidents intended,[22] this result has ironically been good for the fortunes of the GOP. In this sense, to understand the Rehnquist Court's place in American politics, it is important to distinguish between the ideological interests of social conservatives and the electoral interests of the GOP. Time and again, the Rehnquist Court has issued decisions that address some of the central concerns of conservatives within the Republican coalition without going so far as to issue majority opinions that would threaten to permanently drive away the party's more moderate supporters. In turn, Republicans have at times shaped their reaction to this Court's decisions—or those of lower courts—as a means to appeal to more moderate swing voters. At other times, the Republican response has been designed to rally the party's conservative base.

Appealing to Swing Voters:
Abortion and Affirmative Action

In considering this distinction, it is useful to review the first President Bush's response to the Rehnquist Court's 1992 decision in *Planned Parenthood v. Casey*, certainly the most disappointing ruling for all social conservatives. Recall, in that decision, a sharply split Court chose not to eradicate *Roe v. Wade*, deciding instead to endorse some portions of Pennsylvania's anti-abortion law while still maintaining the principle that women had a right to choose to terminate an unwanted pregnancy. Moreover, the Court majority seemed to suggest that the politics of abortion had played an essential role in its decision to let *Roe* stand. As Justice O'Connor wrote:

> Overruling *Roe's* central holding would not only reach an unjustifiable result
> under stare decisis principles, but would seriously weaken the Court's
> capacity to exercise the judicial power and to function as the Supreme
> Court of a Nation dedicated to the rule of law. Where the Court acts to
> resolve the sort of unique, intensely divisive controversy reflected in *Roe*, its
> decision has a dimension not present in normal cases, and is entitled to rare
> precedential force to counter the inevitable efforts to overturn it and to
> thwart its implementation. Only the most convincing justification under
> accepted standards of precedent could suffice to demonstrate that a later
> decision overruling the first was anything but a surrender to political pres-
> sure and an unjustified repudiation of the principle on which the Court
> staked its authority in the first instance. . . . A decision to overrule *Roe's*
> essential holding under the existing circumstances would address error, if
> error there was, at the cost of both profound and unnecessary damage to the
> Court's legitimacy and to the Nation's commitment to the rule of law.[23]

For social conservatives, the makeup of the 5–4 *Casey* majority was deeply
disturbing.[24] At that time, eight of the Court's nine justices had been appointed by
Republican presidents. The sole Democratic appointee was Justice White, one of
John F. Kennedy's two justices and one of *Roe's* two dissenters. In reaching this mixed
result, moreover, Justices O'Connor, Souter, and Kennedy—all appointed by the two
most recent Republican presidents—had joined forces. Significantly, each of those
three had raised some alarm among conservatives when either President Reagan or
George H. W. Bush announced their nominations to the nation. In other words, conservative willingness to "trust" the particular Republican president had apparently
limited the conservatism of the choices for the Court. President George H. W. Bush's
reaction to the high bench's decision in *Casey* furthered this unease.

Despite the long GOP-led drive to reverse *Roe*, the president did not denounce
the ruling by any means. Rather, Bush stressed that he "was pleased with the Supreme
Court's decision upholding most of Pennsylvania's reasonable restrictions on abortion." He then articulated his position on abortion, which unlike many social
conservatives in his party, allowed for the procedure in cases of "rape or incest or
where the life of the mother is at stake."[25] Bush continued to emphasize this stance
when asked about his position on abortion during the 1992 presidential campaign.
Strikingly, it was a position in clear conflict with the Republican Party's platform,
which proclaimed "that the unborn child has a fundamental individual right to
life which cannot be infringed," and endorsed "legislation to make clear that the

Fourteenth Amendment's protections apply to the unborn children."[26] But Bush didn't seem to care, noting during one question and answer session with voters: "I'm not going to necessarily be bound [by the Republican platform]. I'm the President. I'll say what I'm for and what I'm against."[27]

From the standpoint of the Bush reelection team, there was good reason to resist the Republican platform committee's adamantly pro-life position. In fact, there may have even been joy in the GOP's version of Mudville when social conservatives struck out in *Casey*, since the decision allowed the president to reach out to Republican-leaning pro-choice voters. In contrast, the judicial destruction of *Roe* would have most likely forced the president to highlight a pro-life stance in the midst of the campaign, thereby making it easier for the "new" Democrat Bill Clinton to command the center and attract what would become known as the "soccer mom" vote.[28] A billboard across the street from the Houston Astrodome, the site of the Republican Convention, reminded the Bush team just how many Republicans disagreed with their party's platform. It read: "71% of Our Party Can't Be Wrong! Republicans for Choice." Various public opinion surveys confirmed the billboard's general conclusion. According to one poll, only 22 percent of convention delegates—typically a more conservative lot than the voting public—approved of the plank, and only 19 percent of Republican voters favored outlawing abortion completely.[29]

Moreover, in attempting to downplay the conservative stridency of his party's platform, Bush wasn't doing anything new. Even his hard-charging predecessor had at times sought to ease tensions within the Republican Party over the abortion issue, largely to appeal to women who tended to vote for the GOP but considered themselves socially moderate or liberal. Indeed, presidential candidates typically act in such a fashion when confronted with an issue that potentially may split their electoral alliance. Given Republican strengths among men,[30] Bush only needed to minimize the gender gap to capture the White House for Republicans once again. It was a strategy that was greatly aided by the Court's decision in *Casey*, which effectively took the abortion issue off the list of top concerns for voters. Despite this assistance, Clinton easily defeated Bush in a three-man race.[31] Nevertheless, the point is clear. The *Casey* decision may have been a disappointment to conservatives, but it was a godsend to Republican strategists hoping to capture the White House for the fourth consecutive election, truly a rare feat in American history.[32]

President George W. Bush has pursued a similar strategy when responding to decisions that have disappointed conservatives but pleased Republican Party strategists who believe that a "Big Tent" theme is essential for the GOP to clearly emerge as America's majority party. On abortion, he has sought—like his father before him—to deemphasize his pro-life positioning, preferring instead to highlight a "culture of life." Here's how he answered a question on abortion in the final debate with Senator Kerry:

> I think it's important to promote a culture of life. I think a hospitable society is a society where every being counts and every person matters. I believe the ideal world is one in which every child is protected in law and welcomed to life. I understand there's great differences on this issue of abortion, but I believe reasonable people can come together and put good law in place that will help reduce the number of abortions. . . . What I'm saying is, is that as we promote life and promote a culture of life, surely there are ways we can work together to reduce the number of abortions: Continue to promote adoption laws—that's a great alternative to abortion; continue to fund and promote maternity group homes. I will continue to promote abstinence programs. . . . All of us ought to be involved with programs that provide a viable alternative to abortion.

In a follow-up question, moderator Bob Schieffer asked Bush directly about the *Roe v. Wade* decision: "[Senator Kerry earlier] said that you had never said whether you would like to overturn *Roe v. Wade*. So I'd ask you directly, would you like to?" In response, Bush refused to take the bait, telling Schieffer: "What he's asking me is will I have a litmus test for my judges, and the answer is no, I will not have a litmus test. I will pick judges who will interpret the Constitution, but I'll have no litmus test." Bush's avoidance of discussing *Roe* is not a new strategy. Just like his father's campaign in 1992, the Bush team was apparently concerned that advocating the overturn of *Roe*—or even discussing the decision—would be destructive to their candidate's electoral chances, as pro-choice women (in particular) would be much less inclined to vote for him.[33] (Indeed, a search of the weekly compilation of presidential documents reveals no public mention of the word "Roe" by the president in his first four years in office.) In the end, this strategy seemingly paid off. In his early study of the election results, political scientist Barry C. Burden finds "tentative support for the popular 'security mom' thesis." In other words, Bush did particularly well with white women concerned about security but seemingly less concerned about the end of *Roe v. Wade*.[34]

This doesn't mean that President Bush never talks about abortion. He does. But he usually does so by discussing the issue in terms of a "culture of life" and the more popular ban on partial-birth abortion. For example, his response to the abortion question in the final debate included: "Take, for example, the ban on partial-birth abortion. It's a brutal practice. People from both political parties came together in the Halls of Congress and voted overwhelmingly to ban that practice. It made a lot of sense. My opponent, in that he's out of the mainstream, voted against that law."[35]

On the campaign trail, Bush consistently referred to the partial-birth ban in similar fashion.[36]

Bush also made a very strong statement on *Roe* during the second debate without mentioning the ruling by name. In response to a question on selecting Supreme Court justices, President Bush said in part:

> I would pick somebody who would not allow their personal opinion to get in the way of the law. I would pick somebody who would strictly interpret the Constitution of the United States. Let me give you a couple of examples. . . . Another example would be the Dred Scott case, which is where judges years ago said that the Constitution allowed slavery because of personal property rights. That's personal opinion. That's not what the Constitution says. The Constitution of the United States says we're all—it doesn't say that. It doesn't speak to the equality of America. And so I would pick people that would be strict constructionists. We've got plenty of lawmakers in Washington, DC. Legislators make law. Judges interpret the Constitution.[37]

Although most in the audience likely missed the significance of Bush's words, they certainly attracted the attention of ardent social conservatives, who have long viewed *Roe* as the twentieth century's *Dred Scott*. In fact, Associate Justice Antonin Scalia—the justice President Bush once noted as the type of jurist he would select for the Court if presented with the opportunity—has repeatedly made this comparison in his opinions on abortion cases.[38] And following the debate, noted conservatives expressed their pleasure with the president's use of the 1857 decision. For example, the Reverend Louis P. Sheldon, chairman of the conservative Traditional Values Coalition, called Bush's answer "a very poignant moment, a very special gourmet, filet mignon dinner." "Everyone knows the Dred Scott decision and you don't have to stretch your mind at all. When he said that, it made it very clear that the [*Roe*] decision was faulty because what it said was that unborn persons in a legal sense have no civil rights." Conservative constitutional scholar Douglas Kmiec and Eleanor Smeal, president of the liberal Feminist Majority, both agreed that Bush was attempting to reach out to his conservative base with his reference to *Dred Scott* (although the Bush campaign denied any abortion-related significance).[39]

Bush's strategy seemingly worked, as pro-life voters turned out at the polls in strong numbers for his reelection, although some of these voters might have been motivated more by related "moral" issues. According to the influential Reverend Rick Warren, author of the best-selling *The Purpose Driven Life*, there were "five non-negotiable issues" in this area: abortion, same-sex marriage, stem-cell research,

Table 2.3. Opinions on Abortion

Abortion should be . . .	Total %	Bush %	Kerry %
Always legal	21	25	73
Mostly legal	34	38	61
Mostly illegal	26	73	26
Always illegal	16	77	22

Note: Percentages compiled from the National Election Pool exit poll.

human cloning, and euthanasia.[40] Although the exit poll only included questions about the first two, answers on abortion likely provide a good barometer—at least at the extremes—for positions on stem-cell research, human cloning, and euthanasia. (For example, a voter who thinks abortion should always be illegal is more likely to be opposed to embryonic stem-cell research.) And here, there was a clear increase for the pro-life position from four years earlier, especially for the most conservative stance on the issue. Specifically, in 2004, 16 percent of voters said abortion should be illegal in all circumstances, a 3 percent increase from four years earlier. In real numbers, this clearly pro-life group was approximately 13.7 million voters in 2000 and 19.6 in 2004, a 43 percent increase. In comparison, in 2000, 23 percent of voters said abortion should always be legal. In 2004, that figure fell to 21 percent. In real numbers, this clearly pro-choice group was approximately 24.2 million voters in 2000 and 25.7 in 2004, a 6 percent increase. At the same time, the percentage of voters holding a more moderate position on abortion—either mostly legal or mostly illegal—remained fairly stable from 2000. Then, 33 percent of voters thought abortion should be legal in most circumstances and 27 percent thought it should be mostly illegal. In 2004, those figures stood at 34 percent and 26 percent, respectively.

  The president has pursued a similar strategy on affirmative action, at times making clearly conservative statements but at other times taking a more moderate position. For example, in January 2003, when the Supreme Court heard oral arguments on the University of Michigan affirmative action cases (*Gratz* and *Grutter*),[41] the president stressed: "At their core, the Michigan policies amount to a quota system that unfairly rewards or penalizes prospective students, based solely on their race."[42] But following the Court's "liberal" ruling in *Grutter*, the president seemingly altered course, issuing a statement that virtually echoed the one his father released following *Casey*. On the same day the Court announced its support for the diversity principle in affirmative action programs, President Bush "applauded" its rulings. To him, the Court deserved such praise "for recognizing the value of diversity on our Nation's campuses." He added: "Diversity is one of America's greatest strengths.

Today's decisions seek a careful balance between the goal of campus diversity and the fundamental principle of equal treatment under the law."[43]

Leading conservatives, however, were not so pleased, stressing a stance more in line with the president's original position. Abigail Thernstrom, for example, could not find enough words to express her disappointment with the *Grutter* decision, noting that she was "in a rage," "beside myself," "in meltdown," and "totally dismayed." She also called the *Grutter* decision "disgusting," adding that the Court "should be ashamed of itself."[44] With such diverging words in mind, the obvious question is, Why would a supposedly conservative president—even a compassionate one—react in a fashion in clear conflict with his most ardent supporters?

Here again, the Court's decision favored Republican politics by disappointing conservative principles. The Bush White House no doubt designed the president's reaction to reach out to minority voters—particularly Hispanic voters—who Republican strategists believe are essential to creating a "Big Tent" GOP. In this sense, Pete Wilson's advocacy in 1994 of the divisive Proposition 187—which restricted illegal immigrants from using certain public services—provided the president with a ready example of how the Hispanic community might respond to the aggressive pursuit of racially conservative policies. Through his support of Proposition 187, Wilson had become persona non grata in California's Hispanic community, partially contributing to the near decimation of the party in the Golden State for close to a decade. For Bush to attract the Hispanic vote in 2004, then, it was helpful that the Court, in a sense, took the affirmative action issue off the national agenda for the next twenty-five years. While some conservatives will continue the fight in the courts and in the states—predicted and no doubt inspired by Justice Scalia's dissent—others have reached the end of the line. To California's Ward Connerly of anti-affirmative action Proposition 209 fame, "the battle will continue." But to Thernstrom, it's time to "move on."[45] While it is unclear whether affirmative action made the difference in 2004, Bush did attract more Hispanic voters to his candidacy than he had four years earlier.[46] Although this figure is in dispute, according to exit polls, the president garnered 44 percent of the Hispanic/Latino vote, a nine-point increase from 2000.[47]

Rallying the Base: Gay Marriage

While Bush's stance on affirmative action was clearly an effort to emphasize the "compassionate" nature of his conservatism, his reaction to the Court's "liberal" 2003 decision striking down Texas's sodomy law allowed him to appeal to the core of the Republican base. In many ways, this attempted balancing on judicial issues is similar to that of previous Republican presidents, in particular Richard Nixon and George H. W. Bush. But in contrast to these two predecessors (especially the latter), George W. Bush has made great strides in buttressing conservative support.[48] Such support was also crucial to his reelection effort. As noted above, Bush's political strategist, Karl Rove, has stressed that one of the main reasons why his candidate failed to capture the popular vote in 2000 was due to his "inability to rally enough religious conservatives to the polls."[49]

In this sense, the Court's decision in *Lawrence* presented a political opportunity for the president. While the Court's ruling was no doubt a liberal victory, the elevation of gay rights on the national agenda mobilized conservative voters. As Ken Connor, president of the Family Research Council, noted: "There are two issues that are non-negotiable for the base: the sanctity of life and the sanctity of marriage."[50] And while President Bush was reserved in the first few days after the Court's *Lawrence* decision, this initial reticence soon gave way to a campaign to find a way to outlaw gay marriage (even though the decision only involved Texas's sodomy law). Perhaps significantly, Bush made his strongest statement on the matter just days after televangelist Pat Robertson made a plea to the Almighty, that, in Robertson's words, he might replace three justices of the Supreme Court: "One justice is 83 years old, another has cancer, and another has a heart condition. Would it not be possible for God to put it in the minds of these three judges that the time has come to retire? With their retirement and the appointment of conservative judges, a massive change in federal jurisprudence can take place."[51] After Robertson's plea in July 2003, the conservative campaign to ban gay marriage was energized by the Massachusetts high court decision ordering the state to allow same-sex couples to marry and the open defiance of traditional marriage laws by officials across the county (most notably by San Francisco mayor Gavin Newsom). In response, President Bush announced his support for a constitutional amendment defining marriage as the union between a man and a woman.

If *Lawrence* had been a single event, the issue of gay rights would likely not have played much of a role in the 2004 presidential election. However, the arrival of gay marriage on the national scene ratcheted up the debate, putting Democrats on the defensive. In fact, after the election, some Democrats blamed Mayor Newsom, a fellow Democrat, for escalating the importance of same-sex marriage in an election year. As California senator—and former San Francisco mayor—Dianne Feinstein put it: "I believe it did energize a very conservative vote . . . So I think that whole issue has been too much, too fast, too soon." Representative Barney Frank of Massachusetts, an openly gay member of the House, concurred, suggesting that San Francisco's "spectacle weddings" were a primary reason why the eleven state bans of same-sex marriages passed so easily.[52] In truth, John Kerry also opposed gay marriage. However, four factors likely clouded his position for most voters: his opposition to a U.S. constitutional amendment defining marriage as a union between a man and a woman; his opposition to the 1996 Defense of Marriage Act; his consistent support for civil unions; and his refusal—against the advice of former President Clinton—to support state bans on gay marriage.[53]

The Bush campaign also had an unclear position on the appropriate legal status for same-sex couples, reportedly because of a concern that the president would "become too closely identified with the effort" to ban gay marriage "or come across as harsh on the issue." While Bush did clearly advocate for the amendment to the Constitution, Vice President Dick Cheney—who has a lesbian daughter—did not. Just before the Republican Convention—which adopted a platform that included both a strong pro-amendment plank and an anti–civil union plank—Cheney noted that he thought the matter "best be handled" at the state level. Moreover, a week before the election, President Bush departed from the platform. In a high profile interview with Charles Gibson of *Good Morning America*, Bush explained: "I don't think we should deny people rights to a civil union, a legal arrangement, if that's what a state chooses to do so." When Gibson noted that the Republican platform opposed civil unions. The president responded: "Well, I don't."[54] It was another example of Bush's use of his father's strategy on social issues.

Nevertheless, voters saw a stark difference between the two candidates on the issue of gay marriage. Of the 37 percent of voters who opposed any legal recognition of same-sex couples, 70 percent supported the president's reelection. In comparison, of the 25 percent of voters who supported gay marriage, 77 percent backed John Kerry. Of those 27 percent who supported civil unions—seemingly the position of both candidates by Election Day—52 percent voted for Bush and 47 percent for Kerry, a close reflection of the overall popular vote of 50.7 percent to 48.3 percent.

As noted above, social conservative activists have pointed to the president's support for a constitutional amendment banning gay marriage as an essential component of his victory. For example, Tony Perkins, president of the conservative Family Research Council, asserts that values voters made the difference for Bush in Ohio. Perkins reaches this conclusion after comparing the number of Ohio's values voters with those in Pennsylvania, a state with "a very similar voter demographic." Significantly for him, values voters made up 23 percent of the Buckeye State's voting

Table 2.4. Opinions on Policy toward Same-Sex Couples

Choices	Total	Bush	Kerry
Support same-sex marriage	25	22	77
Support civil unions	35	52	47
No legal recognition to gay couples	37	70	29

Note: Percentages compiled from the National Election Pool exit poll.

population but only 18 percent of the Keystone State's voting population. According to Perkins, "had Bush garnered only 18 percent rather than 23 percent of voters for moral values in Ohio he would have lost a raw number of 139,807 votes—enough for Kerry to have carried Ohio . . . and the presidency." He continues:

> While there are a number of factors affecting the votes in both states, there were two glaring differences between the two states. First, Ohio had a marriage amendment on the ballot and Pennsylvania did not. Ohio voters had an extra incentive to go to the polls and vote for the pro-family, pro-life candidate since they were also voting to protect the institution of marriage. Another factor is that in Pennsylvania, Arlen Specter, a decidedly pro-abortion senator, was on the ballot with Bush. Pro-family/life voters were something less than inspired to go to the polls when the only choice they were given for the Senate race was between two pro-abortion candidates. This was especially demoralizing when the pro-life candidate, Pat Toomey, was defeated in the Republican primary by a coalition of President Bush and Pennsylvania's other Republican senator, Rick Santorum. The message here is clear: pro-family issues win elections.[55]

Family values may win elections, but Perkins's analysis does not prove this point; largely because he assumes that those additional values voters in Ohio—5 percent more than in Pennsylvania—would have simply not shown up at the polls if they had been presented with Pennsylvania's election scenario.[56] Such a display of disaffection is possible, but it cannot be assumed.

After all, the senate candidate in Ohio was George Voinovich, an opponent—along with the state's other leading Republicans—of the same-sex referendum and hardly an eager advocate for the end of *Roe v. Wade*.[57] Ohio's values voters may have turned out in large numbers to support the same-sex ban, but at least two multiple regression analyses by political scientists conclude that the "presence of gay marriage referenda on the ballot had no impart on turnout."[58] In Ohio and Pennsylvania, two of the three battleground states rich with electoral votes, turnout was up 10 percent and 8.1 percent, respectively.[59]

An Issue That Wasn't: The Pledge of Allegiance

Another Supreme Court–affected issue that threatened to appear as an electoral concern involved school prayer; specifically the issue of whether Congress's 1954 addition of the words "under God" in the Pledge of Allegiance violated the First Amendment's Establishment Clause. The pledge issue had been a "hot button" issue in an earlier race for the presidency between another George Bush and another Massachusetts Democrat. In 1988, a central component of George H. W. Bush's attack of the "liberal governor from Massachusetts" was Dukakis's veto, "as governor, [of] a bill requiring public schoolteachers to lead children in the pledge of allegiance to the flag."[60] In 2004, the Supreme Court considered the constitutionality of the pledge based on similar legislation from California. However, in *Elk Grove Unified School District v. Newdow*, the Court majority dismissed the case after concluding that the respondent lacked legal standing to sue. In doing so, the Court effectively removed the pledge issue from the campaign. According to Susan Jacoby, "Democratic Party officials were privately delighted with the decision, because it relieved John Kerry . . . of any obligation to take a stand on the case." Nevertheless, George W. Bush still repeatedly attacked Kerry as the "liberal Senator from Massachusetts" (see chapter 5).[61]

CONCLUSION

Along with his maneuvering on the culture war issues, President Bush's lower court appointments also likely served as a vehicle for mobilizing conservatives to the voting booth. Indeed, in his first term, Bush displayed a strong willingness to expend political capital on appointments by selecting thoroughly conservative jurists to the lower courts.[62] As New York senator Chuck Schumer explained: "Bush said during the [2000] campaign that he was going to pick judges in the mold of Scalia and Thomas, but I thought it was just campaign talk. Then it became clear that that was exactly what he meant."[63] Given his record on lower court appointments, some in conservative circles have even proclaimed their faith that Bush will deliver in a similar fashion if he has an opportunity to fill a High Court vacancy. As Roberta Combs, president of the Christian Coalition noted: "The president has made great selections on the Circuit Court, and I trust his judgment on the Supreme Court."[64] Others are not so devoted. As Pat Robertson put it: "With Souter's nomination, there was a 'Don't worry, everything will be fine' approach. I don't think we in the conservative movement will accept that approach again, and I don't think the White House will try it. They know the Supreme Court is their lasting legacy."[65]

In the end, President Bush's ability to deliver on the Supreme Court will no doubt determine his historical standing with social conservative voters. And as he begins his second term, it appears that he will have a few vacancies to fill. Whether he attempts to fill them with nominees who hold views similar to Justices Scalia and Thomas—the two most conservative of the nine sitting justices—is already a major source of speculation in the nation's capital as advocacy groups from both ends of the ideological spectrum prepare for the next confirmation battle.[66] As Jack Goldsmith, a Harvard Law School professor and former member of the second Bush administration, reasons: "An entire generation of lawyers have been reared and trained in Justice Scalia's philosophy. So the Bush administration is likely to be more successful than its predecessors in finding reliably conservative nominees."[67] If Goldsmith is correct, President Bush may well produce the thoroughly conservative Supreme Court that social conservatives have been striving for since the 1960s. That success, however, may end up disrupting the Republican alliance. Put another way, the culture war is seemingly here to stay.

NOTES

1. For a discussion of the recent politics of values generally, see, James Davison Hunter, *Culture Wars: The Struggle to Define America* (New York: Basic Books, 1991); and John Kenneth White, *The Values Divide: American Politics and Culture in Transition* (New York: Chatham House, 2003). See also, Gertrude Himmelfarb, *One Nation, Two Cultures: A Searching Examination of American Society in the Aftermath of Our Cultural Revolution* (New York: Vintage, 2001); and John Micklethwait and Adrian Wooldridge, *The Right Nation: Conservative Power in America* (New York: Penguin Press, 2004).
2. Jeffrey Toobin, "Ashcroft's Ascent: How far will the Attorney General go?," *New Yorker*, April 15, 2002, 50–63, 63.
3. Although different exit poll wording makes it difficult to tell if evangelical Christians made up a greater share of the electorate than in 2000, political scientist John Green's polling showed that President Bush increased his share of the evangelical vote by 5 percent from 2000, from 71 percent to 76 percent; Green cited in Laurie Goodstein and William Yardley, "Bush Benefits From Efforts to Build a Coalition of the Faithful," *New York Times*, November 5, 2004; see also, John C. Green, "The American Religious Landscape and Political Attitudes, A Baseline for 2004," available at www.pewforum.org
4. Thomas B. Edsall, "Exit Poll Data Inconclusive on Increase in Evangelical Voters"; and Alan Cooperman and Thomas B. Edsall, "Evangelicals Say They Led Charge for the GOP," *Washington Post*, November 8, 2004.
5. David D. Kirkpatrick and Laurie Goodstein, "Group of Bishops Using Influence to Oppose Kerry," *New York Times*, October 12, 2004. Leo quoted in Goodstein and Yardley, "Bush Benefits from Efforts to Build a Coalition of the Faithful."
6. Moreover, the two Kerry states (Michigan and Oregon) were the only ones where the same-sex ban did not pass by more than 20 percent of the vote.
7. David Brooks, "The Values-Vote Myth," *New York Times*, November 6, 2004; and Charles Krauthammer, " 'Redneck Vote' is a Liberal Myth," *New York Daily News*, November 12, 2004.
8. Krauthammer, " 'Redneck Vote' is a Liberal Myth." Thomas Frank, *What's the Matter with Kansas? How Conservatives Won the Heart of America* (New York: Metropolitan Books/Henry Holt & Company, 2004); on the other hand, some liberals expressed concern about losing a "values" election, which raises questions about why they might want

to advance this "myth." As Reverend Thomas Reese, editor of the Jesuit magazine *America*, explained, "John Kerry could have been more effective at portraying his goals—fairer wages, better health care—as 'moral values.' " Reese added: "The Democratic Party seems almost embarrassed talking about family issues or religion." Reese quoted in "Liberals Dismayed by 'Moral Values' Claims," *New York Times*, November 9, 2004.

9. Kreitzer quoted in "Liberals Dismayed by 'Moral Values' Claims," *New York Times*, November 9, 2004. See also, Adam Nagourney, "Baffled in Loss, Democrats Seek Road Forward," *New York Times*, November 7, 2004.

10. Charlie Cook, "A Shift, But Far From a Transforming One," *National Journal*, November 13, 2004, 3486.

11. See Jim Rutenberg, "Poll Question Stirs Debate on the Meaning of 'Values'," *New York Times*, November 6, 2004.

12. See, however, Goodstein and Yardley, "Bush Benefits From Efforts to Build a Coalition of the Faithful."

13. See, however, Morris Fiorina, Samuel J. Abrams, and Jeremy C. Pope, *Culture War? The Myth of a Polarized America* (New York: Pearson Longman, 2005); and Philip A. Klinkner, "Red and Blue Scare: The Continuing Diversity of the American Electoral Landscape," *The Forum* 2 (2004), no. 2, article 2, 1–10.

14. "Portrait of the Electorate," *New York Times*, November 10, 1996.

15. The Democrats also won the District of Columbia in each of these six presidential races.

16. Frank, *What's the Matter with Kansas?*, 6–7.

17. *Planned Parenthood v. Casey*, 505 U.S. 833 (1992). For more on the Rehnquist Court, see Thomas M. Keck, *The Most Activist Supreme Court In History: The Road to Modern Judicial Conservatism* (Chicago: University of Chicago Press, 2004); and Mark Tushnet, *A Court Divided: The Rehnquist Court and the Future of Constitutional Law* (New York: W.W. Norton, 2005).

18. For some women, however, access is quite limited. For a discussion of the recent politics of abortion, see William Saletan, *Bearing Right: How Conservatives Won the Abortion War* (Berkeley: University of California Press, 2003).

19. Kennedy quoted in Ethan Bronner, *Battle for Justice: How the Bork Nomination Shook America* (New York: W.W. Norton, 1989), 90.

20. To be sure, Republicans held a majority in the Senate when Reagan nominated O'Connor in 1981, and therefore, Democratic support was not necessary to secure confirmation. For reaction to the O'Connor nomination, see Elder Witt, *A Different Justice: Reagan and the Supreme Court* (Washington, DC: Congressional Quarterly, 1986), 37–43

21. Robert H. Bork, "Adversary Jurisprudence," in *The Survival of Culture: Permanent Values in a Virtual Age*, Hilton Kramer and Roger Kimball, eds. (Chicago: Ivan R. Dee, Publisher, 2002), 196, 217, and 221.

22. See, however, Christopher Lasch, *The True and Only Heaven: Progress and Its Critics* (New York: Norton, 1991).

23. *Planned Parenthood v. Casey*, 505 U.S. 833 (1992), 836. Justice Souter was apparently responsible for this section of the opinion; see David J. Garrow, "Justice Souter Emerges," *New York Times Magazine*, September 25, 1994. On Justice Souter, see also, Thomas M. Keck, "David H. Souter: Liberal Constitutionalism and the Brennan Seat," in *Rehnquist Justice: Understanding the Court Dynamic*, Earl M. Maltz ed. (Lawrence: University Press of Kansas, 2003).

24. Conservatives found some solace with the three dissenting justices. For example, Justice Scalia spoke in clear terms on what he thought the Court should have done with *Roe*: "We should get out of this area, where we have no right to be, and where we do neither ourselves nor the country any good by remaining," *Planned Parenthood v. Casey*, 833, 1002.

25. Bush, "Statement on the Supreme Court Decision on Abortion," June 29, 1992, *Weekly Compilation of Presidential Documents*.

26. 1988 Republican Party platform.

27. Bush, "Question-and-Answer Session in Secaucus, New Jersey," *Weekly Compilation of Presidential Documents*, October 22, 1992.

28. See, for example, Robert Reinhold, "Weakness in a GOP Citadel Threatens Bush in California," *New York Times*, August 5, 1992.

29. Photo of billboard, *New York Times*, August 15, 1992; figures in R. W. Apple, Jr., "Behind Bush's Mixed Abortion Signals," *New York Times*, August 15, 1992.

30. On the importance of the male vote in electoral politics today, see, for example, Ruy Teixeira and Joel Rogers, *America's Forgotten Majority: Why the White Working Class Still Matters* (New York: Basic Books, 2000).

31. Bush did effectively reduce the Republican gender gap to 1 percent. However, his weakness among male voters, for a Republican, cost him the election. In the end, he won 38 percent of the men's vote, and 37 percent of the women's vote.

32. There have only been four times in American history when one political party has captured the White House in four consecutive elections.

33. I elaborate on this point in a paper entitled, "A Nearly Perfect Fit? Abortion, the Rehnquist Court, and the GOP," delivered at the 2003 American Political Science Association Annual Meeting. Jeffrey Rosen makes a similar point in "How the Election Affects the Court: Supreme Mistake," *New Republic*, November 8, 2004.

34. Barry C. Burden, "An Alternative Account of the 2004 Presidential Election," *The Forum* 2 (2004), no. 4, article 2, 4.

35. George W. Bush, "Presidential Debate in Tempe, Arizona," *Weekly Compilation of Presidential Documents*, October 13, 2371, 2377–2378.

36. See, for example, George W. Bush, "Remarks in Vienna, Ohio," *Weekly Compilation of Presidential Documents*, October 27, 2628–2634.

37. George W. Bush, "Presidential Debate in St. Louis, Missouri," *Weekly Compilation of Presidential Documents*, October 8, 2307.

38. Most recently, he opened his 2000 dissent in a Nebraska partial-birth abortion case with: "I am optimistic enough to believe that, one day, *Stenberg v. Carhart* will be assigned its rightful place in the history of this Court's jurisprudence beside *Korematsu* and *Dred Scott*. The method of killing a human child—one cannot even accurately say an entirely unborn human child—proscribed by this statute is so horrible that the most clinical description of it evokes a shudder of revulsion," *Stenberg v. Carhart*, 530 U.S. 914.

39. Peter Wallsten, "Abortion Foes Call Bush's Dred Scott Reference Perfectly Clear," *Los Angeles Times*, October 14, 2004.

40. Alan Cooperman and Thomas B. Edsall, "Evangelicals Say They Led Charge for the GOP," *Washington Post*, November 8, 2004.

41. *Grutter v. Bollinger*, 539 U.S. 244; and *Gutter v. Bollinger*, 539 U.S. 306.

42. George W. Bush, "Remarks on the Michigan Affirmative Action Case," *Weekly Compilation of Presidential Documents*, January 15, 2003, 71.

43. President Bush continued by noting: "My Administration will continue to promote policies that expand educational opportunities for Americans from all racial, ethnic, and economic backgrounds. There are innovative and proven ways for colleges and universities to reflect our diversity without using racial quotas. The Court has made clear that colleges and universities must engage in a serious, good faith consideration of workable race-neutral alternatives. I agree that we must look first to these race-neutral approaches to make campuses more welcoming for all students. Race is a reality in American life. Yet like the Court, I look forward to the day when America will truly be a color-blind society. My Administration will continue to work toward this important goal." Bush, "Statement on the Supreme Court Decision on the Michigan Affirmative Action Cases," *Weekly Compilation of Presidential Documents,* June 23, 2003, 803.

44. Thernstrom quoted in "Voices in the News," June 29, 2003, *National Public Radio*; and in Chuck Noe, "Supreme Court Split on Colleges' Racial Discrimination," Newsmax.com, June 23, 2003.

45. Connerly and Thernstrom quoted in Nina Totenberg, "Split Ruling on Affirmative Action: High Court Rules on Race as Factor in University Admissions," *National Public Radio,* June 23, 2003.

46. See also, Carolyn Curiel, "How Hispanics Voted Republican," *New York Times,* November 8, 2004; and Kirk Johnson, "Hispanic Voters Declare Their Independence," *New York Times,* November 9, 2004.

47. See however, Darryl Fears, "Pollsters Debate Hispanics' Presidential Voting," *Washington Post,* November 26, 2004. See also, Adam Clymer, "Bush 2004 Gains among Hispanics Strongest with Men, and in South and Northeast, Annenberg Data Show," December 21, 2004, available at www.annenbergpublicpolicycenter.org.

48. See, for example, Adam Nagourney, "Bush, Looking to His Right, Shores Up Support for 2004," *New York Times,* June 30, 2003.

49. Toobin, "Ashcroft's Ascent," 63.

50. Conner quoted in Nagourney, "Bush, Looking to His Right."

51. Pat Robertson, "Operation Supreme Court Freedom," www.PatRobertson.com. See also, Pat Robertson, "Supreme Court: Time for a Change," July 17, 2003, www.PatRobertson.com

52. Dean E. Murphy, "Some Democrats Blame One of Their Own," *New York Times,* November 5, 2004.

53. "September: Bill Clinton Weighs In," *Newsweek,* November 15, 2004.

54. Adam Nagourney and David D. Kirkpatrick, "Urged by Right, Bush Takes on Gay Marriages," *New York Times,* July 12, 2004; Republican Party platform, 83; Robin Toner, "Cheney Stakes Out His Position on Gay Marriages," *New York Times,* August, 25, 2004; Elisabeth Bumiller, "Bush Says His Party is Wrong to Oppose Gay Civil Unions," *New York Times,* October 25, 2004.

55. Tony Perkins, "Washington Update," November 5, 2004, www.frc.org. See also, David Finkel, " 'It's a Victory for People Like Us'; Bush Emphasis on Values Drew Ohio Evangelicals," *Washington Post,* November 5, 2004.

56. Perkins also arrives at the figure of 139,807 votes by simply subtracting 5 percent from Bush's election night total. However, Bush didn't win all values voters in Ohio. He won 85 percent of them. As adjusted—and using the official results—the figure falls to 121,496. Bush won Ohio by 118,775 votes. This is still enough votes to support Perkins's point, but again the point is based on a faulty assumption.

57.   Alan Johnson, "Issue I is Bad Idea for Ohio, Taft Says," *Columbus Dispatch*, October 14, 2004. On Voinovich and abortion, see Michael Barone and Richard E. Cohen, *The Almanac of American Politics* (Washington, DC: National Journal, 2004), 1252.

58.   Alan Abramowitz, "Terrorism, Gay Marriage, and Incumbency: Explaining the Republican Victory in the 2004 Presidential Election," *The Forum* 2 (2004), no. 4, article 3, 3; see also, Burden, "An Alternative Account of the 2004 Presidential Election," 6–7.

59.   Michael P. McDonald, "Up, Up and Away! Voter Participation in the 2004 Presidential Election," *The Forum* 2 (2004), no. 4, article 4, 3.

60.   Harvey C. Mansfield, Jr., *American Constitutional Soul* (Baltimore: The Johns Hopkins University Press, 1991), 65.

61.   *Elk Grove Unified School District v. Newdow*, 542 U.S.____; Susan Jacoby, "Ideas; Where politics shouldn't go," *Newsday*, July 11, 2004. See also, Timothy Noah, "Lay Off Massachusetts," October 14, 2004 at www.slate.com

62.   See, for example, David M. O'Brien, "Ironies and Disappointments: Bush and Federal Judgeships" in *The George W. Bush Presidency: Appraisals and Prospects*, Colin Campbell and Bert A. Rockman, eds. (Washington, DC: CQ Press, 2004); and Sheldon Goldman et al., "W. Bush Remaking the Judiciary: Like Father Like Son?" *Judicature* (May–June 2003): 282–309. See also, Jess J. Holland, "Bush, Senators make pact on judges," *Philadelphia Inquirer*, May 19, 2004.

63.   Schumer quoted in Jeffrey Toobin, "Advice and Dissent: The fight over the President's judicial nominations," *The New Yorker*, May 26, 2003, 44.

64.   Combs quoted in Nagourney, "Bush, Looking to His Right."

65.   Robertson quoted in Toobin, "Advice and Dissent," 48.

66.   See, for example, Robin Toner, "Changing Senate Looks Better to Abortion Foes," *New York Times*, December 2, 2004; and Sheryl Gay Stolberg, "Prepping for the Next Big Battle: The Supreme Court," *New York Times*, December 8, 2004.

67.   Goldsmith quoted in Jeffrey Rosen, "Can Bush Deliver a Conservative Supreme Court?," *New York Times*, November 14, 2004.

3

THE ECONOMY
AND DOMESTIC POLICY

Donald W. Beachler

WAS IT THE ECONOMY?

In 1992, Bill Clinton's political advisor James Carville sought to distill his candidate's message down to a single phrase as the Arkansas governor challenged the incumbent president, George H. W. Bush. The first President Bush was widely regarded as an able practitioner of foreign policy after expelling Saddam Hussein from Kuwait in 1991, but a sluggish economy was weakening his political standing. Carville coined the phrase, "It's the Economy, Stupid," and Clinton went on to win a three-way race for the presidency against Bush and independent billionaire Ross Perot, who garnered an impressive 19 percent of the popular vote. Discontent with the economy helped Clinton become the first Democrat in sixteen years to win a presidential election.

In 2004, Democrats hoped to capitalize on sluggish job growth to unseat another incumbent Republican president named Bush, who, unlike his father, seemed to evoke almost equal degrees of loathing and adulation in the electorate. The presidency of George W. Bush had been characterized by several extraordinary events. The attacks of September 11 galvanized the vast majority of the public behind the president as he attacked Al Qaeda in Afghanistan. The booming stock market of the 1990s crashed and corporate scandals were thought to be damaging to a GOP widely perceived to be the party of big business. Despite the widespread economic misgivings extant in 2002, George W. Bush played a prominent role in the 2002 congressional campaign that saw the Republicans gain seats in the House and recapture a majority in the narrowly divided Senate. In the 2002 midterm elections, held about fourteen months after the attacks of September 11, the president and the Republicans were able to use concern about terrorism to surmount economic difficulties that historically cause political damage to the party occupying the White House.[1]

By 2004, George W. Bush had launched a controversial war on Iraq. The explicit justification was to depose the Iraqi regime of Saddam Hussein, who the administration claimed had weapons of mass destruction that could be turned over to terrorists or that Saddam could use against the United States or its allies. The United States prevailed easily in the war and Saddam was captured at the end of 2003, but no weapons of mass destruction were found, and the United States found itself battling an insurgency that claimed far more American lives than had been lost in the original three-week campaign that ousted Saddam. Democrats hoped that the controversial nature of the Iraq War would help shake Bush's luster as the national unifier and induce the public to consider the economic circumstances in the country.

Bush faced a unique economic challenge as he faced reelection in 2004. Though the country had emerged from recession, for a variety of reasons, the economy was producing far fewer jobs than in previous recoveries. While job creation continued throughout 2004, Bush faced the electorate as the first president since Herbert Hoover, in 1932, to run for another term while presiding over a net loss of jobs in the country. Unlike Hoover, Bush was not governing a nation in a depression, but Democrats believed that the loss of jobs and the rising number of citizens without health insurance provided them with the opportunity to unseat an incumbent wartime president.

Democrats should have learned from 2000 that the economic state of the country is not the sole determinant of the outcome of presidential elections. All of the statistical models that rely on economic data predicted a substantial Gore victory in the 2000 presidential election. The state of the economy has been a key variable in many quantitative models that attempt to predict presidential election outcomes.[2] In 2000, Americans had experienced several years of high GDP growth, record stock market surges (though the market had begun to retreat in 2000), the lowest unemployment rate in decades, and in the spring of 2000, 60 percent of the country rated the economy as good or excellent. Yet, while Al Gore did win a narrow victory in the popular vote in 2000, he of course lost the electoral college by a narrow margin after the disputed counts in Florida were resolved.[3] At a minimum it was clear that a bad economy would not, by itself, determine the outcome of the 2004 presidential election.

This chapter will examine the key domestic issues of the 2004 presidential elections; the economy, health care, taxes, and the federal budget deficit. It will also attempt to explain why John Kerry could not take advantage of slow job growth to defeat George W. Bush. Before proceeding to an overview of the key issues in the campaign, it is important to place the United States in a global perspective by explaining the very different political and economic context in which American elections take place.

FIRST THINGS FIRST: THE UNITED STATES AS A DIFFERENT POLITICAL ECONOMY

As did the rest of the developed world in 2004, the United States combined a capitalist or market economy with a democratic electoral system. Political parties that wish to be rewarded by the voters, and governments that wish to be reelected, must preside over a period of relative economic prosperity. Voters use the ballot box to punish poor economic performance. In a market economy, growth depends upon the investment decisions of the private sector. All governments must induce investment from capitalists if they wish to succeed in a democratic capitalist society.[4]

Despite the need to create conditions for private sector growth there is still a great deal of variation in the politics and economic policies of various capitalist democracies. The balance of power between capital, labor, and government varies widely across different political systems. Levels of taxation and government-provided or government-mandated social services vary greatly from country to country. For example, in many European countries the government mandates that workers receive five or six weeks of annual paid vacation. In the United States, there are no legally mandated minimum vacations and the average worker receives just thirteen days paid vacation each year.[5] In most European nations, workers receive paid leave when they give birth or adopt a child. In the United States, certain workers are legally entitled to unpaid leave for twelve weeks.

The United States occupies a unique position among economically developed countries with respect to taxation and the level of government benefits provided to citizens. While they often complain of high taxes, Americans pay relatively low taxes compared to their Canadian and European counterparts. For example, in 2001 it was estimated that Americans paid taxes equivalent to about 31 percent of the entire economy as measured by Gross Domestic Product. By contrast, Canadians paid over 40 percent, the French nearly 50 percent, and the Swedes nearly 56 percent of GDP.[6] While they retain far greater portions of their income, Americans live in a nation where one-fifth of children are raised in poverty, more than double the rate in most other wealthy nations. The gap between rich and poor is much greater than in most European nations.[7]

The dual results of America's exceptional path are well summed up by Andrew Hacker at the conclusion of his 1997 book, *Money*. Hacker states that, "America's chosen emphasis has been on the offering of opportunities to the ambitious. . . . America has more self-made millionaires and more men and women who have attained $100,000 than any other country. . . . Less is left for those who lack the opportunities to or the temperament to succeed in competition. The United States has a greater percentage of its citizens in prison, on the streets, and more neglected children, than any of the nations with which it is appropriately compared."[8]

The United States is different from most developed market nations because it has never had a strong party of the left. This phenomenon, often called "American Exceptionalism," has meant that business in the United States has had more power than in other countries. As was previously noted, labor unions, which can act as a countervailing power to business, are also weaker in the United States. Politicians, such as John Kerry, Al Gore, and Bill Clinton, who are regarded as being on the "left" in the United States, take positions on issues that would mark them as conservatives in most European countries. The fact that John Kerry was not in favor of government-sponsored or government-mandated health insurance for every citizen would make him unelectable as a conservative party candidate in many European countries.[9]

Given the relatively small differences between the two major American political parties, the campaign would inevitably consist of slogans that would be careful not to upset powerful business interests or to disrupt the convoluted financial structure of American health care. Given the strong aversion of most Americans to tax increases, candidates have incentives to promise more than they can possibly pay for without incurring considerable debt. In this regard, Kerry and Bush did not disappoint in the 2004 presidential election.

HEALTH CARE

The United States occupies an ambiguous position in the world with respect to its health care policies. While many Americans enjoy access to excellent doctors, first rate medical facilities, and benefit from the finest medical research, the United States is the only nation with an advanced economy that does not provide universal health care coverage to all of its citizens. No nation spends a higher percentage of its Gross Domestic Product (GDP) on health care than does the United States. Despite the fact that 15 percent of U.S. GDP was devoted to health care, by 2003, 45 million Americans, or 15.6 percent of the population had no health insurance of any kind.[10] Most European countries provide coverage to all of their citizens while devoting about 10 percent of their economies to health care. While some universal health care systems such as the National Health Service in Britain have well-publicized problems such as waiting lists for non-emergency treatment, others like France and the Scandinavian countries do not suffer from such problems.

The United States ranks twenty-fourth in the world in infant mortality (measured as a percentage of children who die before their first birthday). Slovenia and the Czech Republic, comparatively poor European countries who were hampered by decades of communist economics, have lower infant mortality rates than the United States. For African Americans, the rates are much higher than for whites, and when black Americans are considered as a separate group, they rank fortieth in the world in infant mortality, behind nations such as Belarus, Macedonia, and Cuba.[11]

In 1993, Bill Clinton proposed a complex, difficult to comprehend health plan that aimed to both control costs and provide universal health insurance in the United States through a combination of government and private insurance programs. Fierce opposition from business groups, the insurance industry, and the plan's own complexities all contributed to its unraveling as Clinton was unable to get a Congress that had Democratic majorities in the House and Senate to even vote on any proposal that would have guaranteed health insurance for all Americans.[12]

Given the complexities of the American health care system and the political risks in various reforms, it is not surprising that neither George W. Bush nor John Kerry offered a health care program to the electorate that would cover all the uninsured. There was, however, a substantial difference between the policies offered by the two candidates to increase the number of Americans with health insurance. The president proposed spending $70 billion over ten years to help the uninsured purchase policies. While the $1,000 limit for individuals and the $3,000 limit for families was only a fraction of what health insurance policies would cost, the president indicated that this was as far as he was willing to go in the direction of using the federal government to assist the uninsured.[13] Like many Republicans, George W. Bush argued that reforms that limited doctors' liability in malpractice cases would reduce medical costs and, thereby, make health insurance more affordable. It was difficult to estimate the number of Americans who might gain access to insurance if patients' rights to collect large punitive damage awards against physicians were restricted, but the nonpartisan Congressional Budget Office estimates that a 30 percent reduction in malpractice costs would reduce health care spending by 0.5 percent.[14]

John Kerry proposed spending $650 billion over ten years to increase the percentage of Americans with health insurance. The Democratic nominee proposed spending more than twice as much as the president to subsidize the health care premiums of low-wage citizens, and offered federal subsidies that would make insurance more affordable to small business and individuals. Kerry argued that he could pay for his larger health plan by rolling back the portion of the Bush tax cuts that benefited individuals earning more than $200,000 a year.[15]

Independent analyses of the two candidates' health care plans indicated that the impact of the two plans would be distinctly different. The Kaiser Family Foundation study estimated that the Bush proposal would enable about 1.8 million of the 44 million uninsured to obtain health insurance. Kenneth Thorpe of Emory University estimated that over 26 million Americans would be able to obtain health insurance under the Kerry plan.[16] If they were able to wade through the heated rhetoric about Kerry's war record or the president's and vice president's lack of one, Kerry's alleged flip-flopping, speculation about Dick Cheney's place on the ticket, and assorted campaign trivia, Americans were presented with an interesting policy choice on health care. Were they willing to repeal the portion of the Bush tax cuts for households earning over $200,000 per year to fund health insurance for 26 million Americans? (Two analysts interviewing voters in West Virginia found that many voters who supported the notion of a national health care system were uncertain as to how Kerry's health plan would work.[17]) Of course, health care would not be the only issue even for those who closely followed the election, so the tax cut and health care tradeoff was not answered directly by the election results.

In November 2000, after several years of economic prosperity, and ten months before the attacks of September 11, 2001, 15 percent of voters listed health care issues as most important to them.[18] In 2004, despite the rise in the number of the uninsured, just 8 percent of voters chose health care as the most important issue.[19] The poll result, which was based on a somewhat different set of questions than the 2000 exit poll, does not indicate that Americans did not care about health issues. We can only conclude that most did not regard them as most significant.

THE ECONOMY

Not all voters cast their ballots on the basis of issues. In 2000, 62 percent said that issues were most important in deciding how to cast their votes, while 38 percent regarded the personal characteristics of the candidates as most important. (Unfortunately the issues and character question was not asked in the 2000 exit poll.) In the 2000 election, exit polls asked voters which issues mattered most to them. Seventy-six percent of respondents listed a variety of domestic issues. Jobs and the economy were first with 18 percent, 15 percent mentioned education, and another 15 percent listed various aspects of health care. Taxes and Social Security were each listed first by 14 percent of voters. Only 12 percent of respondents listed world affairs as the most important issue.[20]

In 2004, with terrorism a continuing concern and the Bush administration's Iraq policy a source of ongoing controversy, it was inevitable that traditional economic policy issues would not be as prominent as in the preceding election. Yet, an economy with slow rates of job growth provides an issue to the party challenging the incumbent.

Economic events are often beyond a president's power to control and capitalist economies have cycles of boom and bust that are often difficult for government to manage. Still, government policies can have an impact on the economic lives of its citizens. For example, since the administration of Calvin Coolidge (1923–1929), average annual job growth has been higher under Democratic than Republican presidents.[21] For a president's electoral fortunes, timing may be more important than overall job growth. Jobs grew at a slower annual average rate under Ronald Reagan than they did under Jimmy Carter. Reagan was blessed with a growing economy when he ran for reelection in 1984, while Carter was beset by economic problems when Reagan challenged him in 1980.

Presidents are not wholly, and may not even be largely responsible for the state of the American economy, but economic issues certainly loom large in American elections.[22] A president may get blamed when the economy does not do as well as citizens expected and they are quick to claim credit when things go well. This fact was encapsulated by James Carville, Bill Clinton's principal campaign consultant in 1992, when he summed up the campaign's message in the now famous slogan, "It's the Economy, Stupid."

The truth of Carville's message was certainly evident to President Bush, who could reflect upon his father's experiences on national tickets. After winning election as Ronald Reagan's vice president in 1980, the Reagan–Bush team won a landslide reelection in 1984 when 41 percent of voters said that their family finances were better than four years ago. Just 19 percent of 1984 voters claimed that they were worse off financially than in 1980. In 1988, George H. W. Bush soundly defeated Michael Dukakis, as those who considered themselves to be better off (44 percent) were more than double those who claimed to be worse off (17 percent). In 1992, Bill Clinton defeated the first President Bush amid the lingering effects of recession when just 19 percent of voters said their families were better off than in 1988, and 34 percent said they were worse. Of the 34 percent who said their financial situation had declined since 1988, just 13 percent voted for the incumbent president in 1992.[23] In 1996, the only American presidential election of the last seven without a Bush on the Republican ticket, Bill Clinton easily defeated Bob Dole amid an improving economy.[24]

While economists stated that technically the recession had ended in 2001, the subsequent recovery saw slow job growth in many areas of the country. George W. Bush faced the unenviable prospect of running for reelection having been president during a net loss of over a million jobs. Bush was in danger of becoming the first president since Herbert Hoover to be president for a term in which no new jobs were created. Some of the worst job losses were in the key battleground states of the Midwest. In June 2004, Ohio, which Bush won by 3 percent of the vote in 2000, lost jobs for the eighth time in the preceding ten months.[25] Industrial states such as Ohio, Michigan, and Pennsylvania had all experienced severe job losses in the Bush years. By the summer of 2004, Ohio had lost 281,000 jobs in the preceding four years.[26]

The job anxieties of Americans were exacerbated by fears of outsourcing. For the past few decades, blue-collar Americans had lost millions of factory and mill jobs as their employers either relocated to take advantage of cheap labor, or closed because they could not compete with foreign firms that sometimes paid factory labor less than fifty cents an hour. Despite the pain of dislocation inflicted on millions of blue-collar workers, the dominant wings of the Democratic and Republican parties supported free trade. Major newspapers, the major banks, and the majority of economists also argued that, in the long run, the country was better off with free-trade policies. Public opinion polls, however, often showed that the majority of Americans, including a majority of Republicans, did not support trade policies that cost American jobs.[27] In the summer of 2004, a *New York Times*/CBS News poll found that 69 percent of registered voters agreed with the statement that "trade restrictions are necessary to protect domestic industries."[28] On the issue of trade, the opinions of the majority could not prevail against mostly unified elite opinions.

Fears of lost jobs due to global wage competition were ameliorated somewhat in the Clinton years by the rapid job growth that allowed many displaced workers to find jobs even if they were in the service sector and paid less than lost manufacturing jobs. However, a slowing economy in the 2000s left workers less sure about future job prospects. The fear of a global economy was exacerbated as service and professional jobs also began to go offshore or be "outsourced." Outsourcing of professional jobs undermined a basic premise of globalization advocates in the 1990s. Both Bill Clinton, an ardent free trader, and most of his Republican opponents argued that Americans need not fear the loss of manufacturing jobs overseas because displaced workers could be retrained for more skilled jobs that paid better than those jobs that had been lost.[29] In this rosy view of the American economic future, yesterday's steelworkers were tomorrow's computer programmers.

Early in the new century more skilled professional jobs began to be outsourced abroad. Nations like India had highly skilled computer programmers, engineers, and accountants who could perform work for which Americans had traditionally been paid well, but at a fraction of the cost. There was talk that Indian radiologists would soon be reading X-rays for a fraction of the fees that an American physician would receive for a similar service. The continued loss of manufacturing jobs combined with the outsourcing of some professional positions ensured that jobs and the economy would be of concern to many voters in 2004.

By the summer of 2004 there was enough concern about free trade that the president decided not to seek congressional ratification of the Central American Free Trade Agreement (CAFTA) until after the election. By postponing consideration of CAFTA, which John Kerry had criticized, the president spared himself the wrath of economically insecure workers on at least one issue. He also allowed Republican senators and representatives to avoid voting on an issue that was likely to be controversial in some states.

The Bush administration was generally supportive of the free-trade status quo. Bush did, however, enact tariffs on imported steel in an effort to assist an industry concentrated in such important electoral college battleground states as Pennsylvania, Ohio, and West Virginia.[30] These tariffs, which were a drastic departure from the general philosophy and practice of the Bush administration, were lifted after the World Trade Organization declared them to be an unfair restraint on trade. With the exception of steel, the administration did not seem to object to a global marketplace. Gregory Mankiw, the president's chief economic advisor, argued that despite the job losses, in the long run Americans benefited from the displacement of jobs to low-wage labor markets because they could purchase cheaper consumer goods. On his campaign website, the president argued that it was important to help Americans gain skills needed to acquire jobs being created in the United States. He also stated that, "The answer to outsourcing is to make America more competitive in the global market place, not isolate ourselves from it. The president's pro-growth and job training policies are helping American workers and companies do just that."[31] Republicans argued that those who claimed that trade policies were creating a larger gap between the rich and the poor were fomenting class warfare.

During his twenty years in the Senate, John Kerry had sought to create a moderate image on economic issues. Seeking to portray himself as a pro-business Democrat, Kerry had been a solid supporter of the free-trade regime favored by economic and political elites. Kerry had voted for the North American Free Trade Agreement (NAFTA) and the Permanent Normal Trade Relations (PNTR) agreement with China, despite the vehement protests of labor unions who argued that millions of American jobs would be lost to competition from low-wage labor.

Despite his free-trade record, Kerry made a partial election year conversion when he denounced American corporations that were taking jobs overseas. During the primary campaign, Kerry denounced "Benedict Arnold CEOs" who were betraying American workers to increase their profits. After he secured the nomination, Kerry no longer used the Benedict Arnold label, but he did argue that he would seek to end tax breaks that encouraged companies to relocate abroad. Kerry also stated that he would enforce provisions of trade treaties that required nations that had access to American markets to respect the rights of workers to organize unions, and to enforce their own environmental laws.

As Kerry sought to curry favor with business and workers in hard-hit states such as North Carolina, Ohio, Pennsylvania, West Virginia, and Wisconsin, he was quite vague about what policies might actually save American jobs. On his campaign website Kerry promised to, "review all our existing trade agreements to ensure that our trade partners are living up to their labor and environmental obligations and that trade agreements are enforceable and balanced for America's workers. He will consider necessary steps if they are not."[32] Kerry's platform was essentially to consider taking unspecified actions in the event that a review determined that other nations failed to meet criteria that Kerry never specified.

While it was unclear what might actually be done about protecting American workers from global wage competition, the debate was at least joined and John Kerry offered to provide some assistance on the issue even after he stopped denouncing corporations that outsourced jobs as economic traitors. Senator Ernest Hollings, an eighty-two-year-old Democrat from South Carolina, had long opposed trade agreements that he believed cost blue-collar jobs. Because of his view that free trade undermined the middle-class lifestyle of blue-collar Americans, Hollings was denounced by most Republican and Democratic politicians, newspapers, and academics. As he put it, "As soon as I said that we should protect our standard of living they came around like Pavlovian jackasses jumping up and down and saying 'protectionist, protectionist.' "[33] In 2004, John Kerry, while not adopting an outright protectionist position, supported the notion of Hollings and others that trade agreements must demand certain labor and environmental standards.[34]

For many voters the concern about the economy was not simply the net loss of jobs, but the quality of the jobs being created, as relatively well-paid jobs were sometimes replaced by jobs that offered far lower salaries. For example, in the key battleground state of Ohio the average annual salary of jobs lost between January 2001 and January 2003 was $41,287. The average annual wage for jobs created in that period was $29,418.[35] The continued loss of industrial jobs in key midwestern states was a threat to the living standards of blue-collar workers.

The electoral college meant that the inevitably uneven nature of economic growth could pose problems for, and also present opportunities to, the president. Some of the battleground states were the biggest job losers in the Bush years. Between March 2001 and June 2004, Ohio lost 219,000 jobs and Michigan experienced a net loss of 213,000 jobs. In Pennsylvania, 74,000 jobs disappeared. Florida was Bush's best big state in terms of job gains. In the first three and one-half years of the Bush administration, Florida had a net gain of 260,000 jobs. Changes in employment are not the only determinants of presidential voting, but in Pennsylvania and the Midwest, the uneven economy made the president's job harder, while in closely contested Florida, he could argue that he had presided over a period of prosperity.[36]

In the spring of 2004, the Bush administration started receiving the positive job numbers they had long desired. In March and April, job growth was in the 350,000 range and the May job growth met the 150,000 per month figure that is needed to keep pace with an expanding labor market. The unemployment rate remained at the 5.6 percent figure it had been at since January. The stagnant unemployment rate in the face of job growth was a result of more workers entering the labor force.[37]

As of early June, the Bush administration faced a frustrating paradox. Though there was increased job growth in the spring of 2004, the president's approval ratings on the economy declined. For example, in April 2003, when job growth was negligible, 52 percent of voters approved of the president's handling of the economy. By late May of 2004, with much greater job growth, only 44 percent of the public approved of the president's management of the economy. In early June, a Gallup Poll revealed that 47 percent of Americans believed that the economy was improving, while 45 percent believed that it was getting worse.[38] Another polling firm, Rasmussen Reports, reported that in the month of May, 33 percent of Americans said their finances were getting better, while 44 percent reported that their personal finances were getting worse.[39] It was simply unclear how the politics of employment would play out in November.

WHAT KIND OF JOBS?

As the Iraq War dragged on with mounting American casualties and photos of abused Iraqi prisoners, the president's overall job approval rating declined. As some citizens' opinions of the president declined, they also gave him negative ratings on the economy. Others argued that voters were concerned about the quality of many of the jobs being created. Many people believed that too many new jobs paid low wages and offered meager benefits.[40] As the economy has been transformed from one where General Motors has been replaced by Wal-Mart as the largest private employer, many Americans feared that well-paid manufacturing workers were being replaced by retail workers who were paid poorly and did not receive the health insurance and pension benefits that unionized workers enjoyed. In the summer of 2004, Stephen S. Roach, the chief economist at the investment bank Morgan Stanley, estimated that 81 percent of the total job growth in the preceding year was in lower wage sectors of the economy.[41] The administration argued that there was no conclusive evidence about the quality of jobs being created.[42]

In an opinion piece in the *New York Times*, Roach noted that between March and June of 2004, 495,000 part-time jobs were created. These part-time jobs accounted for 97 percent of the jobs created in this period. Roach related the jobs problem to the ongoing globalization trends. "Under unrelenting pressure to cut costs, American companies are now replacing high-wage workers with like quality low-wage workers abroad. . . . It was only a matter of time before the globalization of work affected the United States labor market. The character and quality of job creation is changing before our very eyes. Which poses the most important question of all, what are we going to do about it?"[43] Roach's claims were buttressed in August by an analysis that indicated that most new job creation was taking place in low-paying fields such as clerical work, retail sales, and hotels. In the first seven months of 2004, there were no new net jobs created in industries that paid in the top fifth of wages, while 477,000 jobs were created in industries that paid in the bottom fifth of wages.

The Bush administration faced further political problems with the economy in June and July when job growth slowed to just 112,000 in June, while only 32,000 new jobs were created in July. The July figures, which were at least 100,000 jobs short of the numbers predicted by most economists, meant that as of the report issued in early August, the economy had lost over one million jobs during the Bush presidency.[44]

As they have for decades, labor unions worked hard in 2004 to turn their voters out for the Democratic presidential ticket. Andrew Stern, president of the Service Employees International Union (SEIU), said that it was difficult to motivate blue-collar workers who had not voted before because the Democrats had not really addressed what Stern called the "Wal-Mart economy." Stern meant that Kerry, like Bush, had not addressed the issue of low-wage jobs that did not offer health insurance to workers.[45] The constraints that a polity with so much business power places on political candidates meant that there was little real discussion of the concerns of many working Americans.

One additional factor making Americans grouchy about the economy was the rise in prices of a variety of goods including two basics in most Americans' budgets: milk and gasoline. As of mid-2004, there were still enough unemployed workers that there was little real growth in workers' wages. Wages, especially for working-class people, were not keeping up with price increases. In the words of Ethan Harris, chief economist at Lehman Brothers, "Joe Six-Pack is under a lot of pressure. He got a lousy raise; he's paying more for gasoline and milk. He's not doing that great. But proprietors' income is up. Profits are up. Home values are up. Middle-income and upper-income people are looking pretty good."[46]

The impact on politicians of the economic problems of the people at the bottom half of the income scale is probably lessened by the class disparities in voter turnout.

Table 3.1. Income and Voter Turnout, 1972–1996

Year	Overall Turnout (%)	Income (%)	
		Bottom 5th	Top 5th
1996	49.0	38.7	72.6
1992	55.2	42.0	78.0
1988	50.1	42.2	73.7
1984	53.1	44.7	74.7
1980	52.6	45.7	76.2
1976	53.5	46.7	74.1
1972	55.2	49.2	79.7

Source: Tom DeLuca, "Joe the Bookie and the Class Cap in Voting," *American Demographics* (November 1998), 27.

Those who are least successful in the economy are far less likely to vote than those at the upper end of the economic scale. As table 3.1 shows, from 1972 through 1976, those in the top fifth of income earners were far more likely to vote than those in the bottom fifth. It is of course hard to know which comes first.[47] Do low-income voters vote less because they feel their concerns are not represented in the narrow two-party American political system, or are their concerns not as fully addressed because they vote at lower rates? Because the difference in voter turnout between rich and poor citizens is much greater in the United States than in other developed democracies, it is likely that the absence of a party of the left reduces turnout among low-income voters and this in turn further reduces the concerns politicians have for them.[48]

While job growth was slow in most of 2004, there was job creation. George W. Bush, like any incumbent president, sought to claim credit. John Kerry continually pressed the argument that the jobs were not of the same quality as those that were lost.[49] In June, Republicans were hopeful that citizens would soon appreciate what, in the view of the president's backers, was good economic news. Republican Senator James Talent of Missouri said, "The economy has really turned. . . . It just takes awhile longer for that to filter through to folks."[50] Others argued that while more jobs were being created, consumers were feeling the pinch of higher gasoline and other consumer prices at a time when there was a slight rise in interest rates.[51]

In mid-June, Kerry proposed raising the minimum wage to $7.00 an hour by 2007. Kerry might have gained more support if he had emphasized this issue more. A Florida amendment to raise the minimum wage to $6.15 by April 2005, garnered 72 percent of the vote, even as George W. Bush was winning the state. In Nevada, a similar $1 boost in the minimum wage received 68 percent of the vote even though George W. Bush won the state's five electoral votes.

An old southern lawyer's tale tells of the advice given to a new attorney. If the facts are on your side, argue the facts. If the law is on your side, argue the law. If neither are on your side, change the subject. Undoubtedly, the Bush administration preferred to talk about gay marriage, Osama bin Laden, and John Kerry's alleged inconsistencies rather than economic displacement in 2004. In the end, that was to prove an effective strategy.

TAXES

Tax cutting has been a key part of Republican policy since the presidency of Ronald Reagan. Before Reagan, Republicans were as likely to emphasize balanced budgets and were reluctant to cut taxes unless they were accompanied by matching cuts in federal spending. By 2004, the president and most Republicans in Congress regarded tax cuts as far more important than balancing the federal budget.

George W. Bush proposed, and saw enacted, a series of large tax cuts in the first three years of his presidency. The tax cuts included the elimination of the estate tax, or as Republicans preferred to call it, the "death tax." Tax rates were cut and a number of tax credits including an expanded child credit were added to the tax code. The Bush administration argued that the tax cuts provided needed stimulus to a sluggish economy that continued through the first three years of the administration. Bush officials argued that joblessness would have been higher without the tax cuts.

While all Americans who paid federal income taxes benefited to a degree from the Bush tax cuts, the steep cuts in higher income tax rates and the abolition of the estate tax (only the wealthiest 2 percent of Americans who died left estates that were subject to federal estate tax in 2001) meant that most of the benefits of the Bush tax cuts went to wealthier citizens. Liberal groups like Citizens for Tax Justice showed that a household with $22,000 would receive a $99 tax cut from the 2003 Bush plan, while a family earning $1,082,000 would get a tax reduction of $30,287.[52] The Bush administration argued that since upper-income taxpayers pay the bulk of federal income taxes, it was only fair that they should receive the largest tax cuts.

Opponents of Bush tax policy argued that the president's tax plan would cause federal budget deficits to soar. Indeed even without including the money "borrowed" from the Social Security Trust Fund, the administration ran federal budget deficits in the range of $400 billion annually. The Citizens for Tax Justice estimated that the tax cuts would add over $3 trillion to the national debt between 2001 and 2010.[53] The Bush administration argued that the deficits were attributable mainly to a war on terrorism and an economic slowdown. They also hoped that a growing economy would provide more tax revenue as more citizens would be working and higher corporate taxes would generate additional revenues. Some conservatives believed that high federal budget deficits were a barrier to liberals who could not plausibly finance increases in federal spending on health care, education, and the environment that were a vital part of their agenda.

While promising to repeal the Bush tax cuts for those making over $200,000, Kerry also proposed tax breaks for specific groups of Americans. He argued that the child care tax credit should be increased from $3,000 to $5,000 per year and that the credit should be extended to stay-at-home parents. Kerry also proposed extending the tax credit to low-income families who were not recipients because they do not pay federal income taxes.[54] Of course, like Bush, he had no plausible explanation of how he would pay for future tax cuts.

THE DEFICIT? WHAT DEFICIT?

From the perspective of 2004, it is striking to recall one of the questions that was asked in exit polls in the 2000 presidential election. Voters were asked what their priority was for the annual budget surpluses that the federal government was running and that many forecasters believed were the wave of the future. (For the record, 28 percent favored a tax cut, 24 percent wanted to reduce the national debt, and 35 percent wanted to strengthen Social Security.)[55] In 2000, the notion of federal budget surpluses was a new concept to nearly all Americans. The United States government had not run a surplus in thirty years and the deficits of the 1980s and early 1990s were, in relative terms, the largest peacetime deficits in American history.[56] In 2000, the government projected that the federal government would have trillions of dollars in surpluses in the next two decades. In 2004, there were no questions asked about how to dispose of looming federal budget surpluses.

For many years large budget deficits were seen as bad for both economic and moral reasons. It was long believed that if the federal government borrowed a great deal of money, interest rates would rise because of competition for available funds. These higher interest rates would make it more difficult for consumers to borrow money and for businesses to take on new loans for the creation and expansion of enterprises. Reduced consumer spending and slower rates of business investment mean less job creation. Running large annual deficits was also thought to be morally irresponsible because it meant that one generation lived beyond its means and burdened future generations with the debt and interest accumulated by previous excess consumption. Prodded by the independent candidacy of H. Ross Perot, who described the debt and deficits as the crazy aunt who lives in the basement who nobody will talk about, the budget deficit was a major political issue for all three major candidates in the 1992 presidential election.

The first President Bush and Bill Clinton had both paid a steep political price because they raised taxes as part of measures to reduce federal government budget deficits. George H. W. Bush was never forgiven by some conservative Republicans for breaking his pledge to not raise taxes. Clinton's increase in taxes was widely thought to be one of the factors that contributed to the Democrats' electoral catastrophe in 1994 that brought the Republicans to a majority in the House of Representatives for the first time since 1954. The actions of both presidents and rapid economic growth in the 1990s brought an end to the annual federal budget deficits that were added to the national debt each year.

By 2004, the United States was again running large annual budget deficits. The Bush tax cuts, the economic recession, an aging population, and increased military expenditures in the wake of the September 11 attacks and the invasion of Iraq were largely responsible for the soaring deficits. For fiscal year 2004, the Congressional Budget Office projected that the federal government would run a deficit of $477 billion. This figure did not include over $100 billion in surplus Social Security funds that were drained out of the trust fund for that retirement entitlement and spent in 2004. The federal government spends the Social Security surplus each year and issues, what are in effect IOUs to the Social Security Trust Fund. The 2004 deficit was the largest in U.S. history, though the budget deficits of the 1980s were a larger percentage of GDP.[57] Of fifteen major economies, the United States had the second-largest deficit (Japan was the largest) measured as a percentage of GDP.[58]

Given the large budget deficit and the role the issue had played in 1992, the absence of much discussion of budget deficits in 2004 is notable. One possible explanation is that voters simply do not care that much about deficits. It is hard for the average citizen to see how budget deficits impact their life. Paul O'Neill, the Bush administration's first treasury secretary, alleged that Vice President Cheney told him that Ronald Reagan proved that deficits do not matter.[59] What Cheney presumably meant was that Reagan had been reelected in a landslide in 1984 despite running large budget deficits.

While strong economic growth brings more revenue to government coffers, deficit reduction generally entails the painful choices of cutting spending or raising taxes. Jack Kemp, a former congressman and the GOP vice presidential nominee in 1996, referred to such choices as root canal economics. The websites of both major party presidential candidates presented their deficit reduction proposals in very general terms. Neither candidate could credibly claim to pay for his proposals, let alone reduce the budget deficit. Majorities of Americans often want tax cuts, government spending on a variety of popular programs, and reductions in the deficit. Contradictory attitudes about the budget deficit might be summed up by an old religious saying that everybody wants to go to heaven, but nobody wants to die.

Table 3.2. The Most Important Issues for Voters in 2000 and 2004

Issues 2000	Total (%)	Bush (%)	Gore (%)	Issues 2004	Total (%)	Bush (%)	Kerry (%)
Economy/jobs	18	37	59	Moral values	22	80	18
Education	15	44	52	Economy/jobs	20	18	80
Social security	14	40	58	Terrorism	19	86	14
Taxes	14	80	17	Iraq	15	26	73
World affairs	12	54	40	Healthcare	8	23	77
Healthcare	8	33	64	Taxes	5	57	43
Medicare/RX drugs	7	39	60	Education	4	26	73

APPLES AND ORANGES:
DID THE ECONOMY MATTER?

It is difficult to assess the importance of the economy in 2004 compared to the 2000 presidential election, because the exit polls gave voters different sets of questions for each election. Table 3.2 lists the issues presented to the voters and the percentage of those who said each was the most important issue for them in 2000 and 2004. Only the category of world affairs was listed under foreign policy in 2000 and just 12 percent selected it as the most important issue. Given the choice of Iraq and terrorism, just over a third of the electorate chose these two foreign policy concerns in 2004. This increase in foreign policy as an important issue is unsurprising given the attacks of September 11, 2001, and the U.S. invasion and subsequent occupation of Iraq.

Voters were not offered a choice of moral values as an issue in the exit poll in 2000, but in 2004, 22 percent of them selected it as the most important issue. Despite the job creation problems the United States encountered during the first Bush administration, the number of voters selecting jobs and the economy as the most important issue increased by only 2 percent between 2000 and 2004. Those selecting jobs/economy as the most important issue supported Kerry by a margin of 80 to 18 percent. The reasons more voters did not vote on economic issues are dealt with in the following section of this chapter, which explores the Kerry campaign's inability to exploit what traditionally would have been a golden opportunity for a candidate challenging an incumbent president.

KERRY'S FAILURE

Kerry was the choice (80 to 18) among the 20 percent of voters who listed the economy as the most important issue, but in the national exit poll of all voters 49 percent trusted Bush on the economy and 45 percent trusted Kerry. Fifty-two percent of voters rated the economy "not good" or "poor," while 47 percent rated it as "good" or "excellent." Neither candidate was trusted by a majority of the electorate to manage the economy. Nationally, 49 percent of voters said they trusted Bush to handle the economy, while 44 percent said they trusted Kerry to do so. The questions were asked separately about each candidate, so voters had the ability to answer affirmatively or negatively about both Bush and Kerry if they so desired. It is also not clear from the polls whether the unwillingness of a majority of voters to accord trust to either candidate was a function of their assessment of these two particular candidates or whether they simply did not believe that a president can do much to impact the economic well-being of Americans. Whatever the case may be in this regard, John Kerry was not going to win the presidency on the basis of economic discontent when more voters trusted Bush to handle the economy.

Even in an economically hard-hit state like Ohio, Kerry did not appear to gain much from the weak state of the economy. Exit polls indicated that 41 percent of voters rated the economy in Ohio as either excellent (3 percent) or good (38 percent). Thirty-six percent of the Ohioans who said their state's economy was not so good voted to reelect George W. Bush. In fact, just 24 percent of Ohio voters selected the economy as the most important issue, just 2 percent above the national average. Youngstown State University Professor John Russo explained that many blue-collar voters do not believe that either Republican or Democratic politicians will do much to alleviate those damaged or threatened by the free-trade orthodoxy embraced by the political elites of both parties. According to Russo, residents of deindustrialized towns "see very little difference between Republicans and Democrats, so they will vote on social issues. There is a sense government officials aren't going to do very much at all."[60]

Kerry's inability to convince voters that he could do better than Bush on the economy was even evident in California, a state he won handily. In California, a Democratic stronghold in the last four presidential elections, 46 percent of voters trusted Kerry to handle the economy. The same percentage trusted Bush on the economy even though Kerry won the state by more than a million votes.

As is usually the case, economic despair and prosperity were spread unevenly around the United States. John Kerry was hampered by the fact that in several battleground states, majorities of voters thought the economy to be in good shape. For example, majorities of the voters in Nevada (74 percent), Arizona (63 percent), Florida (60 percent), and Colorado (56 percent) thought the economy in their state was good or excellent. Despite initial high hopes of winning some of these states, Kerry lost them all. With a majority of voters in all four states trusting Bush to handle terrorism, but not Kerry, it is, in retrospect, hard to imagine how Kerry might have won in these states where voters believed that the economy was doing well.

The state of West Virginia indicates the degree to which economic perceptions may be irrelevant to a state's electorate. Before 2000, West Virginia was one of the most reliable Democratic states in presidential elections. George W. Bush surprised political commentators by winning West Virginia's five electoral votes by a comfortable 6 percent margin in 2000. Democrats were eager to retake the state in 2004. Just 28 percent of West Virginia's voters had a positive evaluation of the state's economy (19 percent below the national average). Still, 57 percent of the state's voters trusted Bush to handle the economy, while just 42 percent said the same of Kerry. Also in West Virginia, 71 percent of households owned a gun (30 percent above the national average) and 48 percent of the electorate was made up of white evangelical or born-again Christians (25 percent above the national average). Fifty-nine percent of voters from gun-owning households, and 66 percent of white voters who described themselves as evangelical or born-again Christians voted for Bush. In West Virginia, at the very least, we can say that a majority of voters had no faith that John Kerry would make things better and that socially conservative voters like gun owners and white evangelical or born-again Christians gave a socially conservative bent to the electorate. In the end, George W. Bush carried the state by a decisive 56 to 43 percent margin.

CONCLUSION

Given the ambiguity and dispute over the poll data on issues, it is impossible to make an absolute judgment about the role of the economy in the outcome of the 2004 presidential election. What is of course obvious is that John Kerry was unable to exploit the weak job creation numbers to oust George W. Bush from the presidency. The strong mobilization of Republican voters meant that Bush bested Kerry in the percentage of voters who trusted him to handle the economy, though neither candidate could gain a majority of voters on that question.

Several factors may explain Kerry's inability to exploit the slow rate of job creation. On the trade issue, Kerry did not have a record that differed from that of George W. Bush. If displaced workers in the Midwest perceived themselves to be victims of free-trade policies, they would have had to apportion the blame equally between John Kerry and George W. Bush.

Many voters may believe, as do many economists, that a president has a limited ability to impact the direction of the national economy. If the voters believe that no president can master the economy, then they may look to other issues such as foreign policy or moral values. It was clear that these were issues that George W. Bush preferred to focus on.

John Kerry did not maintain a steady focus on the economy as a political issue. Even in months with poor job creation numbers, Kerry did not stick to the economy as his main issue.[61] Kerry's inability or unwillingness to focus on a single message may have diluted any positive gains he might have made from exploiting the negative job creation of the first three and half years of Bush's first term.

Of those who showed up at the polls, less than three in ten reported that their own situations had deteriorated while George W. Bush was in office. Whatever their overall opinion of the economy, 32 percent of voters said that their own families' finances were better than four years ago, 28 percent said worse, 39 responded that they were in about the same financial position as they had been four years earlier. In 2004, there was, for the United States, a high voter turnout of about 60 percent of the eligible electorate.[62] It is, of course, impossible to know if the 40 percent who did not vote would have answered differently, though we do know that lower-income people are generally underrepresented in the electorate.

Finally, the Kerry campaign may not have been able to communicate effectively with voters about the economy. Sitting in a diner in Elyria, Ohio, Democratic congressman Sherrod Brown said of a waitress, "She probably makes $18,000 a year and the Democrats don't know how to talk to her. Democrats assume that workers know we're better on the economic issues than the Republicans. . . . We have to talk about all these issues to her, to make crystal clear which side we're on. If we don't, she'll vote on abortion and the guys in the plants will vote their guns."[63]

NOTES

1. On the 2002 elections, see Gary C. Jacobson, "Terror, Terrain, and Turnout," *Political Science Quarterly*, 188: 3 (2003), 1–22. Also see, Donald Beachler, "Ordinary Events and Extraordinary Times: The 2002 Congressional Elections," in Jon Kraus, Kevin J. McMahon, David M. Rankin, eds., *Transformed By Crisis: The Presidency of George W. Bush and American Politics* (New York: Palgrave Macmillan, 2004).
2. James E. Campbell and James C. Garand, eds., *Before the Vote: Forecasting American National Elections* (Thousand Oaks, CA: Sage, 2000).
3. For a discussion of Gore's loss despite the favorable economic conditions in 2000, see James E. Campbell, "The 2000 Presidential Election of George W. Bush: The Difficult Birth of a Presidency," in Kraus, McMahon, and Rankin, eds. *Transformed by Crisis*.
4. Charles Lindblom, *Politics and Markets: The World's Political Economic Systems* (New York: Harper Collins, 1980).
5. *World Almanac and Book of Facts, 2004*.
6. Ira Katznelson, Mark Kesselman, and Alan Draper, *The Politics of Power: A Critical Introduction to American Government*, Fourth edition (New York: Wadsworth, 2002).
7. Andrew Hacker, *Money: Who Has How Much and Why* (New York: Scribner, 1997).
8. Ibid.
9. The literature on American Exceptionalism is vast. For one particularly good explanatory essay, see Martin Shefter, "Trade Unions and Political Machines: The Organization and Disorganization of the Working Class in the 19th Century," in Martin Shefter, ed.,

Political Parties and the State: The American Historical Experience (Princeton, NJ: Princeton University Press, 1993).

10. "Income Stable, Poverty Up, Numbers of Americans Without Health Insurance Rise," Press Release, U.S. Census Bureau, August 26, 2004.

11. The infant mortality rate is presented annually in the *World Almanac and Book of Facts*. The data presented here is from the 2004 edition.

12. Theda Skocpol, *Boomerang: Health Care Reform and the Turn against Government* (New York: W.W. Norton, 1997).

13. Robin Toner, "Biggest Divide: Maybe It's Health Care," *The New York Times*, May 14, 2004, A18.

14. David E. Rosenbaum, "Debate on Malpractice Looms for Senate," *The New York Times*, December 20, 2004.

15. Toner, "Biggest Divide, Maybe It's Health Care."

16. Paul Krugman, "Medical Class Warfare," *The New York Times*, July 16, 2004.

17. John B. Judis and Ruy Texeira, "Movement Interruptus," *The American Prospect*, 16: 1 (2004).

18. The 15 percent figure was derived by adding the percentage of those who answered health care and those who listed Medicare and prescription drugs. www.cnn.com/Election2000/epolls.US.P000.html

19. Exit poll numbers are available at www.cnn.us.com/US/2004/pages/results/president

20. www.cnn.com/Election/2000/edpolls/us?P000.html

21. David Leonhart, "Bush's Record on Jobs: Risking Comparison to a Republican Ghost," *The New York Times*, July 3, 2003.

22. The economic aspects of presidential elections are discussed in James E. Campbell, *The American Campaign: U.S. Presidential Campaigns and the National Vote* (College Station: Texas A & M University Press, 2000). See chapter 6.

23. Milton C. Cummings, Jr., "Political Change Since the New Deal: The 1992 Presidential Election in Historical Perspective," in Harvey L. Schantz, ed., *American Presidential Elections: Process, Policy and Political Change* (Albany: State University of New York Press, 1996).

24. On 1996 and presidential elections and economics generally, see Walter Dean Burnham, "Bill Clinton: Riding the Tiger," in Gerald M. Pomper, ed., *The Election of 1996: Reports and Interpretations* (Chatham, NJ: Chatham House Publishers, 1997).

25. Peronet Despeignes, "Weak Job Picture in Crucial States May Cost Bush," *USA Today*, July 20, 2004.

26. John Byczkowski, "Ohio Joblessness Rose During June," *Cincinnati Enquirer*, July 17, 2004.

27. *The New York Times*, 2000 Survey.

28. *The New York Times*, July 25, 9.

29. For a well-articulated version of this concept, see Robert Reich, *The Work of Nations: Preparing Ourselves for 21st Century Capitalism* (New York: Vintage, 1995).

30. Dick Polman, "Bush's Steel Tariff is an Early Bit of Politicking," *The Philadelphia Inquirer*, March 13, 2002.

31. www.georgewbush.com

32. www.johnkerry.com

33. Elizabeth Becker, "A Senator Once Isolated on Trade Now Finds a Chorus," *The New York Times*, June 1, 2004, A12.

34. Ibid.

35. Sabrina Eaton, "The Key to the State's Votes is the Economy," *Cleveland Plain Dealer*, March 21, 2004.

36. Table, "The Jobs Picture," *The New York Times*, August 15, 2004.

37. Louis Uchitelle, "Healthy Growth of 248,000 Jobs Reported in May," *The New York Times*, June 5, 2004, A1.

38. "Cursed by Lagging Perceptions," *The Economist*, June 12, 2004, 27.

39. www.Rassmussenreports.com, June 16, 2004.

40. Jonathan Weisman, "Economy Provides No Boost for Bush," *Washington Post*, June 10, 2004, A1.

41. Edmund L. Andrews, "A Growing Force of Nonworkers," *The New York Times*, July 18, 2004.

42. Ibid.

43. Stephen S. Roach, "More Jobs, Worse Work," *The New York Times*, July 22, 2004, A21.

44. David Leonhardt, "Slow Job Growth Raises Concerns on U.S. Economy," *The New York Times*, August 7, 2004.

45. David Broder, "SEIU Chief Says the Democrats Lack Fresh Ideas," www.washingtonpost.com, July 27, 2004.

46. Eduardo Porter, "Hourly Pay in U.S. Not Keeping Pace with Price Rises," *The New York Times*, July 18, 2004, 21.

47. Tom DeLuca, "Joe the Bookie and the Class Gap in Voting," *American Demographics* (November 1998).

48. Jan Leighley and Jonathan Nagler, "Socio-economic Class Bias in Turnout," *American Political Science Review* 86 (1992), 725–736.

49. Robin Toner, "Kerry Opens Two Week Drive on the Economy," *The New York Times*, June 14, 2004.

50. David Leonhardt, "The Slump Has Ended, But Not the Gloom," *The New York Times*, July 4, 2004, Section 4, 1.

51. Ibid.

52. See the CTJ website at www.ctj.org

53. Nedra Pickler, "Kerry Would Increase the Child Care Tax Credit," *Associated Press*, June 16, 2004.

54. www.johnkerry.com

55. CNN 2000 poll, op. cit.

56. For the deficit politics of the first year of the Reagan administration, see William Greider, *The Education of David Stockman and Other Americans* (New York: Dutton, 1982).

57. "The Budget and Economic Outlook," January 2004, www.cbo.gov

58. *The Economist*, July 10, 2004.

59. Ron Suskind, *The Price of Loyalty: The Education of Paul O'Neill* (New York: Simon and Schuster, 2004).

60. "The View from Ohio: The Politics of Resentment," *Manufacturing News*, 21: 11 (2004), 9.

61. Robin Toner, "Kerry in Midwest Tour, Laments Lost Jobs," *The New York Times*, July 3, 2004.

62. Mark Danner, "How Bush Really Won," *The New York Review of Books*, January 5, 2004. Available at www.markdanner.com

63. Harold Meyerson, "Buckeye Blues," *The American Prospect*, 15: 10 (2004), 14.

4

REAGAN'S POLITICAL HEIR

George W. Bush, Values, and the War on Terror

John Kenneth White

In many respects, George W. Bush bears more of a political resemblance to Ronald Reagan than he does to his own father. And to win reelection in 2004, President Bush leaned on the grand coalition Reagan formed nearly twenty-five years ago. Back in 1979, the Reagan coalition was emerging as a powerful and potent force. Signs of its birth were already apparent in the 1978 midterm elections when Republicans added sixteen seats in the House and three in the Senate. Jimmy Carter—a Democrat who had been elected president in 1976 thanks to the Watergate scandal—was proving to be an ineffectual leader. While Carter had not lost his capacity for truth-telling, Americans wanted something more. In 1978, 70 percent believed "the government cannot be regularly trusted to do what is right"; 74 percent said "government is run for a few big interests"; and 79 percent thought "government wastes a lot of tax dollars."[1] Republicans took advantage of this hostility by advocating the "Kemp–Roth" tax plan—a massive cut in federal taxes they claimed would *add* revenues to the federal coffers. Republicans were thinking anew and, in Abraham Lincoln's phrase, were "disenthralling themselves" from their long-standing balance-the-budget dogma. Supply-side economics was becoming an important chapter in the new Republican gospel.

Republican rethinking about government was cheered by a disillusioned electorate. By 1979, a majority began to seriously question whether the present was better than their past and, more ominously, whether the future would hold the promise of better days ahead.[2] A majority also came to believe that "important national problems such as energy shortages, inflation, and crime could not be solved through traditional American politics."[3] And this was *before* the Iranian hostage crisis sharpened the image of Jimmy Carter as a tepid commander-in-chief with a country that was seriously off on the wrong track.

American dismay with life outside their homes was coupled by a sense that something was amiss inside them as well. Ronald Reagan's pollster, Richard Wirthlin, found 68 percent agreed with the statement that "families are weaker now than they were several years ago." Of these, 45 percent blamed a lowering of parental standards and widespread permissiveness; another 31 percent cited two-parent working families.[4] Other data compiled by Wirthlin found a widespread sense of personal anomie:

- Two of three Americans agreed that "everything changes so quickly these days that I often have trouble deciding which are the right rules to follow."
- A majority believed we were "better off in the old days when everyone knew just how they were expected to act."
- Seventy-one percent felt "many things our parents stood for are going to ruin right before our eyes."
- Nearly eight-in-ten believed "what is lacking in the world today is the old kind of friendship that lasted for a lifetime."
- One-in-two said they felt "left out of things going on around me."[5]

Enter Ronald Reagan. In many ways, Reagan was the quintessential man of the 1950s. He resembled the spiffily dressed salesmen of that era: nice pressed suit, perfectly knotted tie, a white handkerchief in the breast pocket, and shoes spit-polished and shined to reflect his sunny optimism. Reagan had a certain "father knows best" quality, and his personality seemed drawn from the popular father figures of television's golden age: Ozzie Nelson (*The Adventures of Ozzie and Harriet*), Ward Cleaver (*Leave It to Beaver*), and Jim Anderson (*Father Knows Best*). Pollster Wirthlin found that Reagan's authoritative, father-like persona appealed to voters. In particular, Reagan supporters regretted the loss of deeply cherished values, especially those associated with the business ethic of hard work and high yield. Those with a higher sense of service to country, a lower support of the welfare state, a greater desire to decrease the role of government, and a lower sense of pacifism, strongly favored Reagan over Carter.[6]

Thus, Ronald Reagan and his campaign team launched what became known as the "strategy of values."[7] Reagan proclaimed his party was "ready to build a new consensus with all those across the land who share a community of values embodied in these words: family, work, neighborhood, peace, and freedom."[8] From these values sprang others that formed the centrality of Reagan's appeal: self-esteem, patriotism, self-realization, and religiosity. This "values strategy" had two objectives: (1) securing Reagan's victories in 1980 and 1984, and (2) establishing a framework for governance. Accomplishing these objectives would not be easy. A June 1980 Wirthlin poll found 51 percent of voters called themselves Democrats, 30 percent were Republicans, and 19 percent were independents.[9] To win, Reagan would have to get overwhelming Republican support, attract large numbers of independents, and procure a substantial number of Democrats. Wirthlin warned that unseating Carter "will be extremely difficult, even unlikely."[10]

Despite the odds, the values strategy worked. Reagan won and in so doing assembled a new coalition that included southern whites, blue-collar ethnics, bornagain Christians, Roman Catholics, and westerners. Of these, southern whites, bluecollars, and Catholics once formed the backbone of the Democratic New Deal–era majority built by Franklin D. Roosevelt. All were won over by Reagan's antigovernment message. For years, Reagan had preached a message of government restraint. In 1976, for example, he warned: "Thousands of towns and neighborhoods have seen their peace disturbed by bureaucrats and social planners through busing, questionable education programs, and attacks on family unity."[11] Four years later, Reagan made the same antigovernment criticisms: "Government has grown too wasteful, too unresponsive, too uncaring to people and their problems."[12] As president, Reagan's message did not waver. In his 1981 Inaugural Address, he famously declared: "Government is not the solution to our problems. Government is the problem."[13] Speaking before a joint session of Congress during his frenetic first one hundred days in office, Reagan told legislators, "We can no longer afford things simply because we think of them."[14] Reagan wanted government programs replaced by initiatives from religious groups, community and professional organizations, and volunteer groups. In Reagan's view, these "mediating institutions" had been supplanted by "puzzle palaces on the Potomac" that were engaged in an ongoing assault on prevailing local community values.

The Reagan Revolution resulted in a wholesale shift in public thinking. In 1936, at the height of the New Deal, pollster George Gallup found 56 percent favoring a concentration of power in the federal government; 44 percent wanted authority centered in the states.[15] By 1981, the figures were reversed: 64 percent wanted power concentrated in the state governments; 36 percent preferred more federal control.[16]

Anticommunism was another key ingredient of Ronald Reagan's appeal. Throughout his acting and political careers, Reagan professed a profound antipathy toward communism. As he once told an interviewer: "Coming out of the cage of the

Army [after World War II] . . . a series of hard-nosed happenings began to change my whole view of American dangers. Most of them tied in directly with my own bailiwick of acting. . . . From being an active (though unconscious) partisan in what now and then turned out to be communist causes, I little by little became disillusioned or perhaps, in my case, I should say reawakened."[17] By 1964, this former Democrat-turned-Republican was on the mashed-potato circuit campaigning for Barry Goldwater. Reagan used as his text a talk he had given for years to employees of General Electric, sponsor of the television program he hosted, *Death Valley Days*. In it, he railed against communists and Democrats, whom he believed were too supine in the face of the Soviet threat: "The specter our well-meaning liberal friends refuse to face is that their policy of accommodation is appeasement, and appeasement does not give you a choice between peace and war, only between fight and surrender."[18]

In his never-give-up fight against communism, Reagan stressed the importance of Judeo-Christian values to combat it. He told television interviewer David Frost in 1968 that Jesus Christ was the historical figure he most admired.[19] Eight years later, while challenging Gerald R. Ford for the Republican presidential nomination, Reagan inserted a section into the Republican platform titled "Morality in Foreign Policy," which read: "Honestly, openly, and with firm conviction, we shall go forward as a united people to forge a lasting peace in the world based upon our deep belief in the rights of man, the rule of law, and guidance by the hand of God."[20] In a memorable 1983 address, Reagan damned the Soviet Union as an "evil empire," saying it was "the focus of evil in the modern world."[21]

Reagan's words resonated: in 1983, 73 percent said that the "real problem with communism is that it threatens our religious and moral values."[22] Christian fundamentalists vigorously agreed with these sentiments and became strong Reagan backers. In 1980, the Moral Majority bought newspaper advertisements that read: "We cannot afford to be number two in defense! But, sadly enough, that's where we are today. Number two. And fading!"[23] Reagan received 61 percent support from white evangelicals that year; in 1984, that figure increased to 81 percent. George H. W. Bush got 81 percent of the born-again vote in 1988, and a less impressive (but still substantial) 61 percent backing in his failed 1992 reelection effort.

Catholics, too, were inspired by Reagan's anticommunist rhetoric. For decades, the Roman Catholic hierarchy had likened communism to self-avowed atheism. In 1978, that struggle culminated with the election of the Cardinal of Krakow, Karol Jozef Wojtyla, to the papacy. Pope John Paul II had spent decades tormenting the communist regime in his native Poland. Like him, many American Catholics stood shoulder-to-shoulder with their imprisoned eastern European cousins behind the Iron Curtain. Patrick J. Buchanan, a Catholic high school student during the late

1940s, recalled one especially memorable incident:

> When the Communist regime in Budapest announced in 1948 the coming
> trial for treason of Josef Cardinal Mindszenty, the Primate of Hungary who
> had resisted both the Nazis and the communists, there was enormous
> anguish. Cardinal Mindszenty was constantly in the prayers of the nuns and
> the school children, and when the newspapers displayed, months later, the
> shocking picture of the drugged and broken prelate as he "confessed" at one
> of Stalin's ugliest "show trials," the Catholic world was stunned. We did not
> need any classroom discussion about Marxism to recognize the evil of com-
> munism; it was written all over the tortured face of the Catholic priest.[24]

Ronald Reagan's antigovernment, antitax, and anticommunist messages merged
to form a powerful elixir. A new coalition was being born, but how long would it last?
Before Reagan took office, Richard Wirthlin advised: "Certainly, the people and the
pundits will start asking whether the Reagan administration constitutes a juncture in
American history when the role of the federal government was changed and a 'new
beginning' was commenced along the lines of your approach to governance."[25] The
answer to Wirthlin's question was found in the election returns. In 1980, Reagan
received 51 percent of the popular vote and 489 electoral votes. By 1984, the Reagan
coalition had become a political behemoth: Reagan won 59 percent of the ballots and
an astounding 525 electoral votes. Four years later, George H. W. Bush became the
first vice president since Martin Van Buren to ascend directly to the presidency—in
essence, creating a third Reagan term. Thus, the Reagan coalition won three straight
presidential victories—something that had not been done since Franklin Roosevelt's
back-to-back wins in 1932, 1936, and 1940. This was an extraordinary achievement,
especially considering that Roosevelt's third term was won thanks to the onset of
World War II.

The Reagan coalition was certainly a mixed lot. John Judis writes that it
"consisted of seemingly incompatible constituencies—pro-choice suburbanites from
New Jersey alongside small-town fundamentalists from Alabama, anti-communist
Chinese-Americans from California alongside nativist white North Carolinians."[26] As
table 4.1 shows, southern whites, Catholics, and high school graduates were strong
Reagan–Bush backers. Other groups, including westerners, first-time voters, rural voters, and men were being added to the Republican presidential roundup. Middle-
income voters, who had felt the pangs of inflation and were hostile to new taxes, also
voted Republican. White Protestants, who had been in the GOP tent since the 1930s,
remained so. While Republicans and conservatives were overwhelmingly loyal, many
independents and Democrats were attracted to the Republican ticket. Independents

Table 4.1. The Reagan Coalition, 1980–1988 (in percentages)

Group	Reagan Vote 1980	Reagan Vote 1984	Bush Vote 1988
Southern whites	61	71	67
Catholics	50	54	52
White Protestants	63	72	66
Westerners	53	61	52
Rural areas	55	67	55
Republicans	86	92	91
Independents	55	63	55
Conservatives	73	82	80
First-time voters	N/A	61	51
High school graduate	51	60	50
Men	55	62	57
Income $30,000–$49,999	59	59	56

Source: Marjorie Connelly, "Portrait of the Electorate," *New York Times*, November 10, 1996, 28. Data is based upon the CBS News/*New York Times* 1980, 1984, and 1988 exit polls.

gave both Reagan and Bush solid majorities, while one-in-four Democrats voted for Reagan in 1980 and 1984, and one-in-five backed Bush in 1988.[27]

GEORGE W. BUSH AND REAGAN: A SPIRITUAL CONNECTION

As noted above, George W. Bush has much in common with Ronald Reagan. Like Reagan, the younger Bush emphasizes the importance of Judeo-Christian values. For example, when asked during a presidential debate to name his favorite philosopher, Bush took his GOP opponents and questioners aback when he replied, "Christ, because he changed my heart."[28] As president, Bush has frequently returned to religious themes. A July 4, 2001, speech in Philadelphia is typical: "Without churches and charities, many of our citizens who have lost hope would be left to their own struggles and their own fate. And as I well know, they are not the only ones whose lives can be changed and uplifted by the influence of faith in God."[29] This is quite unlike Bush's father, who rarely invoked the Almighty, conforming to the Northeast Yankee tradition of "not wearing your religion on your sleeve."

Of course, there were differences. Unlike Reagan, Bush wanted a more active federal government in the nation's domestic life. During the 2000 campaign, he called for an initial tripling of government funding for a values-based school curricula that promoted character formation, more government money for internet filters at schools and public libraries, and government support for several faith-based programs. Bush's support for a constitutional amendment banning gay marriage and his eagerness to embrace the Christian Right's social agenda differs from Reagan who accepted the support of the Christian Right but hardly ever used his authority to advocate its social agenda. Bush, on the other hand, has established the Office of Faith-Based Initiatives in the White House, something Reagan would have probably opposed since he believed that charity was best left in private, nongovernmental hands.

Still, the similarities between Reagan and the younger Bush were remarkable. Like Reagan, Bush acknowledged during his 2000 presidential campaign that the sexual license of the go-go 1960s needed to be replaced with the traditional family values often associated with the sedate 1950s. In a speech that could have easily been given by Reagan, Bush declared:

> The real problem comes, not when children challenge the rules, but when adults won't defend the rules. And for about three decades, many American schools surrendered this role. Values were "clarified," not taught. Students were given moral puzzles, not moral guidance. But morality is not a cafeteria of personal choices—with every choice equally right and equally arbitrary, like picking a flavor of ice cream. We do not shape our own morality. It is morality that shapes our lives.[30]

By explicitly rejecting the sexual freedom during the "Make Love, Not War" era, Bush offered himself as a Reagan-like father figure—someone who, unlike the morally deficient Bill Clinton, would set an example that complemented his values rhetoric. Thus, Bush promised to "return the highest standards of honor to the highest office in the land," saying this was "a charge I plan to keep."[31] This promise found many takers: three-quarters thought Bush had high personal and moral standards, and 70 percent said he shared the moral values they tried to live by.[32] By a five-to-one margin, Bush was viewed as having higher moral standards than Clinton, and an astounding 81 percent of Republicans cited his moral character as a "very important" reason for backing him.[33] Overall, 43 percent said they would be more likely to support Bush over Democrat Al Gore because he would bring morality and ethics back to the White House.[34]

Reagan and Bush's values strategies were complemented by their anti-tax messages. Like Reagan, George W. Bush has a powerful aversion to taxes, and Bush had won the overwhelming support of voters who considered tax cuts a priority for the new budget surplus. In 2001, he won quick congressional approval of a $1.2 trillion, eleven-year tax cut that was more comprehensive than the Reagan tax cuts of 1981. Upon signing the bill, a proud Bush declared: "Tax relief is the first achievement produced by the new tone in Washington, and it was produced in record time."[35] Unlike Reagan—especially during his gubernatorial years—Bush was uncompromising when it came to taxes. Undoubtedly, he recalled the difficulties his father faced after breaking his infamous "read my lips, no new taxes" pledge. For example, at an early stage in the 2001 tax debate, Bush stubbornly resisted the urge to compromise with congressional Democrats, telling White House director of legislative affairs Nick Calio: "Nicky, we will not negotiate with ourselves, ever."[36] In 2003, Bush got a Republican-controlled Congress to pass an unprecedented second round of tax cuts totaling $350 billion, even though he had begun a long and expensive war in Iraq.

But even as Bush was keeping his Republican base happy, the political utility of tax cuts was waning. According to a 2003 Harris poll, a mere 8 percent said they would benefit "a lot" from a tax cut; 51 percent answered "only a little"; and 34 percent said "not at all."[37] A *Los Angeles Times* survey found that half believed reducing the federal deficit (which had ballooned under Bush) would be the most effective method of stimulating the economy; only 37 percent believed tax cuts were more helpful.[38] Americans, it seemed, wanted government to balance its budgets (a message that formed the core of independent Ross Perot's third-party candidacy in 1992). At the same time, they also wanted government to regulate the excesses of the marketplace. These included reigning in the practices that created the Enron, Adelphia, and other corporate scandals that became news headlines in 2002. One poll found 75 percent having less confidence in the stock market thanks to the Enron scandal; 74 percent were less confident in corporate America; 53 percent were less confident in the Republicans in Congress; and 48 percent were less confident in the Bush administration—all courtesy of Enron.[39]

The terrorist attacks of September 11, 2001, pushed the headlines of corporate greed off the front pages and gave George W. Bush and the Republicans a renewed sense of purpose. It was about time. Ever since the Cold War ended with a whimper on December 25, 1991, the day Mikhail Gorbachev gave up his post as president of the Soviet Union, Republicans had struggled in presidential politics. Nationalist Republicans—tough-minded warriors ("peace through strength" was their motto) and tenacious summit negotiators (Reagan's Soviet mantra was "trust, but verify")—received a much-needed boost.

Prior to the September 11 attacks, foreign policy had receded as a factor in presidential elections. Bill Clinton had been elected twice without much public attention to foreign policy, and George W. Bush likely benefited from its absence as an issue.[40] If foreign policy had been more prominent in 2000, Al Gore may have won, since his expertise was vastly more extensive than that of Texas's governor.[41] According to the 2000 exit poll, 35 percent of voters felt Vice President Gore was better suited to handle a potential world crisis; 27 percent believed Governor Bush was the best candidate to handle such a crisis. Another 29 percent agreed both candidates were up to the challenge. But 47 percent of voters also felt that the U.S. military under Clinton had become weaker, and these voters supported Bush 72 percent to 25 percent over Gore. Displaying electoral shades of Reagan, of the 14 percent who felt that strong leadership mattered the most in a candidate, Bush had a 30-point advantage over Gore.

Less than a year after a contentious 2000 election, Osama bin Laden's brazen attacks put foreign policy uppermost among the public's concerns. And Bush's rhetoric kept it there. Using the earthy language of the Wild West, Bush initially declared that he wanted al Qaeda's mastermind "dead or alive."[42] But Bush did more than make Osama bin Laden the most wanted man in the world. He drew a bright line between the freedom-loving West and the Mideast terrorists. Standing before a joint session of Congress shortly after the September 11 attacks, Bush declared: "Every nation, in every region, now has a decision to make. Either you are with us, or you are with the terrorists."[43] In numerous speeches, he consistently portrayed the U.S. cause as one that would enhance the values of freedom, religious tolerance, and a belief in progress, while castigating the terrorists as "evil-doers"—words reminiscent of Reagan's infamous "evil empire" speech. As Bush ominously declared, "The terrorists' directive commands them to kill Christians and Jews, to kill all Americans, and make no distinctions among military and civilians, including women and children."[44]

But the war on terror—important as it is—hardly compares to the Cold War. The Cold War touched nearly all nation-states; it penetrated all aspects of social and economic life; it was costly; and it involved widespread public sacrifices. The war on terror involves shadowy organizations that transcend nation-states; it does not involve broad-based public sacrifice (there is no draft); and it has not permeated into the social and cultural fabric. Three years after the September 11 attacks, a Zogby International poll finds only 25 percent are anxious about a terrorist strike on U.S. soil. Instead of worrying about terrorism, 40 percent fret about being able to pay their bills; 37 percent are concerned about an uncertain economy; 18 percent stay awake trying to find a job; and 38 percent are troubled by a deterioration of moral values.[45]

While the Iraq War has consumed much of the public debate, a growing number of Americans do not see a link between it and the war on terror. By late 2003, only 46 percent saw Iraq as a major part of the war on terror; 48 percent said it was either a minor part of the war on terror or separate from it.[46] One year later, Americans were evenly split as to whether Bush's decision to invade Iraq had been a mistake: 47 percent said yes; 51 percent, no.[47]

A DIMINISHED COALITION

A few months before the November 2004 election, Republican National Chairman Ed Gillespie declared, "The party of George W. Bush is very much the party of Ronald Reagan."[48] In some ways, George W. Bush's victory over John F. Kerry demonstrates the continued utility of the Reagan coalition. Most of the top groups supporting Bush were ones that once backed Ronald Reagan and George H. W. Bush (see table 4.2).

Especially noteworthy was the decisive support Bush received from those aged thirty-five to forty-nine. These voters constituted the Reagan generation, those born between the years 1955 and 1969, whose first presidential votes were cast between 1976 and 1988. According to a study by Mason–Dixon Polling and Research, the Reagan generation was instrumental to Bush's margin of victory (see table 4.3). These voters cast solid majorities for Bush, while those in all other age groups supported Kerry. Young voters, in particular, were strongly pro-Democratic. According to a Zogby International post-election poll, 62 percent of those aged eighteen to twenty-four backed Kerry. An equal percentage of first-time voters also voted for Kerry.[49] Political

Table 4.2. The Reagan Coalition Redux: 2004 Bush Strengths in Rank Order

Group	Bush Percentage
Republicans	91
Very conservative	89
Conservative	84
Born-again	65
Attend church daily	64
Rural	64
Investor class	61
Attend church once a week	60
Protestant	60
White	59
Married	58
With children under 17 years of age	57
Income of $75,000 or more	56
Age 30–49 years old	56
Less than high school	56
Age 35–54 years old	55
Some college	55
Private employee	54
Men	53

Source: Zogby International, post-election poll, November 3–5, 2004.

Table 4.3. The Reagan Generation vs. All Other Age Groups (in percentages)*

State	Reagan Generation Vote for Bush	Reagan Generation Vote for Kerry	All Other Age Groups Vote for Bush	All Other Age Groups Vote for Kerry
Florida	56	43	49	50
Ohio	59	40	48	51
Iowa	56	43	48	51
Nevada	56	43	49	50
New Mexico	54	45	48	51

Source: Jonathan Pontell and J. Brad Coker, "The Invisible Generation Elects a President," *The Polling Report*, November 29, 2004, 7.

Note:* The Reagan Generation refers to ages 35–49 years old.

scientists believe new voters hold the nation's political future in their hands. Once new voters become committed to a party—a process that occurs fairly quickly—they become, in the phrase used by political scientist V. O. Key, "stand-patters."[50] Rarely do voting habits become altered—a fact of party life that has been reinforced by today's bitter red vs. blue partisanship. The continuance of support from first-time Reagan voters was good news for Bush. But the future suggests that the Democrats might benefit from the first-time Kerry voters.

Some believe that the Reagan/Bush coalition may temper the support it has lost from young and first-time voters by the emergence of a growing investor class. According to a Zogby International post-election poll, 26 percent say they personally own stock on the New York Stock Exchange or NASDAQ, while another 44 percent say they own a 401K or some other pension plan. When all respondents are asked if they considered themselves to be a member of the "investor class," 27 percent answered yes. And of these, 61 percent voted for Bush; 37 percent backed Kerry.[51] Some believe that as young voters enter the workforce and become vested in the country's economic markets, their party preferences will shift to the Republicans. Only time will tell, though history suggests otherwise.

There can be no doubt that it was the war on terror that clinched Bush's reelection. During the fall campaign, Vice President Dick Cheney scared voters by darkly warning that if they made the "wrong choice"—that is, voting for John Kerry—then, "the danger is that we'll get hit again [by terrorists] and we'll be hit in a way that will be more devastating."[52] Former house speaker Newt Gingrich hailed Cheney's bluntness, saying, "Dick Cheney has understated the difference in danger to the United States between a Bush and a Kerry presidency."[53] Cheney's remarks were among the most dire offered since 1964, when Lyndon B. Johnson ran television advertisements featuring a nuclear bomb exploding and implied that Barry Goldwater would lead the country into a nuclear exchange with the Soviet Union. Reagan also used the fear theme, most famously in his campaign's 1984 "Bear in the Woods" commercial. In 2004, the Bush–Cheney campaign revived it once again with a TV spot showing a pack of wolves on the verge of attack. As the narrator told viewers:

> In an increasingly dangerous world. . . . Even after the first terrorist attack on America. . . . John Kerry and the liberals in Congress voted to slash America's intelligence operations. By six billion dollars. . . . Cuts so deep they would have weakened America's defenses. And weakness attracts those who are waiting to do America harm.

In truth, the Swift Boat Veterans—with their own ads attacking Kerry's medal-winning service in the Vietnam War—and the Democratic candidate himself aided the Bush–Cheney campaign in this regard. As Mark Danner writes, Kerry:

> did not prove himself a very creative or resourceful candidate, and the Bush campaign was ruthless and brilliant in seizing on his missteps—his mention of a "global test" for United States intervention abroad, for example, and his unfortunate statement that "I actually voted for the $87 billion before I voted against it"—and using them to color in vivid tones the picture they wanted to paint of the senator. Kerry gave them a good deal of help, particularly by focusing on Vietnam, and attempting to make his heroic service as a naval officer there a central part of his campaign while avoiding discussion of his more controversial leadership in the antiwar movement after he returned.[54]

Whether Kerry's assistance was crucial or not, the Bush–Cheney exploitation of fear worked. According to the 2004 exit polls, 19 percent cited terrorism as the most important issue and of these, 86 percent supported Bush. Moreover, a solid majority (54 percent) believed the nation was safer than it had been in 2000, and 79 percent of these voters backed Bush. Overall, 58 percent said they trusted Bush to handle terrorism; only 40 percent trusted Kerry.[55]

While less than a majority of voters (46 percent) believed that the Iraq War had made the United States more secure, these voters supported Bush by an 80-point margin. And 55 percent believed that the Iraq War was part of the war on terrorism, supporting Bush at 81 percent compared with 18 percent for Kerry. Overall, a narrow 51 percent majority approved of the decision to go to war in Iraq, and these voters overwhelmingly voted to reelect the current commander-in-chief. Seventy-one percent of voters were worried about terrorism, and these voters also supported Bush over

Kerry. Of the 19 percent who considered terrorism the second most important issue of the election, following moral values, Bush beat Kerry by 62 points. Bush voters believed strong leadership and a clear stand on issues were the most important qualities in a president, especially during a time of war and terror.

Married women were also especially receptive to Bush's claim that he could keep them and their families safe. In 2004, women gave Kerry a mere 3-point advantage over Bush, whereas in 2000, Al Gore had an 11-point lead. Decades before, Richard Nixon noted the power of fear in political campaigns, saying: "People react to fear, not love. They don't teach that in Sunday school, but it's true."[56] The results of the 2004 election verified the truth behind Nixon's long-ago assertion.

A TWENTY-FIRST-CENTURY
COALITION STRUGGLES TO BE BORN

Despite George W. Bush's win, the Reagan coalition is not nearly as potent as it once was. Contrast George W. Bush's vote in 2004 with the support his father received sixteen years earlier. While the figures are similar, the power of the Reagan coalition translated Bush Sr.'s 53 percent of the popular vote into 426 electoral votes thanks to victories in 40 states. This year, Bush's 51 percent garnered him just 286 electoral votes and 30 states. Bush's puny electoral vote margin ranks among the smallest in history—close to his 271 votes in 2000, Woodrow Wilson's 277 votes in 1916, and Jimmy Carter's 297 votes in 1976. Unlike the comprehensive Reagan and George H. W. Bush victories, the 2004 contest came down to a single state: Ohio. If Ohio's twenty electoral votes had switched from Bush to Kerry, then the Democrat would have become president-elect, and Republicans would be singing the post election blues.

A principal reason the Reagan coalition is losing its clout is that the United States is experiencing profound demographic and societal transformations—changes that will only accelerate in the years ahead. Take family life. Newly released Census Bureau figures show that since 1970, the percentage of households containing five or more people has fallen by half—dropping from 21 to 10 percent.[57] According to Barbara Whitehead, codirector of the National Marriage Project at Rutgers University: "It's clear from [the new Census figures] that compared to the middle of the 20th century, marriage is not nearly a universal status of adulthood. There is," she adds, "much more diversity in living arrangements."[58] The census data clearly show that the father-knows-best era of half a century ago is giving way to one that is perhaps best represented by *Bridget Jones*, a 2001 movie that depicted a single and somewhat youngish heroine. A prolonged single life is certainly a sign of the times. According to the Census Bureau, the number of people living alone has increased from 17 percent in 1970 to 26 percent in 2003.[59] But when couples do decide to merge, marriage is not always the option. From 1960 to 2000, the number of unmarried couples grew tenfold, from fewer than 500,000 to 5,500,000.[60] Simply put, American life today consists of every conceivable household arrangement.

Nonwhites are also writing a new and significant chapter in the twenty-first century story. In the old colonial city of Boston, whites are a minority—a historic first.[61] By 2050, it is estimated that whites will be a minority everywhere.[62] Tiger Woods, whose father is black and mother is Thai, is emblematic of the changing times. In 1997, Woods simultaneously became the first African American and the first Asian American to win the Masters golf tournament. In the Bush family, George P. Bush—son of Florida governor Jeb Bush and his Mexican-born wife, Columba— symbolizes the increased Hispanic influence in U.S. society. According to the 2000 U.S. Census, the Hispanic population grew 58 percent from 1990 to 35.3 million. Hispanics now rival blacks as the nation's most numerous minority.[63]

These stories are portents of even greater changes to come. In 1998 alone, there were 1.3 million intermarriages among whites, Asians, and Hispanics.[64] Pollster John Zogby has described the emerging "Tiger Woods Effect." According to Zogby, the 1860 Census contained only three racial categories: black, white, and "quadroon"— a slave term that described someone of mixed heritage who was at least one-fourth black.[65] In 2000, the census contained nineteen racial categories—including white, black, African American or Negro, American Indian or Alaska Native, Mexican, Mexican American, Chicano, Puerto Rican, Cuban, other Spanish/Hispanic/Latino, Asian Indian, Chinese, Filipino, Japanese, Korean, Vietnamese, other Asian, Native Hawaiian, Guamanian or Chamorro, Samoan, and other Pacific Islander. These categories reflect a melding of many racial cultures. Today, 2.4 percent categorize themselves as multiracial; among children under the age of eighteen, 4.2 percent.[66] As interracial marriages become more commonplace, they are more frequently accepted. According to recent surveys, 75 percent say marriage between blacks and whites is acceptable; among teenagers, the figure is an all-time high of 91 percent.[67]

Changes in skin tone have been accompanied by the growth of non-Christian religious communities. Chief among these are Islam, Hinduism, and Buddhism. Islam is the eighth largest denomination in the United States—bigger than the Episcopal Church, the Presbyterian Church U.S.A., the United Church of Christ, and the Assemblies of God.[68] Currently, there are between 1.5 million and 3.4 million American Muslims.[69] Thanks to an influx of immigrants from Iran, Pakistan, Yemen, Lebanon, and Afghanistan—due to the domestic turmoil that has racked those nations—Muslims are becoming a more visible part of the American landscape.[70] During the past two decades, 2,000 mosques, along with numerous Islamic schools, have been built. Today, there are an estimated 1,200 interest groups, publishers, and radio stations that cater to largely Muslim audiences.[71]

As with Muslims, the number of Asian Indian immigrants has risen dramatically. The first wave began in the 1960s when thousands of students and professionals—many of them Hindus—emigrated from India to the United States. A decade later they were joined by other, less well-educated family members who took jobs as taxi drivers, clerks, small business operators, and factory workers. From 1990 to 2000, the number of Asian Indian migrants rose once more from 800,000 to more than 1.6 million. Many found good-paying jobs in the burgeoning high-technology industries. Among the most successful are Vinod Khosla, cofounder of Sun Microsystems, and Sabeer Bhatia, who started Hotmail.[72]

The number of Buddhists has also sharply increased. Today, there are more than seventy-five forms of Buddhism and five million Buddhists scattered across the United States—thanks to increased immigration from Japan, China, and Vietnam.[73] Kathy Jaekles, a twenty-five-year practitioner, says things have changed since her mother converted to Buddhism when she was a teenager: "People are more accepting and tolerant of Buddhists. I feel freer to tell people I'm Buddhist."[74] She is not alone. A 1997 survey of 750 human resource professionals found 68 percent offered flexible schedules for religious observances.[75]

New religions are just one part of a profound change in the country's spiritual life. Increasingly, many Americans are looking within for spiritual help. The result is an eschewing of so-called mediating institutions—especially religious ones—that had often been previously used to answer life's basic questions: "Who are we? Why are we here?" Over the past four decades, there has been a substantial increase in the number of those who do not attend any church. In 1963, 49 percent told the Gallup Organization they attended church regularly; 50 percent answered "seldom" or not at all.[76] Exit polls in 2000 indicate weekly church attendance had fallen to 42 percent, while 56 percent answered monthly, seldom, or never.[77] In 2004, the figures were much the same despite the efforts of the Bush campaign to bring more churchgoers to the polls: 42 percent said they went to church weekly; 57 percent answered monthly, a few times a year, or never.[78]

More than three decades ago, social demographers Richard M. Scammon and Ben J. Wattenberg coined the phrase "demography is destiny."[79] In many ways, the 2004 election shows signs of an emerging Democratic coalition that is young, less religious, nonwhite, and single. John F. Kerry attracted broad support from these groups (see table 4.4). These groups are likely to become an even more important part of American life, thanks to their growing numbers. Writing in *The American Conservative*, Steve Sailer notes that while George W. Bush carried nineteen states with the highest white fertility rates, John F. Kerry carried the sixteen states with the lowest white fertility rates.[80] These numbers would seem to be good news for Bush and the Republicans. But any rejoicing should be tempered by a National Center for Health Statistics report that showed the average white woman giving birth at a pace

Table 4.4. Kerry Coalition Twenty-First-Century Strengths in Rank Order

Group	Kerry Percentage
African American	92
Age 18–24	62
First-time voter	62
Single	61
Divorced/widowed/separated	60
Attend church on special occasions	60
Hispanic	58
Age 18–29 years old	56
Registered within the last six months	55
Attend church rarely	54
No children less than 17 years of age	51

Source: Zogby International, post-election poll, November 3–5, 2004.

consistent with having 1.83 babies during her lifetime, or 13 percent *below* the replacement rate of 2.1 children per woman.[81] Sailer reports that even excluding vast Alaska, Bush's counties were only one-fourth as densely populated as Kerry's.[82]

One of the best places to see the erosion of the Reagan coalition is Orange County, California. Site of the John Wayne Airport, Disneyland, and the Crystal Cathedral (home to Dutch Reform televangelist Robert Schuller), Orange County was once a bastion of right-wing conservatism. For years, the profoundly anti-communist and conspiracy-minded John Birch Society called Orange County home. Today, the area is increasingly nonwhite in its population and more Democratic in its politics. During the 1990s, Hispanics rose to 31 percent of the county's population and Asians increased to 14 percent, even as the number of whites declined by 6 percent.[83] In 2004, the inevitable happened: the Census Bureau reported that whites had become an official minority (49 percent).[84] Orange County's future can be glimpsed in these statistics: Hispanics comprise 44 percent of those under eighteen years of age; among those over age seventy, three-quarters are white.[85]

The political transformation is just as profound. Today, Orange County is represented in Congress by Loretta Sanchez, a Hispanic who came to office in 1996, by besting Republican incumbent Bob Dornan. Dornan had earned the nickname "B-1 Bob," thanks to his support of the B-1 bomber and other Cold War–era military hardware. As the campaign began, Dornan boasted: "She can't beat me. Bob Dornan is a father of five, grandfather of ten, military man, been married forty-one years. She has no kids, no military, no track record."[86] But on Election Day, voters gave Dornan a shock: Sanchez won by 984 votes.[87] Since then, Sanchez has become an entrenched incumbent; in 2004, she won a fifth term with 60 percent of the vote.

Demography suggests that future congresses will have more Loretta Sanchezes. Already in the upcoming 109th Congress (2005–2006), there are twenty-four Hispanics in the House: nineteen Democrats (including Sanchez) and five Republicans. In 2005, the Senate will welcome two new Hispanic members: Republican Mel Martinez (Florida) and Democrat Ken Salazar (Colorado).[88]

IS DEMOGRAPHY REALLY DESTINY?

While the Reagan coalition is struggling to maintain its majority, its demise is hardly inevitable. Karl Rove, George W. Bush's political guru, maintains that Bush's tenure is reminiscent of William McKinley's. McKinley, it should be recalled, sparked a Republican revival that broke a twenty-year two-party deadlock that often resulted in minority presidents and disputed presidential outcomes (for example, 1876, 1884, 1888, and 1892). Rove's thesis was outlined in the October 2, 2000, issue of *U.S. News and World Report:*

> Under Rove's theory, America is experiencing a "transformational" era comparable to the Industrial Revolution more than a century ago. He sees parallels to the election of 1896, when Republican governor William McKinley of Ohio—"a natural harmonizer," according to one admirer— rode to victory on a belief that the GOP could no longer base its appeal on old divisions from the Civil War because the nation had utterly changed. Today, Rove argues, the "new economy," based on technology, information, and entrepreneurship, is again transforming America, along with a new wave of immigrants from Latin America, Asia, and elsewhere. And the country is eager for a new leader who will, in Bush's inelegant phrase, be a "uniter, not a divider"—just like McKinley was.[89]

In reality, George W. Bush has not lived up to his McKinley-like potential. McKinley's "natural harmonizing" skills created a broad coalition of Northern labor and industrial capital. But Bush has hardly been "a uniter" and his partisan base (both ideologically and in sheer geographic size) has shrunk. While the red states loom large following Bush's victory, it is worth remembering that in four straight presidential elections Republicans have ceded the entire West coast (including Reagan's native California) to the Democrats. Recall that Reagan won every state in the Far West twice. During the same period (1992–2004), Republicans lost every northeastern state, except New Hampshire and West Virginia in 2000, the former because third-party candidate Ralph Nader was a spoiler. Reagan, on the other hand, carried every northeastern state twice, save Maryland, Rhode Island, and West Virginia (which he lost in 1980).[90]

Far from creating a renewed Reagan-like majority based on the transformational demography and economy of the twenty-first century, it seems clear that the base of the Reagan/Bush coalition has shrunk to the South and the interior heartland. Fear of terrorism was crucial to Bush's reelection chances. Another terrorist strike— especially one as massive as September 11 on the U.S. homeland—would revive fears about an invisible enemy and possibly give the Reagan/Bush coalition a jolt of renewed energy. However, such a catastrophic attack could also spawn a Cold War– like McCarthyism, with Americans wondering who is to blame and ascribing it to those holding power. (Democrats would probably escape much damage, as they hold so little political authority.)

It seems clear that with the sole exception of the so-called investor class, the Reagan/Bush coalition has yet to court nonwhite twenty-first-century voters. Hispanics did vote for George W. Bush in greater numbers in 2004 than in 2000, though there is some dispute as to how high that percentage really was. A Zogby International post-election poll found Bush with 41 percent of the Hispanic vote—better than the 35 percent he won in 2000.[91] But there is no sign that Hispanics are moving in large numbers into the Republican Party. Meanwhile, other minorities remain firmly ensconced in the Democratic camp. The 2004 exit poll found Kerry winning 88 percent of the African American vote and a solid 56 percent from Asians.[92]

Yet, George W. Bush has given every sign of wanting to use his second term to create a revived twenty-first-century Reagan coalition. His plans to create private Social Security accounts (thereby spawning more investors) and immigration reform (an obvious overture to Hispanics) are omens for the future. Bush's leadership on these issues will force the opposition Democrats to react. And in so doing, the leadership skills of both parties will be sorely tested.

That's just the point. Demography is not really destiny. For demography to matter, there must be strong issues and leaders to match. A century ago, social commentators described an emerging demography that would change twentieth-century America from a rural, white Protestant, and mostly agricultural society into an industrialized, blue-collar, ethnic, Catholic, and urban one. In 1926, Daniel Chauncey Brewer wrote a book titled *The Conquest of New England by the Immigrant.*[93] Yet, it took a Great Depression and the leadership of Franklin D. Roosevelt to translate this new demography into an electoral majority. And that was twenty-eight years after the election of Roosevelt's cousin, Theodore, in 1904, when immigration and industrialization fueled the first Roosevelt's progressive movement!

Today, the United States is experiencing some of the same feelings that were commonplace a century ago—a sense that the nation people once knew is quickly ebbing away. Patrick J. Buchanan writes in *The Death of the West* how one fan came up to him recently and said, "Pat, we're losing the country we grew up in."[94] The prevalence of foreign-language cable networks such as Telemundo, multilingual election ballots and government documents, and even ATMs that converse with customers in different languages (mostly Spanish) are signs of the times. Another portent of the future is the emergence of new family forms—probably best exhibited by ballot questions asking whether gays should be permitted to receive state marriage licenses.

George W. Bush benefited from a backlash against these dramatic transformations. In that sense, Bush was like Reagan. But Reagan's backlash came from those whom social commentators Richard M. Scammon and Ben J. Wattenberg described in 1970 as "unyoung, unpoor, and unblack"—that is, the *real* majority.[95] Today, that old majority is rapidly becoming a twenty-first-century minority. Nonetheless, that old conservative desire to climb atop the globe and yell "STOP!" was much in evidence in 2004. Among those who believed moral values was the most important issue (22 percent of the electorate and the number one concern), Bush won 80 percent of their votes.[96] To many, the emergence of gay marriage also portended a nation in decline. But even as Americans were rejecting gay marriage, they were forging a consensus around some form of acceptance of homosexual unions: 35 percent favored civil unions; 25 percent thought gays should legally marry; and 37 percent wanted no legal recognition (see chapter 2).

In sum, Bush benefited from a sense that the old rules had been lifted and a new moral freedom was emerging.[97] This new freedom was creating a country that was more expressive in its personal and family choices, but also far less orderly. Bush projected a Reagan-like sense of fatherly order—something many welcomed in an era of overwhelming and vast social and economic transformations. But was this the Reagan coalition's last gasp? Or, will George W. Bush build on what's left of the Reagan Revolution and renew the old coalition once more?

NOTES

1. University of Michigan, Center for Political Studies, National Election Study, 1978.
2. Patrick H. Caddell, "Crisis of Confidence—Trapped in a Downward Spiral," *Public Opinion*, October/November 1979, 5.
3. *Connecticut Mutual Life Report on American Values in the '80s* (Lanham, MD: University Press of America, 1981), 202.
4. Decision/Making/Information, survey for the Reagan for President Campaign, November 4–5, 1981.

5. Richard B. Wirthlin, *Reagan for President: Campaign Action Plan*, June 29, 1980, 35–36.
6. Decision/Making/Information, survey for the Reagan for President Campaign, December, 1979.
7. For more on this see John Kenneth White, *The New Politics of Old Values* (Hanover, NH: University Press of New England, 1988).
8. Ronald Reagan, Acceptance Speech, Republican National Convention, Detroit, July 17, 1980.
9. Decision/Making/Information, survey, June 1980.
10. Wirthlin, *Campaign Action Plan* (document given to author), 12.
11. Quoted in William A. Schambra, "Progressive Liberalism and the American 'Community,'" *Public Interest*, no. 80 (Summer 1985), 46.
12. Ronald Reagan, "A Vision for America," television broadcast, November 3, 1980.
13. Ronald Reagan, Inaugural Address, Washington, DC, January 20, 1981.
14. Ronald Reagan, Address to Congress, Washington, DC, February 18, 1981.
15. Gallup poll, 1936.
16. Gallup poll, September 18–21, 1981.
17. Quoted in Lary May, "Movie Star Politics: The Screen Actors Guild, Cultural Conversion, and the Hollywood Red Scare," in Lary May, ed., *Recasting America: Culture and Politics in the Age of the Cold War* (Chicago: University of Chicago Press, 1989), 125.
18. Ronald Reagan with Richard G. Hubler, *Where's the Rest of Me?* (New York: Karz-Segil Publishers, 1981), 311–312.
19. See Lou Cannon, *President Reagan: The Role of a Lifetime* (New York: Simon and Schuster, 1990), 288.
20. "Republican Platform, 1976," 986.
21. Ronald Reagan, "Remarks at the Annual Convention of the National Association of Evangelicals," Orlando, Florida, March 8, 1983.
22. Yankelovich, Skelly, and White, survey, December 6–8, 1983.
23. Haynes Johnson, *Sleepwalking Through History: America in the Reagan Years* (New York: W.W. Norton, 1991), 196.
24. Patrick J. Buchanan, *Right from the Beginning* (Boston: Little Brown and Company, 1988), 66–67.
25. "Initial Action Plan," Reagan transition document prepared by Richard B. Wirthlin, 1.
26. John B. Judis, "Freed Radicals: Would Reagan Recognize the GOP?," *The New Republic*, September 6, 2004.
27. CBS News/*New York Times*, exit polls, 1980, 1984, and 1988. Twenty-six percent of Democrats backed Reagan in 1980; 25 percent in 1984; and 17 percent supported George H. W. Bush in 1988.
28. Cited in Rich Lowry, "It's Not Personal, Mr. Bush," *Washington Post*, July 1, 2001, B1.
29. Quoted in Mike Allen, "Bush Uses Fourth to Extol Role of Faith," *Washington Post*, July 5, 2001, A2.
30. George W. Bush, "The True Goal of Education," Gorham, New Hampshire, November 2, 1999.
31. See George W. Bush, Speech at Bob Jones University, Greenville, South Carolina, February 2, 2000, and Bush, "The True Goal of Education."
32. ABC News, poll, October 28–31, 1999.

33. Fox News/Opinion Dynamics, poll, August 12–13, 1998, and Yankelovich Partners, Incorporated, poll, June 9–10, 1999.

34. Princeton Survey Research Associates, poll, July 19–23, 2000.

35. George W. Bush, "Remarks by the President in Tax Cut Bill Signing Ceremony," Washington, DC, June 7, 2001.

36. Ronald Brownstein, "Bush Moves by Refusing to Budge," *Los Angeles Times*, March 2, 2003, A1.

37. Louis Harris and Associates, poll, June 10–15, 2003.

38. *Los Angeles Times*, poll, November 15–18, 2003.

39. Greenberg Quinlan Rosner Research, poll, July 22–24, 2002.

40. For more on this see John Kenneth White, *Still Seeing Red: How the Cold War Shapes the New American Politics* (Boulder: Westview Press, 1998).

41. According to the Voter News Service exit poll, 35 percent said Gore could best handle a world crisis; 27 percent named Bush; and 29 percent answered both. Voter News Service, exit poll, November 7, 2000.

42. George W. Bush, "Remarks to Employees at the Pentagon," Arlington, Virginia, September 17, 2001.

43. George W. Bush, Address to a Joint Session of Congress, Washington, DC, September 20, 2001.

44. Ibid.

45. Zogby International, poll, December 1–3, 2004.

46. CBS News, poll, December 21–23, 2003.

47. CNN/*USA Today*/Gallup poll, November 19–21, 2004.

48. Quoted in Judis, "Freed Radicals: Would Reagan Recognize the GOP?"

49. Zogby International, post-election poll, November 3–5, 2004.

50. See V. O. Key, *The Responsible Electorate: Rationality in Presidential Voting* (Cambridge, MA: The Belknap Press of Harvard University Press, 1966), 9.

51. Zogby International, post-election poll, November 3–5, 2004.

52. See Adam Nagourney, "When an Explosive Charge Is Not Handled with Care," *New York Times*, September 9, 2004, A1.

53. Ibid.

54. Mark Danner, "How Bush Really Won, *The New York Review of Books*, January 3, 2005; National Election Pool, exit poll, November 2, 2004.

55. National Election Pool, exit poll, November 2, 2004 and Voter News Services, exit poll, November 7, 2004.

56. Quoted on PBS broadcast, "Nixon: The American Experience," September 24, 1992.

57. See Peter Grier and Sara B. Miller, "Incredible Shrinking U.S. Family," *Christian Science Monitor*, December 2, 2004, A1.

58. Ibid.

59. Ibid.

60. See William J. Bennett, *The Broken Hearth: Reversing the Moral Collapse of the American Family* (New York: Doubleday, 2001), 12, and Tom Smith, "The Emerging 21st Century American Family," National Opinion Research Center, University of Chicago, paper, November 24, 1999, 23.

61. According to the 2000 Census, 297, 580 Bostonians listed themselves as minority or multiracial—many hailing from such places as the Caribbean, Asia, or Africa—whereas

291, 561 Bostonians defined themselves as white. See Stan Grossfeld, " 'It's a Good Life,' " *Boston Globe*, May 6, 2001, E1.

62. See William Jefferson Clinton, "Erasing America's Color Lines," *New York Times*, January 14, 2001.

63. See Eric Schmitt, "U.S. Now More Diverse, Ethnically and Racially," *New York Times*, April 1, 2001, 18.

64. John Zogby, "John Zogby's 21st Century Trends," internet document, January 2001. See www.zogby.com

65. Ibid.

66. See William Booth, "California's Ethnic Diversity Grows," *Washington Post*, March 30, 2001, A3; and D'Vera Cohn and Darryl Fears, "Multiracial Growth Seen in Census," *Washington Post*, March 13, 2001, A1.

67. See Darryl Fears and Claudia Deane, "Biracial Couples Report Tolerance," *Washington Post*, July 5, 2001, A1.

68. Cited in James Davison Hunter, *Culture Wars: The Struggle to Define America* (New York: Basic Books, 1991), 73.

69. The number of Muslims is in dispute partially due to the U.S. Census, which does not ask one's religious affiliation. For more on the varying numbers see Bill Broadway, "Number of U.S. Muslims Depends on Who's Counting," *Washington Post*, November 24, 2001, A1.

70. Muslim immigration to the United States has come in five waves: (1) 1875–1912, (2) 1918–1922, (3) 1930–1938, (4) 1947–1960, and (5) 1967–present. See Yvonne Haddad Yazbeck, *Islamic Values in the United States: A Comparative Study* (New York: Oxford University Press, 1987), 14.

71. See U.S. State Department, "Islam in the United States: A Tentative Ascent, A Conversation with Yvonne Haddad." www.usinfo.state.gov/usa/islam/hadad.htm

72. See Peter Whoriskey, "Boom Bolsters Indian Community," *Washington Post*, May 27, 2001, A1.

73. Cited in Patricia Digh, "Companies Make an Effort to Accommodate Religion," *Career Journal*, September 10, 1999. www.careerjournal.com/hrcenter/shrm/features/ 19990910-digh. html and the U.S. State Department, "Islam in the United States," fact sheet. www.usinfo.state.gov/usa/islam/fact2.htm

74. Quoted in "Soka Gakkai Buddhists Are Diverse Group in Search of Peace and Harmony," *Huntsville Times*, October 21, 2000.

75. Cited in Digh, "Companies Make an Effort to Accommodate Religion," www. careerjournal.com/hrcenter/

76. Gallup poll, December 5–10, 1963.

77. Voter News Services, exit poll, November 7, 2000.

78. National Election Pool, exit poll, November 2, 2004.

79. See Richard M. Scammon and Ben J. Wattenberg, *The Real Majority* (New York: Coward-McCann, 1970), 45.

80. Steve Sailer, "Baby Gap," *The American Conservative*, December 20, 2004, 8.

81. Ibid., 7.

82. Ibid., 8.

83. See Michael Barone and Richard E. Cohen, *The Almanac of American Politics, 2004* (Washington, DC: National Journal, 2003); 283; and Patrick J. Buchanan, *The Death of the West* (New York: Thomas Dunne Books/St. Martin's Press, 2002), 139.

84. Of Orange County's 2.95 million residents, 1.49 million are minorities.
85. Ronald Campbell and Erica Perez, "Minorities Dominate 'Real' Orange County," *Orange County Register*, October 1, 2004.
86. Quoted in "Robert Dornan," Wikipedia, the free encyclopedia, see en.wikipedia.org/wiki/Robert_Dornan
87. Barone and Cohen, *The Almanac of American Politics, 2004*, 284.
88. Nancy Frazier O'Brien, "At 29 Percent of the Congress, Catholics Remain Largest Faith Group," Catholic News Service, November 11, 2004.
89. *U.S. News and World Report*, October 2, 2000, quoted in John B. Judis and Ruy Teixeira, *The Emerging Democratic Majority* (New York: Scribner Books, 2002), 145.
90. Rhode Island voted for Jimmy Carter in 1980.
91. Zogby International, post-election poll, November 3–5, 2004, and Voter News Services, exit poll, November 7, 2000. The National Election Pool exit poll gave Bush 44 percent of the Hispanic vote, but there are indications that number was too high.
92. National Election Pool, exit poll, November 2, 2004.
93. Daniel Chauncey Brewer, *The Conquest of New England by the Immigrant* (New York: G. P. Putnam, 1926).
94. Buchanan, *The Death of the West*, 1.
95. Scammon and Wattenberg, *The Real Majority*, 45.
96. National Election Pool, exit poll, November 2, 2004.
97. For more on this see Alan Wolfe, *Moral Freedom: The Impossible Idea That Defines the Way We Live Now* (New York: W. W. Norton, 2001).

Part III

THE REGIONS

5

THE NORTHEAST

All but One, Blue

Kevin J. McMahon

In the haze of an election lost, some disgruntled Democrats—most with their tongues firmly planted in their cheeks—pondered a new nation encompassing the Blue John Kerry states and America's northern neighbor, Canada. Significantly, this hypothetical United States of Canada could easily link all the continental Blue states together. Driving this possibility was the Northeast, much of which borders Canada. These twelve states plus the District of Columbia provided John Kerry—the hockey-playing, French speaking Democratic candidate—with his base of support.[1] However, it wasn't always this way. In fact, the Northeast's development as a Democratic stronghold represents a dramatic turnaround for the region, long regarded as the most Republican in the country. For example, in the critical election of 1896, Republican William McKinley won all of the Northeast's twelve states while losing the entire South, one midwestern state, and five western states.[2] In 2004, the electoral map was almost reversed as Kerry won all but one of the Northeast's states (plus Washington, DC) while losing all of the South and large chunks of the Midwest and West. This chapter analyzes both the politics of the Northeast and its political transformation within the context of the 2004 presidential election. In doing so, it explores how and why the Northeast has emerged as the nation's bluest region.

GEORGE W. BUSH IN THE LAND OF BLUE

Like the cowboys in the popular Pace Picante Salsa commercials—who grew angry when their chuck wagon cook replaced one of their favorite Texas-made brand foods with one made "in New York City!"—the Bush campaign didn't expect much from the voters of the Big Apple. But nevertheless, as a minority president with his greatest appeal in the reddest parts of America, it is somewhat ironic that three of George W. Bush's most notable first term appearances took place in this city at the heart of Blue America. The first of these appearances occurred in the wake of the 9/11 attacks on the United States. While President Bush seemed to struggle in his public appearances immediately following the shocking events of 9/11, by most accounts he rose to the challenge when he visited the scene of the most tragic of those attacks: the remains of the Twin Towers of the World Trade Center (a.k.a., Ground Zero). As he stood atop a charred fire truck, Bush spoke to members of the rescue and recovery team. Someone in the group, straining to hear his words, shouted "we can't hear you." Through a megaphone, the president boomed: "I can hear you. The rest of the world hears you, and the people who knocked these buildings down will hear all of us soon."[3] While Bush would go on to make many more statements about the events of 9/11, few will be remembered more than this one.

Several weeks later, the president paid New York City a visit once again. This time the occasion was a happier one and where he spoke not a word. It took place at Yankee Stadium in the Bronx, where Bush—a well-known fan of the game—had come to throw out the first pitch to open Game Three of the World Series between New York's Yankees and the Arizona Diamondbacks. Warned by the Yankees' star shortstop Derek Jeter that the crowd would boo if he either failed to throw the pitch from the rubber or failed to reach the catcher, the president walked to the top of the mound, reared back, and threw a perfect strike. Although he had not supported Bush in the 2000 election, one Yankee fan in the stadium that night later recalled that at that moment he was "my representative."[4] It was an emotion many Americans felt toward President Bush following the 9/11 attacks.

On the third occasion, the president spoke many words, to both the throng of his most ardent supporters assembled at Madison Square Garden for the Republican National Convention and to the millions more watching on television in their homes. The speech both began and ended with references to the 9/11 attacks and the city that bore the brunt of that tragedy. In it, the president emphasized the importance of the election for the future safety of the nation and the principle of freedom worldwide:

This moment in the life of our country will be remembered. Generations will know if we kept our faith and kept our word. Generations will know if we seized this moment and used it to build a future of safety and peace. The freedom of many, and the future security of our nation, now depend on us. And tonight, my fellow Americans, I ask you to stand with me.[5]

At the time the president spoke these words, John Kerry was falling in the polls, most likely the result of the harsh Swift Boat Veterans' attack ads that effectively raised questions about his wartime heroics in Vietnam. Perhaps adding to the Democratic candidate's downturn in the polls, the Republican Convention—whether due to President Bush's speech or to some of the many others—was widely reported as more successful than the Democrats' gathering in Boston several weeks earlier. And although Senator Kerry would close in on the president following the debates, he would never recapture a clear lead in the polls.

Despite Bush's performance at these three events—all "in New York City!"—the voters of the Big Apple did not upset expectations on Election Day 2004. The president lost the city by well more than a million votes, earning 23.9 percent. He did improve on his 2000 performance, however. Four years earlier, he captured just 17.7 percent of the city's vote. In that year, moreover, he won a mere 11 percent of the vote in the Bronx, the borough that houses Yankee Stadium, and only slightly more (14 percent) in Manhattan, the borough that includes both Ground Zero and Madison Square Garden. In 2004, he increased his share of the vote in both boroughs, by 4 and 6 percent, respectively. Moreover, as Alan Abramowitz writes, "Bush gained an average of 5.4 percentage points in the three states most directly affected by the September 11th terrorist attacks—New York, New Jersey, and Connecticut—compared with 2.5 percentage points in the rest of the country."[6] Indeed, of the eighteen states where Bush saw his two-party vote percentage decline from four years earlier, five were in the Midwest and eight in the West. In other words, as the president traveled farther away from New York City, he did less well in comparison to his performance in 2000. In the Blue Northeast, Bush improved his two-party vote percentage in nine of its twelve states. But nevertheless, he won only one (also losing the District of Columbia). And Red West Virginia, as explained below, is an odd fit for the region. Thus, when it came to the Northeast, Bush must have felt like Republican Vincent "Buddy" Cianci—the fallen "Prince of Providence"—did in 1980. After losing his bid for Rhode Island's governor's office, Cianci quipped: "Running in Rhode Island as a Republican is like being the Ayatolah Khomeini at the American Legion Convention."[7]

Since Cianci's statement, the fortunes of the GOP candidates seeking the governor's office in Rhode Island and most of the rest of the Northeast have actually improved. Republican gubernatorial candidates can—*and often do*—win in the Blue Northeast. As table 5.1 displays, in the last twelve years, Republicans have controlled the

Table 5.1. Republican Governors in Northeastern States

States	GOP since 1992[†]	2004–05 Occupant	Republican Vote*	Democratic Vote*
Connecticut	10	Republican	56	44
Delaware	0	Democrat	46	51
Maine	2	Democrat	41	47
Maryland	2	Republican	52	48
Massachusetts	12	Republican	50	45
New Hampshire**	8	Rep→Dem	49	51
New Jersey	8	Democrat	42	56
New York	10	Republican	49	34
Pennsylvania	8	Democrat	44	53
Rhode Island	10	Republican	55	45
Vermont	2	Republican	59	38
West Virginia	4	Democrat	34	63
Totals	76	6R, 5D, 1 Split	48.1	47.9

Note: [†]Number of years Republicans have controlled the governor's office from 1992 to 2004 (maximum 12). *Figures from the most recent gubernatorial election. **In 2004, Democratic challenger John Lynch narrowly defeated the Republican incumbent, Craig Benson.

governor's office in Northeastern states more often than Democrats.[8] Moreover, in the last gubernatorial election in these states, Republicans had a slightly larger share of the vote than Democrats, 48.1 percent to 47.9 percent. Republicans who win statewide office in the Northeast, however, most often hold views clearly at odds with the national GOP. Typically, successful Republicans in the Northeast prevail in statewide races by promising to keep the lid on spending, taxes, and crime while also proclaiming a liberal attitude on issues like abortion and gay rights. When these candidates seek to move to the national stage, however, this balancing act usually undermines their chances in the Republican Party, especially if they have their sights set on the presidency. Vice versa, when Red state–style Republicans—like George W. Bush—have represented their party on the presidential ticket in recent years, they have not done very well in the Northeast.

The former Massachusetts Governor William F. Weld provides a perfect example of a Northeast Republican who didn't travel well. Largely credited with reviving the Bay State's economy and amending its spendthrift ways, Weld was a popular governor in the nation's most Democratic state during most of the 1990s, winning reelection by a record margin in 1994. After nearly two terms in the Massachusetts state house, however, Weld left office in April 1997 to accept President Bill Clinton's offer to become U.S. ambassador to Mexico. Weld reportedly agreed to this new challenge with a higher office in mind. According to a close Weld advisor: "By stepping out of elective politics and becoming a strong voice on Latin American drug trafficking and international trade, Weld could position himself as a national candidate after the year 2000 if a strong, independent movement emerges or if the GOP by then accepts a moderate on the ticket."[9] But in the end, Weld never made it to Mexico. He fell victim to an effort to block his Senate confirmation. Significantly, Weld's fiercest critics were not Democrats, but members of his own Republican Party. In short, his liberal views on social matters—which had been a basis for his popularity in Massachusetts—were his downfall in a Republican-controlled Congress. While Weld was pro-choice on abortion, supportive of gay rights, and an advocate of medicinal use of marijuana, conservative members of the GOP were not. Most important, North Carolina senator Jesse Helms, chairman of the Senate Foreign Relations Committee, refused to convene a committee hearing on Weld's nomination, citing the governor's position on drugs as one of the chief reasons why he was not of "Ambassador quality."[10] After Weld withdrew from his battle with Senator Helms— which the governor once called a battle for "the future of the Republican Party"—he pledged to remain a strong voice in the GOP, defending the tradition of Abraham Lincoln and Theodore Roosevelt and reclaiming the party's commitment to "defending individual rights."[11] Former New Jersey governor and EPA administrator Christie Todd Whitman has taken up that fight in a new book entitled, *It's My Party, Too: Taking Back the Republican Party and Bringing the Country Together Again*.[12] But if the 2004 election results are any indication, governors Weld and Whitman's wing of the GOP has already lost to the Jesse Helmses of the party.

Given that President Bush does not fit into the northeastern Republican mold, it is not surprising that he won only one state in the region. In addition, the only state he won in 2000 but lost four years later was in the Northeast (New Hampshire). As noted above, in most northeastern states, voters are still willing to support Republicans at the state level, particularly those who are scrooges on fiscal matters. But at the national level, it is increasingly difficult for the GOP to achieve much success in the region if their candidates hold solidly conservative views on social and cultural matters. As the next section shows, this Republican difficulty in the Northeast has been both evolutionary and dramatic.

AS MAINE GOES, SO GOES?
THE BLUING OF THE NORTHEAST

In the 1980s and early 1990s, trivia buffs had an easy time stumping all but the keenest observers of the political scene with a version of the following question: "Excluding the presidential election of 1964, which state has not voted for the Democratic Party's presidential nominee since 1824?" While most would-be responders would instinctively target their attention on the fire-engine Red states of middle America, the answer lay in the middle of Blue America. More specifically, it lay in Vermont. By the early 1990s, Vermont may have had Howard Dean as its governor and Socialist Bernie Sanders as its congressman, but in more than a century and a half of voting it had only supported the Democratic presidential candidate once. Even in the Democratic Party's headiest years, Vermont had remained true to its Republican roots. For example, in Franklin Roosevelt's historic 1936 landslide victory, only Vermont—along with Maine—voted for Republican Alf Landon. And Vermont, by virtue of giving Landon 56.4 percent of its vote, was the more Republican of the two New England neighbors. If FDR's sweeping victory surprised any, it surprised those in Maine. "Until 1958, Maine held state elections in September . . . [and] the results [there] were taken as a gauge of national partisan movement—hence the saying, 'As Maine goes, so goes the nation.' " Thus, when GOP governor Lewis Barrows captured 56 percent of the vote to win reelection in September 1936, Republicans held out hope that their presidential candidate might defeat the popular FDR. Two months later, when only Vermont joined Maine in support of Landon, Democratic Party chairman James Farley quipped, "As Maine goes, so goes Vermont."[13]

Maine and Vermont's support for Landon highlight a simple fact: for much of its existence, the Republican Party has been rooted in the Northeast. Indeed, from the GOP's formation in 1854 until the election of 1936, its presidential candidate won a majority of the Northeast's twelve states every election save one. The exception was the election of 1912, which pitted Democrat Woodrow Wilson against the two candidates of a divided GOP (President Howard Taft and former President Theodore Roosevelt). Four years later, with the Republican Party united behind Charles Evans Hughes, Wilson won only two northeastern states. In his four races for the White House, FDR did make inroads in the Northeast. Nevertheless, in the ten presidential elections from 1948 to 1988, the Republican candidate won a majority of the Northeast's states seven times.

All evidence suggests, however, that Republican control of the Northeast at the presidential level ended in 1992. In that year, Arkansas governor Bill Clinton won Vermont (easily) and every other state in the region (plus the District of Columbia). In fact, by virtue of both states' substantial support for third-party candidate Ross Perot, Vermont and Maine were two of the least Republican states in the nation (forty-seventh and forty-eighth, respectively). In contrast, South Carolina and Mississippi—the two most Democratic states in 1936 (with FDR winning 98.6 percent and 97.0 percent, respectively)—were the two most Republican states (with George Herbert Walker Bush capturing 48 percent and 49.7 percent, respectively). In 1996, Clinton also won every northeastern state. Symbolically, both he and his wife Hillary also moved to New York following their years in the White House, with the president setting up his office in Harlem and the first lady winning one of the Empire State's U.S. Senate seats in 2000. In that year's presidential race, Al Gore won all but two of the Northeast's twelve states. He lost the traditionally Democratic but culturally conservative West Virginia and the traditionally Republican but socially moderate New Hampshire, the latter by a mere 7,000 votes (with Ralph Nader capturing 22,000 votes). If he had won either state, he would have won the presidency. In 2004, as noted above, John Kerry won all but one of the Northeast's twelve states and the District of Columbia. Moreover, he piled up his biggest victories in his blue backyard, winning his home state of Massachusetts with 62 percent of the vote, and both Rhode Island and Vermont with 59 percent. These results are profoundly telling, suggesting in clear terms the underlying reasons for the bluing of the Northeast.

THE IMPORTANCE OF 1968:
FROM ONE GEORGE TO ANOTHER

In one sense, the Republican Party has displayed a remarkable amount of consistency since World War II. With only one exception, in the last fifteen presidential elections, four familial names have appeared as either the party's presidential or vice-presidential candidate (Dewey, 1944, 1948; Nixon, 1952, 1956, 1960, 1968, 1972; Dole 1976, 1996; Bush, 1980, 1984, 1988, 1992, 2000, 2004).[14] On the other hand, in the course of those sixty years, the party's electoral base has undergone a radical restructuring. Two of the most important elections driving that change occurred during the transformative decade of the 1960s; specifically, 1964 and 1968.

In July 1969, with those two elections fresh in his mind, political analyst Kevin Phillips published a book laying out the forthcoming political fortunes of the GOP. It was a book *Newsweek* called "the political bible of the Nixon era." Entitled *The Emerging Republican Majority*, Phillips offered extensive evidence for why the title would tell the tale of the GOP's future. Beyond Phillips' many maps and charts, the story was a simple one. If the GOP could capture the vast majority of those 1968 voters who cast their ballots for Alabama governor George Wallace, it would emerge as America's majority party. As Phillips understood it, this electoral strategy— commonly known as the "southern strategy"—would require some sacrifice, particularly in the Northeast. But this reality is not uncommon. As political scientist Robert Speel writes: "when a party attempts to expand its base with new groups of voters, it inevitably loses voters from its old base. That the North and the South voted along opposite partisan lines in the presidential elections of 1860, 1896, and 1996 is not merely a coincidence."[15]

Writing in the late 1960s, Phillips thought a "successful moderate conservatism" on the part of the Nixon administration "and the lack of a Wallace candidacy would greatly swell the 1972 Republican vote in the South, West, Border and the Catholic North." Thus, "the upcoming cycle of American politics" was destined to pit "a dominant Republican Party based in the Heartland, South and California against a minority Democratic Party based in the Northeast and the Pacific Northwest (and encompassing Southern as well as Northern Negroes)." Under these terms, Phillips thought the GOP could "easily afford to lose the states of Massachusetts, New York, and Michigan," and predicted that the Democratic Party would find the core of its strength in the ten most Democratic states of 1968 (see figure 5.1).[16] The 1964 Republican presidential candidate Senator Barry Goldwater even suggested that the "country would be better off if we could just saw off the Eastern Seaboard and let it float out to sea."[17]

The basis of the GOP's geographical shift stemmed largely from its move to the right on social and cultural matters—particularly civil rights—and the Democratic Party's corresponding endorsement of "liberal" positions on these issues. As Phillips explains:

> Back in 1960 Richard Nixon had run for President as the candidate of a Republican Party still at least partly controlled, as Henry Cabot Lodge's vice-presidential nomination bore witness, by its traditional Yankee bastion. By 1968, however, things had changed. Not only had the civil rights revolution cut the South adrift from its Democratic moorings and drawn the Northeast towards the Democrats, but it had increased the Southern and Western bias of the GOP to a point—the 1964 Goldwater nomination— where the party had decided to break with its formative antecedents and make an ideological bid for the anti-civil rights South. . . . By the dint of the 1964 election, the Republican Party shed the dominion of its Yankee and Northeastern Establishment creators, while the Democrats . . . sank the foundations of their future into the Northeast.[18]

From our vantage point in 2005, Phillips' forecast for the Republican alliance still stands largely intact. While the Democrats have secured more states than his analysis suggests—particularly California and heartland Illinois—the battle lines of 1968 have not changed much. In fact, the map in figure 5.1 displays just how little the Democrats have expanded the playing field since that pivotal election. Of the nineteen states that John Kerry won in 2004, all but one (Delaware) was a top twenty Democratic state in 1968.[19] The twenty-first most Democratic state in 1968 was Ohio, where Kerry narrowly lost. Moreover, the Northeast supplied Kerry with

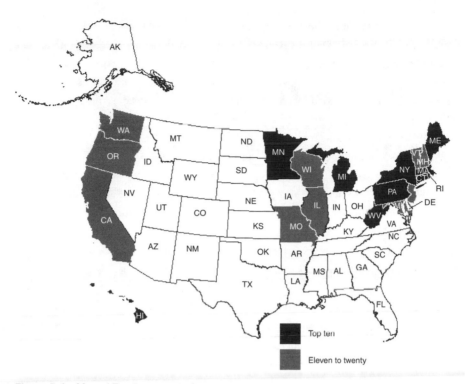

Figure 5.1. Map of Top Democratic States, 1968

Table 5.2. Distinguishing the Blueness of the Kerry States (Northeastern states in *italics*)

Blueness	Kerry States	Electoral Votes
Navy Blue (over 55%)	*District of Columbia*, Illinois, *Maryland*, *Massachusetts*, *New York*, *Rhode Island*, and *Vermont*	94
Pastel Blue (52.5 to 55%)	California, *Connecticut*, *Delaware*, Hawaii, *Maine*, and *New Jersey*	88
Barely Blue (less than 52.5%)	Michigan, Minnesota, *New Hampshire*, Oregon, *Pennsylvania*, Washington, and Wisconsin	80

twelve of his twenty victories (the District of Columbia included), nearly half of his electoral vote total (see table 5.2).[20]

The bluing of the Northeast at the presidential level has occurred gradually. In the five elections between 1972 and 1988, Republicans won a majority of the twelve states four times. And in 1976, Jimmy Carter only narrowly won the region, capturing seven states to Gerald Ford's five.[21] Nevertheless, the 1980 election was a turning point for the region. Despite Ronald Reagan's northeastern success in that year (winning nine of the twelve states), the strength of Republican representative John Anderson's independent bid for the White House revealed in clear terms the region's direction in future presidential contests. Robert Speel explains the Anderson effect in Vermont:

> In 1980, John Anderson's presidential candidacy fit well with Vermont's moderate-to-liberal Republican tradition. . . . Through his campaign [Anderson] emphasized his conservative positions on fiscal and budgetary matters, his liberal views favoring personal privacy on abortion and religion, and his opposition to hawkish defense and military views of the world. Anderson's call for discipline, responsibility, and avoidance of simple solutions for complex problems, combined with his ideological views, gained him much support among Yankee and well-education voters in Vermont, who for years had been voting for like-minded Republican candidates. As national Republican presidential candidates drifted away from such views, these voters increasingly switched to the Democrats, especially when alternatives like Anderson were not available.[22]

In other words, just as Democrat George Wallace served as a gateway for socially conservative Democrats (mainly from the South) to move into the Republican fold, John Anderson's defection from the GOP convinced many northeastern Republicans to do the same. As the next section shows, this defection continues.

ABRA CADABRA: THE DISAPPEARING REPUBLICAN MODERATES

When George W. Bush took the oath of office on January 20, 2001, eight of the Northeast's twenty-four senators were Republican, five of whom considered themselves moderates. Six months into the president's first term, one of the five moderates—Jim Jeffords of Vermont—declared his independence from the GOP.[23] His decision to caucus with the Democrats toppled the Republican majority in the Senate without an intervening election; an event unprecedented in American history. In the midst of the president's reelection campaign, another Northeastern moderate— Lincoln Chaffee of Rhode Island—announced that he could not vote for this George Bush, deciding instead to symbolically write-in the president's father's name. Yet another moderate Republican senator made his way back to Washington only after barely surviving a vigorous challenge from a member of his own party, who charged in a bitter primary fight that the incumbent was not conservative enough to represent either the state or the GOP in the Senate.

That incumbent, Arlen Specter of Pennsylvania, went on to win the general election by a comfortable margin, but his difficulties with conservatives did not end there. Just one day after the president's and his own reelection, he was asked about the future makeup of the Supreme Court, given the number of expected retirements. These questions held special significance for Specter since he was in line to become the next chair of the Senate Judiciary Committee, and, in that capacity, would play an influential role in guiding the president's choices through the confirmation process. In response to a question about the possible selection of "anti-abortion judges," Specter offered President Bush some blunt advice. "When you talk about judges who would change the right of a woman to choose, overturn *Roe v. Wade*, I think that is unlikely. The president is well aware of what happened when a bunch of his nominees were sent up, with the filibuster. . . . And I would expect the president to be mindful of the considerations which I am mentioning."[24] Having been on the front lines of the confirmation battles over Robert Bork (whom he opposed), Clarence Thomas (whom he supported), and President George W. Bush's most controversial lower court appointments (all of whom he supported), Specter knew what he was talking about. Democrats would likely attempt to filibuster a High Court nominee clearly at odds with *Roe*'s central holding (i.e., that a woman has a right to terminate an unwanted pregnancy), especially if that nominee was replacing a pro-*Roe* justice. However, to the social conservatives committed to overturning *Roe*, the pro-choice Pennsylvania senator had crossed the line. Interpreting Specter's comments as a warning to the president, they in turn set out to convince their allies in the Senate—set to be stacked with 55 Republicans in 2005—to deny him of the prized Judiciary Committee chairmanship. Specter countered with a two-week lobbying effort, explaining to his colleagues that he had merely been suggesting to the president the best way to avoid a filibuster fight, not instructing him on the types of nominees he should choose. In the end, Specter survived. But many speculated that he had done so only by renouncing his independence;[25] that as Chairman of the Judiciary Committee he might—to borrow a phrase from Bruce Springsteen—"end up like a dog that's been beat too much."

Specter's maneuverings in the immediate aftermath of the election were in sharp contrast to that of another moderate northeastern Republican, Representative Christopher Shays of Connecticut. Like Specter, Shays had just survived an electoral battle of his own. However, his toughest challenge did not come from within his party, but from his Democratic opponent, Diane Farrell. Farrell's most effective criticism of the congressman was that he had lost his once celebrated independence, insinuating that he had become a patsy for hard-line Republican House leaders like Majority Leader Tom DeLay. In the end, Shays held off Farrell's challenge, capturing 52 percent of the vote to her 48 percent. But two weeks after the election, he set out to reestablish his reputation as an independent voice in the House Republican caucus. After the caucus convened to change a rule that required its leaders to step down from their posts if indicted (in anticipation of such action against DeLay), Shays stepped to the microphones to denounce the vote. He called the rule change a "mistake," and expressed concern that the House Republicans might be abandoning the promises they made during their "revolution" of 1994. "We were going to be different . . . [but] every time we start to water down what we did in '94, we are basically saying the revolution is losing its character." While Shays "feared retribution for broadcasting his opposition," he nevertheless thought that "speaking out is more important than being chairman."[26]

The post-election actions of Senator Specter and Representative Shays are deeply revealing. Particularly during the recent years of narrow partisan majorities in both houses of Congress and ever more ideologically cohesive political parties, Northeast moderates have to walk a fine political line to remain safe in their seats. If they stray too far to the left, they hazard a primary fight from the right. If they wander too far to the right, they risk a tough challenge from the Democrats. In fact, two House moderates from upstate New York cited this tightrope walk as one of the reasons they decided to retire in 2004 instead of seeking reelection. In their place, voters elected a more conservative Republican and a Democrat.[27]

ONE OF THEIR OWN: WHY JOHN F. KERRY WON THE NORTHEAST

John F. Kerry won the Northeast with 55.5 percent of the vote. According to exit polls (detailed in tables 5.3, 5.4, and 5.5), three factors largely explain this comfortable Democratic victory in the region.[28] The first factor centers on the Northeast's metropolitan nature, dominated by the cities—from Boston to Washington, DC—making up the region's megalopolis. Indeed, 20 percent of the region's voters live in big cities and a whopping 66 percent in the suburbs that surround cities. On the other hand, few live in smaller cities (1 percent) and small towns (4 percent). Only 8 percent live in rural communities. The national figures offer a striking contrast: big cities, 13 percent; suburbs, 45 percent; smaller cities, 19 percent; small towns, 8 percent; and rural areas, 16 percent. In many ways, these figures define the divide between the Democrats and the Republicans nationally. In urban areas (30 percent of the vote), Bush's support was limited to 45 percent, while in rural areas (25 percent) his total reached 57 percent. In the suburbs (46 percent), Bush beat Kerry 52 percent to 47 percent, nearly mirroring the breakdown in the overall popular vote.

Second, the Northeast's voters were highly critical of President Bush's performance on the job. Forty percent of the region's voters "strongly disapproved" of the president's work in the White House and 55 percent had an "unfavorable" view of him. On the other hand, only 23 percent gave the president a "strong" approval rating, and just 17 percent had an "enthusiastic" opinion of his administration. Moreover, compared to all voters, slightly more northeasterners said that their vote was a vote against the opposition candidate rather than a vote for the candidate of their choice. Of this 26 percent of northeastern voters, 69 percent voted for John Kerry.

While a majority of northeasterners (53 percent) did have a favorable view of Kerry, the third most important factor that swung the region in his favor had more to do with the policy positions he advanced during the campaign. For example, just 37 percent of northeasterners thought the war in Iraq made the "U.S. more secure," while 58 percent thought the war was "going badly." On economic issues, only 41 percent trusted President Bush to effectively handle the economy, and a plurality (37 percent) thought his tax cuts were "bad for the economy." Perhaps more significantly, 62 percent said Bush "pays more attention to large corporations than ordinary Americans."

On moral and cultural issues, the Northeast set itself apart from the rest of the nation. A full 74 percent of the region's voters supported some type of legal recognition for same-sex couples, either gay marriage (35 percent) or civil unions (39 percent). Just 23 percent did not think same-sex couples should receive any legal recognition. Nationally, that latter figure stood at 37 percent. On abortion, over two-thirds (67 percent) of northeasterners thought abortion should be either always or mostly legal, 12 percent higher than the national figure. These "liberal" positions on these two issues should not be too surprising. Only 10 percent of the region's voters described themselves as evangelical Christians (compared with 23 percent nationally) and 26 percent said they were "liberal" (compared with 21 percent nationally).

On the gun issue, John Kerry had sought to identify himself as a different kind of northeasterner. Clad in camouflage, the Democratic candidate went goose hunting in Ohio near the close of the campaign to display his proclaimed love for the sport. Kerry's actions may have worked with northeasterners; he cut into Bush's 2000 numbers among the region's voters who had a gun owner in their household by 6 percent. But only 27 percent of northeasterners fit into this category, compared to 41 percent nationwide. And elsewhere, voters with gun owners in their household didn't seem to care that Kerry publicly toted a gun (but said he was "too lazy" to carry the dead goose he shot).[29] Bush captured 63 percent of this group nationally, up 2 percent from his 2000 numbers.

George W. Bush did show some strength in the Northeast. For example, he did improve upon his 2000 numbers by 4 percent. Moreover, despite the fact that his opponent was a Catholic from the Northeast, Bush won the Catholic vote in the region, 52 percent to 47 percent. When John F. Kennedy won the presidency in 1960, he captured 78 percent of the Catholic vote nationally and his support among Catholics in the Northeast was fundamental to the Democrats' recapture of the region for the first time since 1944.[30] Despite Bush's success among Catholics, in the end his administration's policies proved too divisive for him to overcome the Northeast's strong sympathy for the Democratic Party's presidential candidate. In a landslide election, the Republican candidate would have been able to rise above the

Table 5.3. Social Forces in Voting Nationwide and in the Northeast, 2004

	Total US in %	Bush US in %	Kerry US in %	Total NE in %	Bush NE in %	Kerry NE in %
Race and gender						
White	77	58	41	78	50	50
Black	11	11	88	11	13	86
Latino	8	44	53	7	28	68
White men	36	62	37	37	52	47
White women	41	55	44	41	47	52
Nonwhite men	10	30	67	11	23	75
Nonwhite women	12	24	75	11	21	77
Demographics						
<$50,000 income	45	44	55	39	34	65
>$50,000 income	55	56	43	61	49	50
No college degree	58	53	47	52	45	54
College graduate	42	49	49	48	40	59
Married	63	57	42	60	49	50
Married with children	28	59	40	28	46	53
First time voter	11	46	53	13	37	62
Union member	14	38	61	18	35	64
Gun owner house	41	63	36	27	55	42
Military service	18	57	41	16	48	51
Community size						
Big cities	13	39	60	20	34	65
Smaller cities	19	49	49	1	40	59
Suburbs	45	52	47	66	48	51
Small towns	8	50	48	4	28	70
Rural	16	59	40	8	37	60

Note: Percentages compiled from the National Election Pool exit poll.

Table 5.4. Religion, Party, and Ideology Nationwide and in the Northeast, 2004

Religion and Religiosity	Total US in %	Bush US in %	Kerry US in %	Total NE in %	Bush NE in %	Kerry NE in %
White Evangelical	23	78	21	10	72	27
Protestant	54	59	40	38	45	54
Catholic	27	52	47	41	52	47
Jewish	3	25	74	5	24	75
Other	7	23	74	8	17	82
None	10	31	67	8	15	82
Attend church weekly	41	61	39	33	52	47
Occasion attend church	40	47	53	45	41	58
Never attend church	14	36	62	14	24	74
Party ID/ideology						
Democrat	37	11	89	41	11	89
Republican	37	93	6	30	88	12
Independent	26	48	49	30	42	55
Liberal	21	13	85	26	11	88
Moderate	45	45	54	48	40	60
Conservative	34	84	15	26	81	19

Note: Percentages compiled from the National Election Pool exit poll.

Democratic leaning of the region. But in 2004, the Northeast made sure that George W. Bush would win no landslide.

THE KEYSTONE STATE: PENNSYLVANIA

In computing their Electoral College math for 2004, most political commentators set their sights on the three big battleground-state prizes: Florida with 27 electoral votes, Pennsylvania with 21, and Ohio with 20. It was not unusual to hear these commentators suggest that whichever candidate won two of these three states would win the White House. In the end, this prediction proved true, as President Bush scored victories in Florida and Ohio. Pennsylvania, on the other hand, went narrowly to John Kerry, 51 percent to 49 percent. Unquestionably, Kerry's win in the Keystone State was driven by his strength in Pennsylvania's two largest cities, Pittsburgh and Philadelphia, and the surrounding suburbs. In western Pennsylvania, Kerry won the Pittsburgh-dominated Allegheny County by nearly 100,000 votes and four of the six counties in the Pittsburgh area. In eastern Pennsylvania, Kerry captured Philadelphia by over 400,000 votes and three of its four suburban counties. With these strong

Table 5.5. Northeastern Voter Evaluation of Issues, Performance, and Leadership

	Total US in %	Bush US in %	Kerry US in %	Total NE in %	Bush NE in %	Kerry NE in %
Economic evaluation						
Natl. economy excellent/good	47	87	13	42	85	14
Natl. economy not good/poor	52	20	79	57	14	84
Bush tax cuts good for economy	41	92	7	32	96	4
Bush tax cuts bad for economy	32	7	92	37	4	94
Trust Bush handling economy	49	93	7	41	95	5
Trust Kerry handling economy	45	12	88	49	7	93
War on terrorism and Iraq						
Trust Bush handling terrorism	58	85	14	50	85	15
Trust Kerry handling terrorism	40	6	93	43	6	94
Approve of Iraq decision	51	85	14	43	80	19
Iraq part of war on terrorism	55	81	18	49	80	19
Things going well in Iraq	44	90	9	35	87	12
Things going badly in Iraq	52	17	82	58	14	85
Policy preferences						
Abortion always legal	21	25	73	29	26	73
Abortion mostly legal	34	38	61	38	36	63
Abortion mostly illegal	26	73	26	18	68	32
Abortion always illegal	16	77	22	11	78	21
Support same-sex marriage	25	22	77	35	20	79
Support civil unions	35	52	47	39	54	46
No legal recognition to gay couples	37	70	29	23	64	36
Govt. do more to solve problems	46	33	66	55	27	71
Most important issue						
Taxes	5	57	43	6	43	57
Education	4	26	73	6	13	85
Iraq	15	26	73	17	19	80
Terrorism	19	86	14	21	83	17
Economy/jobs	20	18	80	20	14	85
Moral values	22	80	18	16	66	31
Health care	8	23	77	8	18	82
Opinion of Kerry/Bush						
Kerry favorable	47	9	90	53	7	92
Kerry unfavorable	51	92	7	45	89	9
Kerry says what he believes	40	5	94	45	4	96
. . . what people want to hear	56	84	15	51	80	18
Strongly approve of Bush	33	94	5	23	89	10
Somewhat approve . . .	20	83	15	22	83	15
Somewhat disapprove . . .	12	18	80	13	18	82
Strongly disapprove . . .	34	2	97	40	1	98
U.S. right direction?	49	89	10	44	91	8
Bush attention to ordinary Americans	41	94	6	34	91	9
Bush attention to large corporations	54	16	82	62	16	83

Note: Percentages compiled from the National Election Pool exit poll.

showings in the Pittsburgh and Philadelphia regions, Kerry held off Bush's dominance in the mainly rural counties in the middle of the state (see figure 5.2). To be sure, this Kerry–Bush division of the state was expected. After all, Democratic consultant James Carville once explained that Pennsylvania was divided into three sections: "Philadelphia in the east, Pittsburgh in the west, and 'Alabama in the middle.' "[31]

The Philadelphia region's support for Kerry is actually a microcosm of the Northeast's political direction in recent years. In the early part of the twentieth century, Philadelphia was well known as one of the nation's most Republican big cities. The four counties surrounding Philadelphia, moreover, remained a bastion of northeastern Republicanism well into the 1980s (and registered Republicans still greatly outnumber registered Democrats).[32] For example, while Democratic presidential candidate Michael Dukakis won 48.4 percent of the Pennsylvania vote in 1988, he won only 38.2 percent in the four suburban counties of Philadelphia (10.2 percent less than his statewide total). Although these counties were trending Democratic at the end of the last century, Bill Clinton did not win a majority of the vote in them in either of his two three-man presidential races. In the strong Democratic year of 1996, he earned 47.7 percent in these four counties (1.5 percent less than his statewide percentage of 49.2 percent). In 2004, while winning just 2.6 percent more than Dukakis's statewide figure and 1.8 percent more than Clinton's 1996 score, Kerry captured a majority of the vote in these suburban counties with 53.2 percent of the vote (2.2 percent *more* than his statewide total). In doing so, he improved on Dukakis's percentage by fifteen points and Clinton's 1996 percentage by five-and-a-half points.[33] Combining these counties together with the City of Philadelphia—which Kerry won with 80.4 percent of the vote—the Massachusetts senator won 62.9 percent of the vote in this section of the state, providing him with 40.8 percent of all his voters in Pennsylvania.

On the other hand, Kerry did not do as well as his Democratic predecessors in the Pittsburgh area.[34] In the six counties making up this section of the state—including the Pittsburgh-dominated Allegheny County—Kerry won 52.2 percent of the vote.[35] While Kerry's total did surpass Clinton's 1996 figure of 51.3 percent, he fell well short of Dukakis's figure of 59.1 percent in 1988. Indeed, excluding the five Philadelphia counties, Kerry's percentage declined statewide in comparison to Dukakis in 1988 and Clinton in 1996. While Dukakis and Clinton won 47.8 percent and 45.5 percent, respectively, outside of the Philadelphia region, Kerry won just 45.1 percent.[36] Kerry's lower figure here is striking, given that Clinton's percentage was likely depressed by the vote for Ross Perot (who won 9.6 percent of the Keystone State vote in 1996). This result suggests that while Kerry was able to convince Perot voters in the eastern part of the state to support his candidacy, he was much less successful in doing so elsewhere in the state.

In some ways, Kerry's difficulties in the vast swath of the state between Pittsburgh and Philadelphia help clarify his failure in the Northeast's only Red state, West Virginia. In his insightful regional breakdown of the United States, political analyst Robert David Sullivan—by ignoring state borders and contiguity—places central Pennsylvania together with all of West Virginia, southern Ohio, western Maryland, and large chunks of eight southern states in a region he calls Appalachia.[37] Sullivan explains that Appalachia is not only the "most rural" of his ten regions, "it is also the oldest, poorest, and least educated." In 2004, "with 61.4 percent of its vote cast for Bush, Appalachia . . . became the most Republican region in the country for the first time since at least 1976 (as far back as Sullivan's county-level data go), and probably for the first time in American history."[38] In turn, Bush easily won West Virginia—56 percent to 43 percent—and nearly won Pennsylvania by excelling in its Red "Appalachia" counties.

Kerry offset Bush's increasing strength in the state's center by improving upon his Democratic predecessors' percentages in the Blue Philadelphia region and maintaining most of Clinton's 1996 and Gore's 2000 percentage in the Blue Pittsburgh region.[39] Pennsylvania was nevertheless a key component in the Bush reelection strategy. And in visiting the state more than any other, the president did improve on his 2000 percentage by two points and captured five counties that Al Gore won four years earlier. Perhaps more importantly, by threatening to win this Gore state, Bush and his team forced the Kerry campaign to maximize its efforts in a state that by Election Day had clearly emerged as essential to a Democratic victory in the Electoral College.

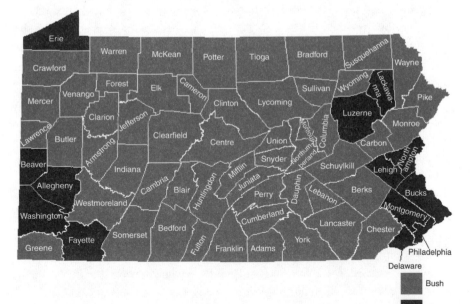

Figure 5.2. Pennsylvania Electoral Map of the 2004 Election

ANOTHER CURSE? THE BAY STATE BLUES

In 1982, they were four of the Commonwealth of Massachusetts' top political dogs, its governor, lieutenant governor, and two U.S. senators. By late 2004, all had run for the presidency . . . and lost. Of course, all four were hoping to follow in the footsteps of Massachusetts' own John F. Kennedy, one with the same last name (and parents) and another with the same initials. Senator Ted Kennedy led off the group in 1980, when he challenged the beleaguered President Jimmy Carter for the Democratic nomination. For a candidate attempting to unseat an incumbent president— something that has never happened since the arrival of the primary system— Kennedy did well, winning several major primaries in the Northeast. But in fact, the strength of his candidacy arguably doomed President Carter in the general election, when he lost in a landslide to former California governor Ronald Reagan. Governor Dukakis was up next. In 1988, he captured the Democratic nomination only to come up short against George Herbert Walker Bush. Many concluded he was the victim of a harsh advertising campaign that he failed to respond to until it was too late, a theme that also helps define the Kerry loss. Batting third: Paul Tsongas, who represented Bill Clinton's toughest competition for the Democratic nomination in 1992. In the midst of Gennifer Flowers's allegations of an extended extramarital affair with Democratic frontrunner Clinton, Tsongas won the New Hampshire primary. Famously, however, the man who finished second claimed victory, tagging himself as the "Comeback Kid." From there, Clinton didn't look back until he was inaugurated the forty-second president of the United States. Twelve years later, in the cleanup spot, there was John Kerry. Of the four, he would achieve the best results on the national election stage. Indeed, according to one close observer of the political scene, "he overperformed his natural vote by four or five percentage points."[40] But nevertheless, he finished behind another George Bush, losing by 2.4 percent of the popular vote and thirty-four electoral votes.

For citizens of the Commonwealth (and all of New England), perhaps it was asking too much. After all, less than a week before Election Day 2004, their beloved Boston Red Sox had won the World Series for the first time in eighty-six years. They had done so, moreover, in dramatic fashion. Before sweeping the St. Louis Cardinals to reverse the fabled "Curse of the Bambino," they had defeated the mighty New York Yankees in a historic seven-game American League Championship Series. Led by the extra-inning heroics of a Ruthian figure—designated hitter David "Big Papi" Ortiz— the Sox battled back from three games to none to beat the Yankees in four games straight, thereby pulling off one of the greatest comebacks in the history of sport.

By the start of that series, those mixing baseball with politics had clearly identified a symbolic connection between the two teams and the nation's two major political parties. The Yankees—who Red Sox president Larry Lucchino referred to as an "evil empire"—were the Republicans. The Red Sox were the Democrats. In truth, more than symbolism distinguished the two teams politically. Yankees owner George Steinbrenner contributed to President Bush's campaign and had once pleaded guilty to felony charges—for which he was later pardoned by Ronald Reagan—for illegally funneling cash to President Nixon. The *Boston Globe*'s Dan Shaughnessy also saw "a Steinbrenner–Dick Cheney connection." As he put it, "they seem to be like-minded guys." And every baseball fan knew that former New York City mayor Rudy Giuliani—one of the president's chief surrogates during the campaign—was the Yankees' biggest enthusiast.

On the Red Sox side, principle owner John Henry was a Kerry contributor who would later campaign with the Massachusetts senator in New Hampshire. Moreover, as Ben McGrath wrote in the *New Yorker:* "Strictly from a management perspective, the Red Sox are progressive, with a front office resembling an activist judiciary, jettisoning tradition at the recommendation of intellectual elites with little practical hardball experience but plenty of theory . . . on their side."[41] There were some difficulties with this distinction. Curt Schilling—the Red Sox ace pitcher who defied injury to win Game Six against the Yankees in a blood-soaked sock—supported the president. And members of the team told each other to "Cowboy Up" in 2003, a phrase more often associated with the Republican candidate. Perhaps Leslie Epstein, the father of Red Sox general manager Theo, summed up the Democratic Red Sox and Republican Yankees political divide best when he said: "I've always been a Red Sox fan. I hated the Yankees so much. To me, rooting for them would be like voting Republican."[42]

Leslie Epstein got to see what those many Red Sox fans who experienced too short a life never did: the Sox as World Champs. It had not happened since 1918, when Jack Kennedy was a mere infant of seventeen months, Tip O'Neill a child of five years, and Bobby Kennedy yet to be born. But on the other hand, six days later, Red Sox fan John Kerry lost the presidency. In the end, it all came down to Ohio. In the streets of Cleveland, in the final moments of the campaign, Kerry leaned on Bruce Springsteen to help rally his supporters to the polls. Downstate near Cincinnati, Red Sox ace Schilling—in defiance of Leslie Epstein's logic—campaigned with the president. Whether or not Shilling made the difference,[43] the last of those four Massachusetts top dogs of 1982 had lost the presidency. Zero for four at the plate is a bad day for any batter. It's much worse for a political party, even over the course of twenty-four years.

There is no new curse. Some commentators say, however, that the Democrats may not have chosen their candidates wisely. Democrat John F. Kennedy was the last Northeasterner to win the presidency, besting Nixon in one of the nation's closest elections.[44] Since that time, the Democratic candidate has won the popular vote four times out of ten. Each of those nominees called the South home.[45] Of those who won the Democratic nomination but lost the popular vote in that span, two were from Massachusetts, two from Minnesota, and one from South Dakota who lost every state save Massachusetts.[46] In two of the last three presidential elections, Massachusetts has been the most Democratic state. In those two elections, it was the only state to give more than 60 percent of its vote to the Democratic candidate. It was one of three states to do the same in 2000. In fact, it has become common for Republicans to belittle the state and its liberal politics. For instance, George H. W. Bush referred to the state as "Taxachusetts." Disgruntled Bay Staters have called it: "Massataxus." In the final debate between George W. Bush and John Kerry, the president made reference to the "Senator from Massachusetts" three times. Here's just one example: "As a matter of fact, your record is such that Ted Kennedy, your colleague, is the conservative senator from Massachusetts."[47] To be sure, John Kerry—largely by virtue of his Vietnam War record—challenged the liberal label, which explains why the president more often referred to him as a "flip-flopper." But in the end, both tags seemed to stick. According to exit polls, 56 percent of voters said that Kerry says "what people want to hear" rather than what "he believes." Of that group, 84 percent voted for the president's reelection. Of the 34 percent of voters who called themselves conservative, 84 percent again supported Bush (a 3 percent increase from the 2000 results). Only 15 percent of conservative voters backed the "Senator from Massachusetts" (see tables 5.4 and 5.5).[48]

Democrats have continued to put their faith in northeasterners despite the decline in the region's Electoral College clout. When JFK captured the presidency in 1960, the Northeast commanded 153 of the 537 electoral votes, 28.5 percent of the nation's total. In 2004, that figure had diminished to 122 of 538 votes, just 22.7 percent of the total. If the Democratic candidates of the 1960s and 1970s had won only the Blue states of 2004, each still would have captured the presidency (albeit by the narrowest of margins with 270 electoral votes). In the 1980s and 1990s, those states would not have been enough to win, providing 262 and 259 electoral votes, respectively. In 2004, they gave Kerry just 252 electoral votes. Since the 1962 reapportionment, moreover, no northeastern state has gained an electoral vote. Half of the twelve have lost votes. Together New York and Pennsylvania have lost 20 electoral votes, ironically the same figure Ohio provided Bush in 2004.

CONGRESSIONAL ELECTIONS

Election Day 2004 was a good one for incumbents in the Northeast. In the region's House races, no incumbent lost. As suggested above, those who faced the most serious challenges were moderate Republicans, most notably Connecticut's Christopher Shays and Rob Simmons and Pennsylvania's Jim Gerlach. In the elections for the Northeast's U.S. Senate seats, there was not even a closely contested race on November 2, 2004. The closest came six months earlier in Pennsylvania, when Arlen Specter held off the conservative representative Pat Toomey by a mere 17,000 votes out of the million cast. Significantly, Toomey's challenge to Specter was widely understood as a battle "for the heart and soul" of the Republican Party in conservative circles and a worst-case scenario among moderates. As Toomey put it:

> Arlen Specter is a liberal. Across the board, he's much more likely to come down on the side of Ted Kennedy than he is on the side of conservatives. The reason I'm running is that there's a real opportunity now for the center right of the Republican Party—commonsense conservatives—to finally govern. We've waited seventy years to have complete control of the elected government in Washington. And we've got that today. We've got a Republican majority in the House, we've got a Republican in the White House, and we've got a Republican majority in the Senate. But, unfortunately, in the Senate it's really a nominal majority. It's not a functioning majority, and it's certainly not a conservative majority. And the reason is that a handful of liberal Republicans who never bought into the Republican conservative ideas in the first place are continuing to side with the Democrats and prevent us from accomplishing so many wonderful things we could be doing.[49]

Toomey's challenge against Snarlin' Arlen—a tag the senator earned due to his often harsh demeanor—had a chance in a closed primary—limited to registered party members who are typically more ideological—in the barely Blue state of Pennsylvania. After all, its junior senator is the conservative Rick Santorum. However, fearing that Toomey would lose in the general election, both the Bush White House and Senator Santorum provided vigorous support to Specter. In the end, this high-level support likely made the difference in the senator's narrow primary victory.

Despite the strength of incumbents, the 2004 House and Senate results are indicative of the bluing of the Northeast with regard to national politics. Since Democrats are likely to target GOP senators from Blue states or Republican House members representing marginal districts, incumbents usually must emphasize their independence from party leaders whenever possible. This is a difficult proposition in a narrowly divided Congress, particularly in the House, where Republican dissent is less tolerated by House leaders who significantly influence funding sources and may encourage primary challenges from more conservative candidates. Nevertheless, compared to the fate of Democrats in the South (see chapter 6), Republicans in the Northeast have managed to hold their own in both the House and the Senate. As indicated by the partisan breakdown in table 5.6, Republicans control 38 percent of the Northeast's House seats and 29 percent of its Senate seats. Moreover, of the twenty-six Republican-represented House districts Al Gore carried in 2000, sixteen were located in the Northeast in 2004. In comparison, the Northeast had only one Democratic-represented district carried by George Bush in 2000. (As might be expected, it was in the Red state of West Virginia.)[50] In 2004, Democrats did win one of those sixteen Republican-held seats, narrowly losing two others. In the district the Democrats won (New York-27), they did so because the popular incumbent Jack Quinn, weary from playing the role of a moderate Republican in a closely divided House, decided to retire from representing his Buffalo-area district.[51] Yet, even with Quinn off the ballot, the race was one of the nation's closest as Democrat Brian Higgins battled against Republican Nancy Naples. True to form, Naples emphasized—with significant assistance from Quinn—her independence from the GOP. In turn, Higgins tried to link his Republican opponent to George W. Bush by running commercials that repeatedly informed viewers that Naples had recently said: "I absolutely support the president." In the end, the election was not decided on election night, requiring a careful counting of all the ballots that resulted in a 3,774-vote Higgins victory.

Table 5.6. Partisan Breakdown of House and Senate Representation in the Northeast

States	2001 Senate	2005 Senate	2001 House			2003 House			2005 House		
			D	R	I	D	R	I	D	R	I
Connecticut	2 D	2 D	3	3		2	3		2	3	
Delaware	2 D	2 D		1			1			1	
Maine	2 R	2 R	2			2			2		
Maryland	2 D	2 D	4	4		6	2		6	2	
Massachusetts	2 D	2 D	10			10			10		
New Hampshire	2 R	2 R		2			2		2	2	
New Jersey	2 D	2 D	7	6		7	6		7	6	
New York	2 D	2 D	19	12		19	10		20	9	
Pennsylvania	2 R	2 R	10	11		7	12		7	12	
Rhode Island	1 D 1 R	1 D 1R	2			2			2		
Vermont	1 D 1 R	1 D 1 I			1			1			1
West Virginia	2 D	2 D	2	1		2	1		2	1	
Totals	16 D 8 R 0 I	16 D 7 R 1 I	59	40	1	57	37	1	58	36	1

CONCLUSION

The Higgins–Naples race says much about the Northeast as a whole. In this Democratic-trending region, Republicans most often must run as moderates to win federal office. At the national level, however, the influence of moderates in the Republican Party has dwindled substantially in recent years. Thus, as a national Republican, President Bush was unlikely to win in most of the Northeast. By simply proving to the region's voters he was a viable alternative, John Kerry was assured of a comfortable victory in nine of the Northeast's twelve states (see table 5.2). Kerry performed even better, also winning the region's two battleground states of New Hampshire and Pennsylvania. In future elections, Democrats will once again look to the Northeast for easy support, but if the 2004 results are any indication, they will likely win the White House only by displaying greater independence from the region's widely perceived "liberal" values.

NOTES

1. On the politics of northeastern states, see generally: Duane Lockard, *New England State Politics* (Princeton, NJ: Princeton University Press, 1959); Josephine F. Milburn and William Doyle, *New England Political Parties* (Cambridge, MA: Schenkman, 1983); Robert W. Speel, *Changing Patterns of Voting in the Northern United States: Electoral Realignment, 1952–1996* (University Park: The Pennsylvania State University Press, 1998); Jeffrey M. Stonecash, ed., *Governing New York State* (Albany: State University of New York Press, 2001); and John Kenneth White, *The Fractured Electorate: Political Parties and Social Change in Southern New England* (Hanover, NH: University Press of New England, 1983). See also, John Leonard, ed., *These United States* (New York: Thunder's Mouth Press/Nation Books, 2003); Alan Rosenthal and Maureen Moakley, eds., *The Political Life of the American States* (New York: Praeger, 1984).
2. At the time, there were forty-five states, and the District of Columbia was not entitled to any electoral votes.
3. Bush quoted in Robert D. McFadden, "After the Attacks: The President," *New York Times*, September 15, 2001.
4. David Fisher quoted in HBO Films, *Nine Innings from Ground Zero*, 2004.
5. George W. Bush, "Remarks Accepting the Presidential Nomination at the Republican National Convention in New York City," September 2, 2004, *Weekly Compilation of Presidential Documents 2004*.
6. Alan Abramowitz, "Terrorism, Gay Marriage, and Incumbency: Explaining the Republican Victory in the 2004 Presidential Election," *The Forum* 2 (2004), no. 4, article 3, 6.
7. Quoted in White, *The Fractured Electorate*, 72. For more on Cianci, see Mike Stanton, *The Prince of Providence: The Rise and Fall of Buddy Cianci, America's Most Notorious Mayor* (New York: Random House, 2003, 2004).

8. In calculating the average during these years, Republicans controlled the governor's office 52.78 percent of the time in these states. Calculation: 76 GOP years/144 total years = 52.78.

9. Dale Russakoff, "From Its Apex, a Political Career Goes South," *Washington Post*, May 3, 1997.

10. Steven Lee Myers, "Helms to Oppose Weld as Nominee for Ambassador," *New York Times*, June 4, 1997; see also, Andrew Miga, "Rocky Road; GOP reps fighting to derail Weld post; Gov. Weld's support of medicinal marijuana use has some conservative House members smoking mad, ready to fight," *Boston Herald*, May 2, 1997.

11. Brian McGrory and Chris Black, "A Stymied Weld Gives Up Fight," *Boston Globe*, September 16, 1997.

12. Christie Todd Whitman, *It's My Party, Too: Taking Back the Republican Party and Bringing the Country Together Again* (New York: Penguin, 2005). For more on the Republican Party, see Lewis L. Gould, *Grand Old Party: A History of the Republicans* (New York: Random House, 2003). See also, Nicol C. Rae, *The Decline and Fall of Liberal Republicans: from 1952 to the present* (New York: Oxford University Press, 1989).

13. Michael Barone and Richard E. Cohen, *The Almanac of American Politics* (Washington, DC: National Journal, 2004), 723.

14. The lone exception is 1964, when Barry Goldwater and William E. Miller made up the GOP presidential ticket.

15. Kevin Phillips, *The Emerging Republican Majority* (Garden City, NY: Anchor Books, 1970; originally published by Arlington House in 1969); and Speel, *Changing Patterns of Voting in the Northern United States*, 18.

16. Phillips, *The Emerging Republican Majority*, 464–466, 29.

17. Goldwater quoted in Kathleen Hall Jamieson, *Packaging the Presidency: A History and Criticism of Presidential Campaign Advertising*, 3rd edition (New York: Oxford University Press, 1996), 179.

18. Phillips, *The Emerging Republican Majority*, 32–33.

19. Delaware was the twenty-fourth most Democratic state.

20. This figure also emphasizes the importance of California in the Democratic Party's election strategy. With 55 electoral votes, the Golden State supplied Kerry with nearly a quarter of his 252 total.

21. Carter also won Washington, DC, and, more importantly, took 108 of the region's 144 electoral votes.

22. Speel, *Changing Patterns of Voting in the Northern United States*, 58–59.

23. See James M. Jeffords, *My Declaration of Independence* (New York: Simon & Schuster, 2001).

24. Mary Curtius, "Judicial Remarks Stir Conservatives," *Los Angeles Times*, November 5, 2004; and Lara Jakes Jordan, "Specter Warns Bush on Picks for Top Court," *Pittsburgh Post-Gazette*, November 4, 2004.

25. See, for example, Maureen Dowd, "Absolute Power Erupts," *New York Times*, November 21, 2004.

26. Carl Hulse, "House GOP Acts to Protect Chief," *New York Times*, November 18, 2004; Gebe Martinez, "GOP Moderates in Congress Get Cold Shoulder," *Houston Chronicle*, November 21, 2004. In the end, Shays' position won the day on this rule

change. Responding to pressure, the House Republican caucus voted to void the "DeLay rule"; see Carl Hulse, "House GOP Voids Rule It Adopted Shielding Leader," and "After Retreat, GOP Changes House Ethics Rule," *New York Times*, January 4, 2005.

27. Republican Randy Kuhl (NY-29) and Democrat Brian Higgins (NY-27) replaced Republican moderates Amo Houghton and Jack Quinn, respectively.

28. The National Election Pool exit poll results are available at www.cnn.com

29. Lios Romano, "Kerry Hunting Trip Sets Sights on Swing Voters," *Washington Post*, October 21, 2004.

30. Phillips, *The Emerging Republican Majority*, 69–73.

31. Quoted in Robert David Sullivan, "Beyond Red and Blue: The New Map of American Politics," *Commonwealth*, 2003; available at www.massinc.org

32. These four counties are: Bucks, Chester, Delaware, and Montgomery. Katharine Q. Seelye, "In Battle for Pennsylvania, Philadelphia Suburbs Probably Hold the Key," *New York Times*, August 24, 2004.

33. Donald W. Beachler, "A New Democratic Era? Presidential Political in Pennsylvania, 1984–1996," *Commonwealth* (1997–1998), vol. 9, 57–71, 60.

34. For possible reasons for this Democratic decline, see John B. Judis and Ruy Teixeira, *The Emerging Democratic Majority* (New York: Scribner, 2002), 94–95.

35. The other five counties are: Beaver, Butler, Fayette, Washington, and Westmoreland.

36. Beachler, "A New Democratic Era?" 60–61.

37. The eight southern states included are (from North to South): Virginia, Kentucky, Tennessee, North Carolina, South Carolina, Georgia, Alabama, and Mississippi.

38. Sullivan, "Beyond Red and Blue," and "Beyond Red and Blue (Again)," *Boston Globe*, November 14, 2004.

39. In 2000, Gore won 61.3 percent and 52.9 percent of the vote in the Philadelphia and Pittsburgh regions, respectively.

40. Newt Gingrich, former speaker of the House of Representatives, quoted in Todd S. Purdum, "An Electoral Affirmation of Shared Values," *New York Times*, November 4, 2004.

41. Ben McGrath, "Down the Stretch," *The New Yorker*, September 20, 2004; Patrick Healy, "Red Sox Leaders Back Kerry in Triple-play Appearance," *Boston Globe*, November 1, 2004.

42. Quoted in Adrian Wojnarowski, "Red Sox GM is Making Boss Squirm," *The Record* (Bergen County, NJ), July 31, 2003.

43. In his electoral analysis on Fox News, conservative commentator Fred Barnes asserted that Schilling had made a difference in Ohio but that Springsteen had not.

44. George Herbert Walker Bush was raised in the Northeast but called Texas home when he captured the presidency in 1988.

45. Georgia's Jimmy Carter (1976), Arkansas's Bill Clinton (1992 and 1996), and Tennessee's Al Gore (2000). Gore won the popular vote but lost the presidency by virtue of his loss in the electoral college.

46. They are: Dukakis (1988); Kerry (2004); Humphrey (1968); Mondale (1984); and McGovern (1972), respectively. Carter did both, winning the popular vote in 1976 and losing it four years later.

47. Quoted in Timothy Noah, "Lay Off Massachusetts," October 14, 2004, at www.slate.com

48. By contrast, of the 21 percent of voters who identified themselves as liberal, 13 percent voted for Bush and 85 percent supported Kerry.
49. Quotes appear in Philip Gourevitch, "Fight on the Right," *New Yorker*, April 12, 2004.
50. Barone and Cohen, *The Almanac of American Politics*, 44–45.
51. See for example, Douglas Turner and Jerry Zremski, "Quinn's Legacy of Contrasts," *Buffalo News*, December 27, 2004.

6

THE SOUTH

Race, Religion, and
Republican Domination

Donald W. Beachler

THE SOUTH AND
CONTEMPORARY AMERICAN POLITICS

The 2004 election continued the recent pattern of Republican dominance of the politics of the American South. For the second straight election, George W. Bush carried all 13 southern states and consequently received all of the region's electoral votes. In 2000 and 2004, Bush won all the southern states despite the fact that a southerner, Al Gore of Tennessee, headed the Democratic ticket in 2000 and North Carolina Senator John Edwards was the Democratic vice presidential choice in 2004. In 2000, Bush's sweep of the South netted him 163 electoral votes. The reapportion ment of House seats following the 2000 census gave the South 168 electoral votes for the 2004 election. The South is by no means the only Republican region of the country, but it is interesting to note that, outside the South, Al Gore won 267 electoral votes compared to 108 for Bush in 2000. In 2004, John Kerry won 252 electoral votes outside the South, while the nonsouthern states captured by Bush provided him with 114 electoral votes. The South put George W. Bush in the White House and it was the South that kept him there.

George Bush's showing in the South in 2004 was even more impressive than in 2000 because he improved on his 2000 margin of victory in every southern state but

North Carolina, where he won by 13 percent of the vote in 2000 and 12 percent in 2004. In Florida, where Bush had prevailed by 537 votes or 0.01 percent in 2000, the president won by 381,000 votes in 2004, for a margin of about 5 percent. Florida was the only southern state where John Kerry got more than 45 percent of the popular vote. In 2004, the Democrats had a number of theories about what might enable them to win electoral votes in the South. It was thought that the loss of tens of thousands of textile jobs in the Carolinas might help there. Virginia, with rapid population growth in the Washington suburbs, was considered to be less southern as it experienced demographic change. In 2000, fearful of backlash against Bill Clinton's impeachment scandal, Al Gore had distanced himself from Clinton. Gore lost Clinton's home state of Arkansas by 5 percent of the vote. In 2004, Kerry welcomed Clinton's assistance and Democrats hoped that the support of the former president would bring them Arkansas's six electoral votes. Despite a last-minute campaign appearance in Little Rock by Clinton, who was recovering from major heart surgery, Kerry lost Arkansas by 9 percent of the vote.

This book focuses on the presidential election of 2004, but the South is also the guarantor of Republican power in the U.S. Congress. There were six open Senate seats in the South in 2004. The Republicans won all six of these contests and were able to narrowly hold on to a seat in Kentucky despite the inept campaigning of Jim Bunning, the Republican incumbent. After the 2004 election, the Republicans held a 22–4 advantage in southern Senate seats. Outside the South there were 41 Democrats and 34 Republicans in the Senate.[1] In the House of Representatives, Republicans had a 92 to 50 margin among Southern delegations, while Democrats had a 153 to 140 majority among representatives from outside the South.[2]

The development of the South into a Republican bastion in presidential and congressional elections took place over several decades. This chapter will begin with an overview of the one-party Democratic South that lasted for nearly a century after the Civil War and then proceed to examine the rise of the Republicans in southern politics.

THE ONE-PARTY DEMOCRATIC SOUTH

The end of Reconstruction in 1877 eliminated any prospect of black equality in nineteenth-century America.[3] In the following years, African American rights were severely undermined as the fourteenth and fifteenth Amendments were left largely unenforced and segregation and disfranchisement became widespread in the South. The right of states to enforce segregation was upheld in 1896 in the famous Supreme Court decision *Plessy v. Ferguson* which promulgated the separate but equal doctrine.

Segregation in the South extended to public education from primary schools to universities, libraries, cemeteries, public transportation vehicles and transit stations, movie theaters, restaurants, and athletic contests.[4] Many southern and border states outlawed interracial marriage until such prohibitions were overturned by the United States Supreme Court in the 1967 decision *Loving v. Virginia*.

In most of the South, blacks were denied access to the ballot box by a variety of mechanisms including literacy tests, poll taxes, grandfather clauses, and extrajudicial intimidation and murder. As the South quickly evolved into a one-party system, the white primary was also developed. Because Democrats won nearly every office in most of the South, blacks could be excluded by measures that permitted only whites to vote in the Democratic primary.[5] By the early years of the twentieth century, few African Americans voted in the South.

The political instrument of white supremacy in the South was the Democratic Party. Because Abraham Lincoln was a Republican and because the radical wing of the Republican Party had pursued policies promoting black equality during Reconstruction, Democrats were able to marginalize the Republicans in much of the South by labeling them as the party of Yankee domination and black equality. By 1900, the South had largely evolved into a one-party system that was to remain undisturbed for nearly fifty years.[6] The renowned political scientist V. O. Key argued that most of the political and institutional arrangements that prevailed in the South during the first half of the twentieth century were centered on questions of race.[7] Candidates sometimes sought political advantage by claiming that they were more committed to preserving white supremacy than were their opponents. The Deep South states of South Carolina, Georgia, Alabama, Mississippi, and Louisiana had the highest black populations and were most committed to the cause of white supremacy and thus to the Democratic Party.

From 1880 through 1944, Democrats had a virtual lock on the electoral votes of the southern states. White voters, in the states with the highest black percentages, were most devoted to the segregationist system and therefore most intensely committed to the Democratic Party.[8] Only twice in this period did any southern states cast their electoral votes for a Republican presidential candidate. In 1920, Warren Harding won Tennessee and Oklahoma. More serious defections from the Democrats occurred when they nominated a Catholic, Al Smith of New York, in 1928. With Smith's religion an issue in the campaign, Republican Herbert Hoover carried seven southern states. The five states in Dixie with the highest black populations (Alabama, Georgia, Louisiana, Mississippi, and South Carolina), and the strongest commitment by whites to segregation, remained loyal to the Democratic ticket in 1928, as did Arkansas.[9]

In each of his four successful campaigns for the presidency, Franklin D. Roosevelt carried all thirteen southern states. In some of the southern states (the outer South) with lower black populations, Republicans received a respectable share of the vote. In some Deep South states, support for the Democrats reached near una- nimity. For example FDR received 98.6 percent of the vote in South Carolina in 1936 and 98.2 percent in 1940. To keep his southern base in line, FDR was reluctant to express overt support for even the most basic civil rights measures. For example, the president refused to take a position on the effort to pass legislation making lynch- ing a federal crime.[10] However, through judicial appointments and the creation of a civil rights section of the Justice Department, FDR did seek to weaken the power of white supremacist politicians of the South.[11]

Southern Democratic sensitivity on the race issue could reach extreme dimensions. In 1936, South Carolina senator Ellison "Cotton Ed" Smith walked out of the Democratic Convention because a black minister offered the invocation. Smith's colorful account of his departure from the convention hall has become infamous. "Bless God, out on that platform walked a slew-footed, blue gummed, kinky headed Senegambian. And he started praying and I started walking. And as I pushed through the great doors, and walked across the vast rotunda it seemed to me that old John Calhoun leaned down from his mansion in the sky and whispered in my ear, 'You did right Ed . . .' "[12]

The United States endured the Depression, experienced the reforms of the New Deal, and defeated the racist fascism of Nazi Germany as a segregated nation. While the South had the most pronounced system of legal segregation, segregation was, as a practical matter, not uncommon in the North. The American armed forces that triumphed in World War II did so as a segregated military. Major League Baseball, the national pastime in the 1940s, permitted only white players at the end of World War II.

Civil Rights and Strain in the Democratic Coalition

The relationship between the South and the Democratic Party showed severe strains in the election of 1948. In early 1948, President Truman proposed legislation that would make lynching a federal crime, ban racial discrimination in employment, and protect black voting rights.[13] Concerned about winning black votes in contested northern states, the Democratic Party, for the first time in its history, adopted a platform embracing civil rights. Southern segregationists were outraged that, in its effort to reelect President Truman, the Democratic Party had explicitly abandoned its commitment to the white South. Several southern delegates left the convention and later convened in Birmingham, Alabama, as the States' Rights Party, to nominate South Carolina's Democratic governor J. Strom Thurmond as its candidate for pres- ident. Thurmond, who later gained fame for serving in the U.S. Senate until he was 100 years old, made the principal priority of the new party clear when he stated that ". . . I am not opposed to the Negro. But I think it in the best interests of law and order, for the integrity of the races, whites and blacks should be kept in separate schools, theaters, and swimming pools. . . . We of the South think it is better not to admit persons of other races into churches, restaurants . . . and other public places."[14]

The commitment of most white southern Democrats to upholding segregation and white supremacy was as strong in 1950 as it had been a half century earlier. The raw racism behind these convictions was stated by even those regarded as the most dignified and genteel southern politicians. Richard Russell of Georgia served his state for thirty-eight years (1933–1971) and today one of the three U.S. Senate office buildings is named after him. Russell was regarded as a scholarly and thoughtful man, yet, he objected to interracial marriage on the grounds that it would lead to a "mongrel race" and all mongrel races were doomed to failure. On the issue of equality between the races, Russell stated that, "Any White man who wants to take the position that he is no better than the Negro is entitled to his own opinion of himself. I do not think much of him, but he can think it."[15]

Despite the fact that there was a Democrat running as a segregationist candidate and a left-wing independent candidacy by former vice president Henry Wallace, Harry Truman was able to defeat Thomas Dewey in the election of 1948. Despite Truman's success, the election of 1948 carried a warning to the Democrats. Thurmond carried four Deep South states, Alabama, Louisiana, Mississippi, and South Carolina. Unlike previous state defections in 1920, and more significantly in 1928, Thurmond won states that had some of the highest black populations in the United States. White voters, who were virtually the entire electorate in these states, put the Democrats on notice that there could be political costs to deviating from the segregationist position that had bonded Democrats and white Southerners for many decades.

Neither political party was particularly eager to take up the cause of civil rights in the 1950s and early 1960s. Other political actors would make political neutrality an increasingly difficult political stance. In 1954, the U.S. Supreme Court declared that segregation was inherently unequal and ruled that racial segregation in public schools was unconstitutional. A year later, led by the young minister Martin Luther King, Jr., blacks in Montgomery, Alabama, launched a boycott of the city's bus system to protest the indignities of segregation on the buses. In 1960, black college students in Greensboro, North Carolina, attracted national attention as they "sat in" at lunch counters where they were forbidden to dine because of their race.[16] Republican Dwight Eisenhower, who was elected president in 1952 and 1956, asserted that laws could not change human hearts with regard to racial issues. Eisenhower stated that he would enforce federal law and did so by sending federal troops to implement federal court orders to integrate Central High School in Little

Rock, Arkansas, in 1957. Eisenhower, however, refused to publicly state his views on the *Brown v. Board of Education* decision. Adlai Stevenson, the Democrat who lost to Eisenhower in 1952 and 1956, was also reluctant to take a stand in favor of civil rights. Stevenson stated that he believed the *Brown* case had been correctly decided, but he opposed using federal troops to enforce school integration.[17]

In the election of 1960, Democrat John F. Kennedy and Republican Richard Nixon sought to win black votes by cautiously supporting civil rights. In the elections of 1952, 1956, and 1960, the South's electoral votes were split between Democrats and Republicans. While race was the defining factor in the region's politics, it is important to note that Republicans were able to win southern electoral votes before the Democrats were identified as the party of civil rights and the party of the over-whelming majority of black voters. At this time, Republicans did well among the growing numbers of middle-class, college-educated voters who voted for the GOP as did similar voters outside the South.[18]

The Republican and Democratic parties were truly differentiated on civil rights most distinctively in 1964. By 1964, President Lyndon Johnson had clearly embraced many of the basic demands of the civil rights movement. Most notably, Johnson had signed the 1964 Civil Rights Act that banned racial discrimination in employment, public facilities, and accommodations. The Republicans nominated Arizona senator Barry Goldwater, the leader of the party's conservative wing. Goldwater voted against the Civil Rights Act and campaigned hard for the votes of southern states. Goldwater's efforts, however, were hampered by his opposition to federal programs that were popular in many parts of the South. Goldwater opposed federal subsidies to farmers, proposed making Social Security contributions voluntary, and favored privatizing the Tennessee Valley Authority, a source of jobs and cheap electricity in several southern states. In losing a national landslide to Lyndon Johnson, Goldwater carried the five Deep South states with the highest proportion of black voters (Alabama, Georgia, Louisiana, Mississippi, and South Carolina). In Mississippi, where few blacks were permitted to vote in 1964, Goldwater won a remarkable 87 percent of the vote. Johnson managed to win, though by relatively small margins, the eight states in the outer South.[19]

By 1968, the white South was in full-scale rebellion against the national Democratic Party that had passed the 1965 Voting Rights Act, the 1968 Fair Housing Act, and a host of social programs that were aimed at helping the poor. The general election in 1968 was a three-way race between Vice President Hubert Humphrey, a strong champion of civil rights, Republican Richard Nixon, and the former Democratic governor of Alabama, George C. Wallace, who had attracted national attention by standing in a doorway at the University of Alabama in a futile attempt to block the admission of black students.[20]

Wallace was known for his flamboyant stands on social and racial issues. Wallace taunted hippy college students who shouted obscenities at him, telling them that there were two four-letter words he was sure that they did not know: SOAP and WORK. As he campaigned across the country, Wallace delighted his supporters by explaining that Alabama did not have riots because in his state the first person who showed an inclination to riot was shot in the head. Wallace mocked the intellectuals who protested the Vietnam War as impractical people who could not park a bicycle straight.[21] A few months before the election, some polls showed Wallace getting a quarter of the vote.[22]

Wallace was a potential threat to Republican Richard Nixon, who sought votes in the South by running as a moderate conservative. Republicans feared that if Wallace won most of the South's electoral votes, the election would be decided in the U.S. House of Representatives, where Democrats had a substantial majority. Nixon presented himself as a candidate who would not repeal civil rights laws, but opposed busing and other measures that involved the federal government in enforcing integration on the South. Earl Black and Merle Black describe Nixon as the candidate of those white southerners who were willing to abandon strict segregation, but did not favor integration.[23] Nixon also appealed to conservative white southerners with his denunciations of the liberal Supreme Court headed by Chief Justice Earl Warren and by promising to restore law and order to a nation that had witnessed a rise in crime and riots in many cities. South Carolina's Strom Thurmond, now a Republican, worked vigorously on Nixon's behalf. Thurmond argued that Nixon was an electable conservative and that a vote for Wallace was a vote to elect the liberal Humphrey to the presidency.

While Nixon narrowly defeated Humphrey in the 1968 election, George Wallace made an impressive showing. Wallace won five southern states (Alabama, Arkansas, Georgia, Louisiana, and Mississippi) and finished a strong second in North Carolina, South Carolina, and Tennessee. Nixon carried seven southern states. Humphrey, with the help of native son Lyndon Johnson, was able to win only Texas. Humphrey's showing in the South was the worst performance of any Democratic candidate since the end of Reconstruction. The election of 1968 marked a new era in southern and national presidential politics. The white South was in open rebellion against the national Democratic Party.

THE EMERGENCE OF
A REPUBLICAN PRESIDENTIAL SOUTH

In the 1970s and 1980s, the southern white electorate evolved away from the Democratic Party. While race was a key, it was not the only factor in the transformation of southern politics. The majority of southern whites deviated from liberal Democratic norms on a number of key issues. Based on National Election surveys, Earl Black and Merle Black found just over half of all white southerners in the 1980s were loyal Republicans. These southern white Republicans favored large defense budgets, believed religion should play a significant role in national life, opposed racial quotas, and were ill-disposed toward gays and lesbians. Over a fifth of the southern electorate was made up of white swing voters who were not firmly committed to one political party. These swing voters were culturally conservative. They were opposed to racial quotas, favored the death penalty, and believed that prayer should be permitted in public schools.[24] Whites were a majority of the electorate in every southern state and most of them were conservative on racial and nonracial issues.

After 1968, the Democrats reformed their presidential nominating process to require that delegates be chosen in primaries or caucuses. These reforms weakened the power of party leaders and elected officials. Because more liberal voters participated in Democratic primaries, between 1972 and 1988 the party often nominated presidential candidates who had difficulties competing in the South.[25] At times, southern Democrats have been able to parlay strong support in their native region into enough support to win the Democratic presidential nomination.[26]

Table 6.1 compares electoral votes won in the South and the rest of the nation in eight presidential elections from 1972 through 2000. In only one of the elections did the Democratic candidate win a majority of southern electoral votes. In fact, in an era when the South was quickly becoming a Republican stronghold, the region was essential in putting Jimmy Carter of Georgia in the White House. The year 1976 deviates from all other elections discussed in this chapter. Since the Civil War, no southerner had been elected president of the United States. Carter appealed to the South to finally elect one of its own to the presidency. (Carter was the first southerner elected directly to the presidency. since Zachary Taylor in 1848.) As a small-town peanut farmer, evangelical Christian, and a politician with an uncanny ability to appeal across racial lines, Carter carried most of the South and narrowly won the presidency in 1976. Although he did not win the southern white vote, Cater carried about 47 percent of the whites and, combined with overwhelming black support, won eleven of thirteen Southern states. One white man in Mississippi likely spoke for many when he explained his vote in 1976, by saying that he voted for Carter because he was ". . . a good old southern boy."[27] By 1980, when Carter was beset by economic and foreign policy problems, he did no better among white voters in his native South than in other regions of the country when he was beaten handily by Ronald Reagan.

Reagan played a great role in consolidating Republican dominance of the South in presidential elections. Reagan was the first Republican president to openly

Table 0.1. Southern and Non-Southern Electoral Votes, 1972–2004

	South		Non-South	
	D	R	D	R
1972 McGovern (D) vs. Nixon (R)	0	147	17	374
1976 Carter (D) vs. Ford (R)	127	20	170	221
1980 Carter (D) vs. Reagan (R)	12	135	37	354
1984 Mondale (D) vs. Reagan (R)	0	153	13	385
1988 Dukakis (D) vs. Bush (R)	0	153	112	273
1992 Clinton (D) vs. Bush (R)	46	117	324	51
1996 Clinton (D) vs. Dole (R)	58	105	321	54
2000 Gore (D) vs. Bush (R)	0	163	267	100
2004 Kerry (D) vs. Bush (R)	0	168	252	114

embrace alliance with the conservative Christian movement, now known as the Religious Right, that fought against legal abortion, gay rights, and for public school prayer and a greater role for religion in public life. Over the course of his political career, Reagan consistently opposed civil rights bills. In 1980, Reagan opened his general election campaign in Mississippi, where he declared his support for states' rights. States rights was long a code word for segregation and white supremacy, and the white crowd in Philadelphia, Mississippi, a town where three civil rights workers had been murdered in 1964, understood Reagan's appeal to their racial conservatism. Reagan also won the approval from a large majority of southern whites with his support for large military budgets and an assertive foreign policy. When he left office, one poll indicated that Reagan was regarded as a racist by about three-fourths of black Americans, but he was popular among a majority of whites, and especially popular among southern whites.[28]

In three presidential elections, Democrats nominated northern liberals who did not fare well in the North or the South. George McGovern and Walter Mondale each carried just one state (McGovern won Massachusetts and Mondale carried

Minnesota, while both of them carried the District of Columbia). George H. W. Bush decisively defeated Michael Dukakis in 1988. Dukakis did win 10 states and 112 electoral votes, but none of them were in the South.

In 1992 and 1996 the Democratic ticket was comprised of two southern candidates, Bill Clinton of Arkansas and Al Gore of Tennessee. In each of the elections the Republicans carried a majority of the southern electoral votes, but Democrats were able to win some electoral votes in the South. In both 1992 and 1996, the Clinton–Gore ticket carried Arkansas, Kentucky, Louisiana, and Tennessee. In 1992, the Democrats also carried Georgia, which reverted to the Republicans in 1996. However, in 1996 Clinton won Florida, which, as the fourth most populous state, was a very desirable target. By winning southern states and coming close in others, Clinton was able to make the Republicans expend resources that had to be diverted away from crucial battleground states outside the South. (Presidential candidates may wish to force their opponents to spend funds in a state even when they believe they have relatively little chance of carrying it. For example, when John Kerry's campaign announced that it was buying television ads in Virginia in May 2004, many political observers believed the campaign was trying to lure the Bush campaign into spending funds in a state that most believed would vote Republican in November.[29])

The most remarkable regional disparity occurred in the 2000 presidential election. In 2000, Al Gore won the nationwide popular vote on his way to becoming the first presidential candidate since 1888 to win the popular vote, but not attain the presidency. Gore also won 72 percent of the electoral votes outside the South. However, Gore failed to carry a single state in the South. Only by winning all thirteen southern states was George W. Bush able to overcome Gore's strength in the Northeast, West Coast, and the upper Midwest. Gore even failed to carry his own state of Tennessee, which had twice elected him to the U.S. Senate and which had, in 1992 and 1996, voted for the Clinton–Gore ticket. Gore's inability to carry a single state in his home region at a time when he was part of an incumbent administration and in a period of peace and prosperity, was largely attributable to a conservative region's rejection of the perceived Democratic permissiveness on issues of sexual morality. In 2004, George W. Bush won the popular vote by a margin of about 2.5 percent. The regional disparities exhibited in 2000 remained as Bush swept the South's electoral votes, but Kerry won 69 percent of the electoral votes outside the South.

THE RACIAL CONTEXT

In explaining southern affection for the Republican Party, some commentators will reflect on southerners or the South as if southern voting patterns were not often a case of black and white. For example, Georgia Democratic senator Zell Miller endorsed George W. Bush for reelection in 2004 and supported Bush's foreign and domestic policies almost without exception. Miller had been the keynote speaker at the Democratic Convention of 1992. That year, Miller had denounced Republicans as the party of the rich and praised Democrats as the party of opportunity for the average person. By 2003, Miller published a book, *A National Party No More*, that purported to explain Democrats' lack of appeal to southerners. Miller argued that since the 1970s, liberals' weakness on defense and support of high taxes had driven southerners from the Democratic Party.[30] Curiously, Miller neglected to distinguish between African American and white southerners. In most elections since 1972, southern whites have favored Republicans by overwhelming margins and been more Republican than white voters elsewhere in the nation. Southern blacks, like blacks elsewhere in the country, voted for Democrats by large majorities.

Table 6.2 demonstrates that only in 1976 was southern white support of Republicans similar to what the GOP gained from white voters elsewhere in the country. Jimmy Carter's 47 percent of the southern white vote in 1976 was by far the best showing by a Democratic candidate in the post-1968 era. Bill Clinton, one of the most successful southern Democrats in presidential politics since Andrew Jackson, lost the southern white vote by a 49 to 34 percent margin in 1992 and 56 to 36 percent in 1996. (The bulk of the remainder of the white vote in 1992 and 1996 went to Ross Perot.) In a battle of two southern candidates, George W. Bush bested Al Gore by 31 percent among southern white voters. Against John Kerry, Bush won southern whites by a 41 percent margin. It is clear that southern white voters are the basis of Republican victories in presidential elections.

It is impossible to determine with precision the extent to which southern white support of Republicans is rooted in the Democrats' support of civil rights and

Table 6.2. White Support for the Republican Presidential Candidate by Region, 1972–2004 (in %)

	1972	1976	1980	1984	1988	1992	1996	2000	2004
Whites in the Northeast	65	50	52	57	54	36	37	44	50
Whites in the Midwest	65	52	55	64	57	39	43	53	56
Whites in the South	76	52	61	71	67	49	56	66	70
Whites in the West	60	54	55	66	58	47	44	51	54

identification with black interests.[31] Certain facts cannot be disputed. Southern white voters deserted the Democratic Party in droves as the Democrats became the party of civil rights. Richard Nixon was greatly aided in his drive for the presidency in 1968 by South Carolina's Strom Thurmond, who only abandoned segregationist policies in the 1970s after they became politically untenable.[32] Republicans benefited from their opposition to bussing and affirmative action. In many elections, the states with the highest black population also had the highest proportion of whites voting Republican.[33]

The racial context of white presidential voting in southern states in 2000 and 2004 is presented in table 6.3. The data presented here indicates that the strongest white support for George W. Bush was, with the exception of Bush's home state of Texas, in the Deep South states that have the highest percentage black populations. Mississippi, the state with the largest proportion of blacks in the United States, had the most racially polarized voting of any state in the nation. It would appear that, at least in 2000 and 2004, white support for the GOP was highest in those states that, historically, were the fiercest defenders of segregation and retain the largest black populations. In 2004, Bush did better with white voters in nearly every southern state. Still, again, with the exception of Texas, Bush did best among southern whites in states with comparatively high black populations. Race is clearly a factor in southern white Republicanism, but, as the next section of this chapter demonstrates, it is not the only explanation for such strong white support for the GOP.

Race apparently matters in other southern elections, sometimes in unusual ways. White voters in conservative regions of Louisiana appear to have opposed the 2003

Table 6.3. Black Population and White Support for George W. Bush

	Black % Population (2000 Census)	White Vote for Bush, 2000 (%)	White Vote for Bush, 2004 (%)
Alabama	26	72	80
Arkansas	16	56	63
Florida	14	57	57
Georgia	29	71	76
Kentucky	7	59	64
Louisiana	32	72	75
Mississippi	36	81	85
Oklahoma	8	62	71
North Carolina	21	68	73
South Carolina	29	70	78
Tennessee	16	60	65
Texas	11	72	73
Virginia	19	60	68

Republican gubernatorial nominee, Bobby Jindal, because he is of Indian descent. Despite his outspoken conservatism, Jindal did worse than expected for a Republican in the areas where Ku Klux Klan leader David Duke did quite well in his 1991 race for governor of the state.[34]

RELIGION AND SOUTHERN POLITICS

In 2004, PBS produced a documentary entitled "The Jesus Factor" about the strong religious faith of President Bush and his relationship to white evangelical Christians. Deeply religious, conservative Christians were regarded as a very important element of the president's political base. Religiosity is a key variable in explaining the political preferences of American voters. In 2000, those voters who attended religious services weekly supported George W. Bush over Al Gore by a 57 to 40 percent margin. Those who reported that they attended religious services more than once a week went for Bush by a 63 to 36 margin. Those who responded that their attendance was seldom, supported Gore 54 to 42 percent. Voters who responded that they never attend religious services supported Gore 61 to 32 percent.

In recent decades conservative, mostly white Christians have become a major influence in American political life.[35] These Christians have mobilized against what they viewed as the excessively secularizing trends in society. They wished to return prayer to the public schools, make abortion illegal in all or most cases, and opposed the agenda of the gay rights movement that sought to gain homosexuals the right to nondiscrimination in employment, to marry, and to serve in the military. Conservative Christians, often known as the Religious Right, also opposed the growing open display and promotion of sexuality in the popular culture.[36]

In presidential elections, the Republican candidates have generally been in accord with most of the positions favored by the Religious Right. Democrats have been very pro-choice, opposed to state-sponsored prayer in public schools, and, while cautious, generally more supportive of gay rights than Republicans. Social issues, sometimes referenced as the culture wars, are a major difference between the two parties in presidential elections.

Because questions about religion and politics were asked quite differently in the exit polls of 2000 and 2004, it is difficult to compare the impact of the Religious Right across two different elections. The 2004 exit polls did ask voters in regional surveys whether they were evangelical or born-again Christians. Table 6.4 examines the concentration and voting patterns of white evangelical/born-again Christians (WEBACs) in each of the four regions.

Table 6.4. White Evangelical Born-Again Christians (WEBACs) and The 2004 Presidential
Election

	Whites as % of Electorate	WEBACs as % of Electorate	WEBACs as % of White Voters	WEBACs % vote for Bush	NonWEBACs % vote for Bush
Northeast	78	10	14	72	40
South	71	33	46	80	47
Midwest	85	25	29	76	43
West	77	19	25	79	40

Table 6.4 indicates that WEBACs were a considerably greater portion of the electorate in the South than in other regions of the country. About one in three southern voters stated that they were WEBACs as opposed to just one in 10 voters in the Northeast, where John Kerry ran very well. Almost half of all white voters in the South described themselves as evangelical or born-again as opposed to a quarter in the West, nearly 30 percent in the Midwest, and about one in seven white voters in the Northeast. WEBACs voted for George W. Bush by the same margin in each region of the country. The greater conservatism of southern white voters appears to be a function of religiosity.

It is clear that what some have dubbed the culture wars and others have called the values divide plays a significant role in southern politics.[37] It might be argued that in recent elections southern politics has been about the two Rs. Race and religion still make the South a distinct region of the country. Other issues, however, do contribute to Republican advantages in presidential elections. National Democrats are more likely to support gun control than are Republicans, to take pro-choice positions on abortion, and to be hostile to the tobacco industry. In his autobiography, *My Life*, Bill Clinton listed abortion, gun control, and tobacco as issues that hurt him in the South in his presidential campaigns.[38]

The Unorganized South: A Brief Note

The weakness of labor unions in the South is another, often neglected factor that harms Democrats and strengthens Republicans in the region. Union workers are more likely to vote for the Democrats than similarly situated workers. All thirteen southern states have unionization rates that are well below the national average. In addition to promoting Democratic candidates among their own members, unions are a key source of personnel for get-out-the-vote operations.[39] In 2000, labor unions played an essential role in helping Al Gore carry the battleground states of Michigan,

Pennsylvania, Iowa, Wisconsin, and Minnesota. The intensive voter mobilization efforts of unions also secured Gore's half-million-vote victory in the popular vote.[40] The South has long had rates of union membership that were lower than states in the Midwest, Northeast, and Pacific Coast. Operation Dixie, a major effort to organize southern workers in the 1940s, failed.[41] The very low rates of unionization in the South (North and South Carolina are the least unionized states in the country) deprives Democrats of an important source of support they enjoy in several other regions of the country.

FLORIDA: THE SOUTHERN BATTLEGROUND STATE

Florida has become an ever more important state in presidential politics as rapid population growth has given the state more electoral votes after every census. In 1969, Florida had ten electoral votes. After the 2000 census figures led to the reapportionment of the U.S. House of Representatives, Florida's electoral votes increased from 25 to 27, the fourth highest in the nation behind only New York (31), Texas (34), and California (55).

Florida gained immense notoriety in 2000 as a result of the disputes over discarded votes, unreadable ballots, and legal wrangling that ended when the United States Supreme Court, in a 5–4 decision in the case of *Bush v. Gore*, ended all recounts and in effect made Bush the president-elect.[42] The final official popular vote in Florida was 2,912,790 for Bush and 2,912,253 for Gore, a margin of just 537 votes. Bush officially carried Florida by less than 0.01 percent of the popular vote.[43] Many Democrats believed that the 97,488 votes garnered by Leftist independent Ralph Nader cost Gore the presidency. With the capture of Florida's 25 electoral votes, George W. Bush had 271 or 1 more electoral vote than the 270 majority needed to become the president of the United States.

The voting problems that had plagued Florida in 2000 were an issue in the months preceding the election in 2004. Because election administration was under the control of Governor Jeb Bush, the president's brother, Democrats were wary of the touch-screen voting machines that replaced the punch card voting system that had produced so much controversy in the previous presidential election. Some Democrats charged that because they produce no paper record of an individual's vote, the touch-screen machines could be easily manipulated in the cause of voter fraud. Florida bans convicted felons from voting for the rest of their lives unless they have proceeded through a cumbersome process to restore their voting rights. Democrats, who had charged that blacks had been unfairly removed from the voting rolls in 2000, were incensed when a list of 48,000 felons contained over 22,000 African

Americans, but only 61 Hispanic names (in Florida, Hispanics vote predominantly Republican in many elections). The list was made public only after a court order. The suspect list was withdrawn in July after a firestorm of publicity.[44] Florida officials decided not to proceed with further purges of felons from the voting rolls based on the statewide list.[45] Some Republicans charged that Democrats gained an advantage because the discarded list contained 18,000 more Democrats than Republicans.[46]

Florida was among the earliest southern states to enter the Republican camp. Dwight Eisenhower won the state in 1952 and 1956, and between 1952 and 1992, Democrats won the state only twice (1964 and 1976). As table 6.5 indicates, from 1972 though 1988, Democratic candidates not only did poorly in Florida, they generally ran well behind their national percentage of the vote.[47] Unlike most other southern states, Florida became a competitive state for Democrats in the 1992, 1996, 2000, and 2004 presidential elections.[48] Aided by demographic changes, Bill Clinton lost the state by only 1 percent of the vote in 1992, and carried the state by about 5 percent in 1996.[49] In the last four presidential elections, Democrats have received about the same percentage of the popular vote in Florida as they have in the nation as a whole.

Florida is, in many ways, a cross-section of the United States.[50] The northern portion of the state borders rural sections of Alabama and Georgia and many white voters there share the conservative values of whites in more traditional southern states. The Hispanic and black populations in Florida are just a few points above the nation average for each ethnicity. Many relatively affluent midwesterners have retired to the Gulf Coast of Florida and made the region south of Tampa predominantly Republican. Retirees and other migrants from the Northeast have made Broward and Palm Beach counties, just north of Miami, very Democratic in presidential elections.

Foreign policy plays a larger role in Florida politics than in most other states. A large Cuban population in Miami-Dade County has traditionally demanded that the U.S. government maintain a harsh policy against the Castro regime. In 2000,

Table 6.5. Florida and the Nation in Presidential Elections, 1972–2004 in %

	1972	1976	1980	1984	1988	1992	1996	2000	2004
US Democratic Vote	37.5	50.1	41.0	40.6	45.6	43.0	49.2	48.4	48.2
Florida Democratic Vote	27.5	51.9	38.5	34.7	38.15	39.0	48.0	48.9	47.1
Difference	−10	+1.8	−2.5	−5.9	−7.1	−4.0	−1.2	+0.5	−1.1

Al Gore would almost certainly have been elected president of the United States if the Clinton administration had not returned Elian Gonzalez, a Cuban refugee orphan, to his father in Cuba. Traditionally Republican Cuban American voters in Florida turned out in large numbers for George W. Bush in an effort to penalize the Clinton administration's handling of the Gonzalez matter.

In 2004, the Bush administration enacted tighter restrictions on Cuban Americans visiting their families in Cuba. Prior to 2004, families were allowed an annual visit to Cuba of unlimited duration. The new policies permitted only one visit of two weeks every three years. The amount of money that could be sent to the island was also restricted and no funds could be sent to anyone who was not an immediate family member. The Bush administration argued that such measures would hasten Castro's decline, but many observers thought the primary purpose of the restrictions was to court votes among Cubans in a pivotal Electoral College state. Others thought that the policies might backfire as younger Cubans and refugees who had come from Cuba since 1980 might resent the restrictions on travel to the island. John Kerry promised that if he were elected he would allow unlimited family visits to Cuba.[51]

Due to the large numbers of Jewish voters in South Florida, American Middle East policy is a bigger concern in Florida than in all but a few other states. Both the Republican and Democratic presidential nominees inevitably compete in their pledges of fidelity to the state of Israel. In recent elections, Jewish voters in Florida, like Jews elsewhere in the United States, have voted heavily Democratic.

Because it is a retirement haven, Florida also has a disproportionate share of elderly voters. In 2000, 14 percent of the national electorate was age 65 or older. In Florida, those over 65 were 20 percent of the electorate. Florida had the highest percentage of elderly voters of any state in the nation. Issues such as the solvency of Social Security and the expansion of Medicare to cover prescription drug benefits have greater resonance in Florida than elsewhere in the United States.

Unlike Al Gore in 2000, John Kerry quickly targeted Florida as an important state in his electoral strategy. By early June, Kerry had visited Florida 20 times in the course of his presidential campaign and it was estimated that Kerry and allied liberal interest groups had spent almost $14 million in the state. The Bush campaign had also spent about $14 million in advertising in Florida five months before the election.[52]

Democratic activists were determined not to permit a repeat of the ballot disqualification fiasco of 2000. Gadsen County, the only black majority county in Florida, had the highest rate of discarded ballots in the state. Twelve percent of the votes cast in Gadsen County were tossed out. Statewide 83 of the 100 precincts with the largest numbers of disqualified ballots had black majorities. A variety of liberal groups, trade unions, and African American ministers placed major emphasis on voter registration and education. They also sought to overcome the fears of many Florida blacks that their votes did not actually matter.[53] In the first four months of 2004, Democrats reversed a long-term trend in Florida by enrolling 105,000 new registrants compared to 58,000 Republicans and 87,000 independents.[54] Because many of the new Democrats were low-income people, Republican officials in Florida doubted that they would actually vote.[55]

The weather probably played a role in the outcome of the 2004 presidential election in Florida. Four hurricanes struck the state in the late summer and early autumn. It would have been unseemly for John Kerry to campaign in the state amid the devastation inflicted by the hurricanes. As the incumbent president, George W. Bush could visit the state in his official capacity, express concern for Florida residents and identify himself with federal relief efforts in the state as he appeared with his brother Jeb, Florida's governor.[56] Election Day exit polling indicated that 87 percent of Florida voters approved of the federal government's response to the hurricanes.

The Bush campaign was also helped by the fact that Florida did not suffer from the economic problems that plagued some other regions of the country. Florida has never been a major manufacturing state and thus was not as affected by the hemorrhaging of industrial jobs that hurt parts of the Northeast and Midwest. Florida saw a net gain of jobs during the first Bush term. While many large states lost hundreds of thousands of jobs between the onset of the recession in March 2001 and November 2004, Florida gained 296,800 jobs.[57] On Election Day, 60 percent of the state's voters rated Florida's economy as good or excellent.

In the end, the outcome in Florida was determined in part by the same factor that destroyed Democratic hopes in several other battleground states. Republicans mobilized more voters than the Democrats' much-publicized efforts. With a massive push, Democrats were able to dramatically increase the vote for their presidential candidate, however. In 2000, Al Gore was credited with just over 2,912,000 votes in Florida. In 2004, John Kerry received more than 3,574,000 votes in the state, an increase of about 662,000 over Gore's 2000 total. In his very tight Florida win in 2000, George W. Bush also received about 2,912,000 votes. Republicans managed to beat Democrats at their own game in 2004, as Bush got 3,955,000 votes in Florida, an increase of over a million votes from his 2000 total. Democrats worked very hard to increase their voter turnout in Florida in 2004. They succeeded in doing so, but Republicans turned out in even larger numbers.[58]

The map indicates that Kerry won the Democratic counties of South Florida, the two major university communities (The University of Florida is located in Alachua County; Florida State is in Leon County, which also contains Tallahassee, the state capital), and a few urban counties that contained Daytona Beach, Orlando,

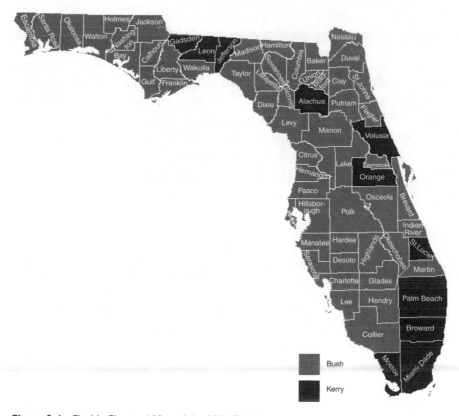

Figure 6.1. Florida Electoral Map of the 2004 Election

and St. Petersburg. With the exception of some rural heavily black counties and Monroe County (Key West), the rest of the state went for George W. Bush, who carried 56 of Florida's 67 counties in an election that was far better run than the widely criticized 2000 election.

The change in the partisan composition of the Florida electorate from 2000 to 2004 helps explain greater Republican success in the state in 2004. In 2000, the voters identified themselves as 40 percent Democratic and 38 percent Republican. In 2004, the electorate was 41 percent Republican and 38 percent Democratic. Not surprisingly, the five-point swing in partisan identification of the Florida electorate matched the Bush gain from a statistical dead heat in 2000, to a comparatively comfortable 5 percent win in 2004. Florida was less Republican than the rest of the South in 2004. Florida again reflected the national popular vote outcome as George W. Bush won 1 percent more of the vote in Florida than in the nation as a whole, and John Kerry received 1 percent less than in the nation as a whole.

Campaign 2004

For Democrats, one of the strategic issues of the 2004 elections was whether to contest any southern state except Florida. Not attempting to win 12 of the 13 southern states was effectively conceding to the Bush campaign about half the electoral votes needed to win the presidency. On the other hand, in a winner-take-all system like the Electoral College, it is a tactical mistake to spend money in states where the candidate has little chance of coming in first. Some Democrats believed that the party should expend its resources in the western states that had fast-growing Hispanic populations. New Mexico governor Bill Richardson, a national figure in the Democratic Party, argued, "I don't think it is realistic for us to have a Southern strategy. . . . We should concentrate on either a Western strategy—a Western/Hispanic strategy—which is basically Arizona, New Mexico, Nevada, and Florida, or we should try to pick off one or two states in the Midwest."[59]

Aided by very strong fundraising after he effectively clinched the Democratic nomination, John Kerry was able to advertise in several southern states in May and June. Arkansas was included in Kerry's first round of ads in crucial battleground states.[60] From the beginning it was clear that Democrats regarded Bill Clinton's home state as Kerry's best opportunity in the South with the exception of Florida. Later the Kerry campaign aired ads in Louisiana and Virginia. Kerry's strategists made it clear that the campaign would reassess his strategy in these states as the fall campaign proceeded, to determine whether their candidate was in fact viable in these states that George Bush had won by 7–8 point margins in 2000.

Kerry's vice-presidential selection process was also influenced by considerations of whether to compete in the South. Kerry was urged by many Democratic politicians to choose North Carolina senator John Edwards, one of his erstwhile rivals for the Democratic presidential nomination. Edwards had received generally positive reviews for his ability to connect with audiences and his emphasis on his working-class roots during the primary season. Some Democrats believed Edwards would help them as they competed in six southern Senate seats in which the incumbent was retiring. The reservations expressed about Edwards centered on the conviction that even with a charismatic southerner as his running mate, Kerry was not likely to carry southern states. In fact, a poll in North Carolina showed a Kerry–Edwards ticket in only a statistical tie with a Bush–Cheney ticket.[61] The poll proved to be wildly optimistic about Democratic prospects in North Carolina, as Bush carried North Carolina by a 12 percent margin.

Kerry might have been able to gain ground on the president in states that had been especially hard hit by manufacturing job losses during the first years of the Bush presidency. Beginning in the 1930s, many southern states were able to entice manufacturing firms to relocate from the North. Part of the inducement to employers was the lower wages and weak union influence in the South as compared to the North.[62] In recent decades many employers have moved overseas or been forced out of business by competition from manufacturers in countries that paid wages that were a fraction of those earned by comparatively low-paid southern workers. Leading politicians in both parties, including Bill Clinton and both presidents Bush, supported the free-trade policies that permitted imports that caused massive manufacturing job losses in states such as North and South Carolina. In the spring of 2004, South Carolina had the third-highest rate of unemployment in the nation in April and the sixth-worst rate in May.[63] In North Carolina, 60,000 manufacturing jobs were lost from 2000 to 2003.[64] Despite the economic problems encountered in many southern states during the early 2000s, John Kerry, as a career supporter of free trade, was not in a position to offer strong alternatives to the polices pursued by the Bush administration. Kerry's strategy was the one often pursued by political challengers. He hoped voters would punish the incumbent for policies they did not like, even if he did not offer a significantly different policy.

For the incumbent president, the reelection strategy for the South could be fairly simple. As a supporter of conservative causes such as banning the vast majority of abortions, opponent of gun control, supporter of school prayer, and a supporter of a constitutional amendment to ban gay marriage, and a self-proclaimed born-again Christian, the president was well positioned on social issues to carry the Republicans' usual large share of southern white votes. As commander-in-chief in a time of war, Bush could expect to do well in a region where the military was quite popular. While polls taken months before an election vary greatly, in most southern states, George W. Bush was ahead of John Kerry in the summer. According to polls conducted in May by Rasmussen Reports, the president led by 21 percent in Alabama, 24 percent in Oklahoma, 10 percent in South Carolina, 8 percent in Tennessee, and 5 percent in Arkansas.[65] Bush hoped to maintain his solid lead in the large majority of southern states so he could concentrate his financial resources and campaign appearances in the closely contested states of the Midwest, where strategists for both parties believed that the election was most likely to be decided.

Kerry's selection of John Edwards as his running mate in early July was not based entirely on his prospective appeal to southern voters. Because of his emphasis on his small-town North Carolina roots, humble origins, and populist championing of those left behind by economic change, Edwards was thought to have broad appeal to rural and working-class voters in the midwestern battleground states.[66] Commentators varied in their views of how much Edwards would aid a northeastern liberal like Kerry in the conservative South.[67] Some argued that he would put several states in play including North Carolina, Virginia, Arkansas, and Louisiana.[68] Political scientist Merle Black argued that Edwards's background as a trial lawyer and opposition to a constitutional amendment banning gay marriage would lead many white southerners to view Democrats as those who would take their money and would not support traditional marriage. On the other hand, Jack Bass, who has written a great deal about southern politics, thought that Edwards's populist idea of two Americas, one powerful and privileged, the other losing ground and excluded from power, would resonate with working-class black and white southerners. Professor Black argued that such populism was outdated in a South that had experienced a large growth in the middle class in recent decades.[69]

Republicans were skeptical of the appeal of a Kerry–Edwards ticket in much of the South, noting that the Democrats were no longer advertising in Arkansas and Louisiana. Both campaigns ran advertisements in North Carolina for the first time, in the wake of the selection of Edwards to the Democratic ticket.[70] Democrats were encouraged when Kerry and Edwards drew 20,000 people to a rally at North Carolina State University in Raleigh four days after Kerry announced his vice-presidential choice.[71] By early August, however, Democrats had essentially conceded North Carolina as it became clear that the presence of Edwards on the Democratic ticket would not bring North Carolina's fifteen electoral votes into the Democratic column.

In several states, social conservatives placed initiatives that would ban gay marriage on the ballot. Republicans again were hopeful that such initiatives would spur a high turnout among conservative voters, especially in contested states such as Arkansas.[72] Bans on same-sex marriage appeared on eleven state ballots in the general election, and were successfully passed in each state. In six states outside the South, support for prohibiting gay marriage ran from a low of 56 percent in Oregon to a high of 73 percent in North Dakota. In the five southern states that voted on the gay marriage issue, opponents of same-sex unions garnered a low of 75 percent in Arkansas and Kentucky to a high of 85 percent in Mississippi. While gay marriage was opposed by majorities around the country, southern conservatism was evident in the higher percentages voting against gay marriage in the five southern states where the issue appeared on the ballot.

August proved to be a difficult month for John Kerry. Swift Boat Veterans for Truth, a group funded in large part by long-time supporters of President Bush, challenged Kerry's claim to have shown courage in battle in Vietnam, and argued that his medals had been gained with false information.[73] The group also criticized the attacks he made on U.S. policy in Vietnam after leaving the military. Kerry was further damaged by a Republican convention that was widely viewed as successful both in bolstering the image of President Bush and in diminishing public opinion of Kerry, who was virulently attacked as a waffler who would leave the nation defenseless against terrorists. As Kerry's position in the polls weakened in September, his campaign decided that for the time being in the South, they would advertise only in Florida.[74] Despite some last-minute forays into Arkansas and occasional campaign stops elsewhere, by the early fall every other southern state was effectively conceded to George W. Bush.

In the end, George W. Bush did win handily in the South in 2004. Bush was viewed as a strong conservative Republican in a region that has become ever friendlier to conservative Republicans. Bush won an impressive 70 percent of southern white votes, while gaining the support of just 9 percent of southern blacks. Bush did much better among southern whites than he did among whites in other regions of the country as he carried 50 percent of whites in the Northeast, 54 percent in the West, and 56 percent in the Midwest.[75]

In examining the 2004 presidential election it is instructive to compare the electorate in the South, where Bush won every state, with the Northeast, where he lost every state except West Virginia, albeit by narrow margins in New Hampshire and Pennsylvania. In the Northeast, 18 percent of voters were union members compared to 7 percent in the South. Forty-nine percent of southern voters reported that they attended church at least once a week compared to 33 percent of voters in the Northeast. Forty-eight percent of southerners reported having a gun in their household compared to 27 percent of voters in the Northeast.

Fifty-nine percent of southern voters approved of the way the president was handling his job while his approval rating was 45 percent among voters in the Northeast. Interestingly, 59 percent of southern voters approved of the decision to go to war in Iraq while 45 percent of northeastern voters approved of this decision. Twenty-four percent of southern voters chose moral values as the most important issue when voting for president and 89 percent of these moral values voters voted to reelect George W. Bush. In the Northeast, 16 percent of voters chose moral values as the most important issue and 66 percent of these voters cast their ballots for the president.

THE SOUTHERN SIX AND
THE BATTLE FOR THE U.S. SENATE

While the presidential campaign understandably got the most media attention, control of the United States Senate was up for grabs in the 2004 elections. As a result of the 2002 elections, there were fifty-one Republicans in the Senate, forty-eight Democrats, and one independent who was officially aligned with the Democrats. A net gain of two seats would have given the Democrats a majority in the Senate. Because incumbents are very difficult to defeat, partisan change is most likely to occur in an open-seat election where there is no incumbent in the general election.

There were eight senators, five Democrats and three Republicans, who chose not to seek reelection in 2004. Democrats appeared to be at a severe disadvantage in seeking to win back the Senate because all five of the Democratic retirees and one of the Republicans who opted not to seek reelection were from the South. Six of the eight open-seat elections were in a region of the country where Republicans were strong and getting stronger. Before November 2004, Republicans already held 17 of the South's 26 seats in the Senate. Democrats faced open-seat Senate elections in Oklahoma, which George W. Bush had carried by a 22 percent margin in 2000, South Carolina (Bush won by 16 percent), North Carolina (Bush by 13 percent), Georgia (Bush by 12 percent), Louisiana (Bush by 8 percent), and Florida, which was, of course, a virtual dead heat in 2000.

Candidate quality is an important determinant of the outcome of congressional elections.[76] Candidates who have held elective office or have name recognition from public service are more likely to win than inexperienced candidates. The Democrats did a good job of recruiting candidates to compete for the open Senate seats in the South. In Oklahoma, Brad Carson, a thirty-seven-year-old former Rhodes Scholar and two-term member of Congress, was the Democratic nominee to replace retiring Republican senator Don Nickles.[77] Carson supported the president's policies on tax cuts and Iraq. In South Carolina, the state education commissioner, Inez Tenenbaum, who had twice been elected statewide by wide margins, was the Democratic candidate to replace retiring thirty-eight-year veteran Democrat Ernest Hollings. In North Carolina, President Bill Clinton's former chief of staff, Erskine Bowles, was the Democratic candidate. In Louisiana, four-term Democratic congressman Chris John, a conservative who had supported George W. Bush on the Iraq War and tax cuts, was the leading Democratic candidate in Louisiana's open primary election. In Florida, Democrats nominated Betty Castor, who was the former state education commissioner. Only in Georgia was the Democratic nominee, African American congresswoman Denise Majette, judged to have no realistic chance of winning.

For Democrats, the challenge was to win with quality candidates in conservative states in a presidential year. With the exception of Florida, none of the southern states with competitive Senate elections were closely contested. South Carolina, Georgia, Oklahoma, Louisiana, and North Carolina were effectively ignored by the Kerry campaign in the last months of the general election. Months before the election, Democrats expressed fears that because there would be no presidential campaigning in many southern states, their Senate candidates would be deprived of get-out-the-vote efforts that could push a candidate to victory in a close election.[78] Democrats hoped, that while John Kerry was unlikely to win most of the southern states with open-seat Senate elections, George W. Bush might be less popular than in 2000 and provide a smaller boost to the Republican Senate candidates than they had initially feared.[79] In fact, Bush won by larger margins in 2004 than in 2000 in every southern state but North Carolina.

Republicans took all six of the southern Senate elections. Only in Florida, where Mel Martinez beat Betty Castor by about 1 percent of the vote, was the election close. The social issues that were thought to have helped Republicans across the country were prominent in the southern Senate races as well. In Oklahoma, Republican Tom Coburn was criticized for saying that doctors who performed abortions should be subject to the death penalty and that lesbianism was rampant in high schools in southeastern Oklahoma. Coburn went so far as to characterize his race against Democrat Brad Carson as a struggle of good against evil.[80] South Carolina Republican Senate candidate Jim DeMint stirred controversy when he said that gays and unmarried pregnant women should not teach in public schools.[81] Both Coburn and DeMint won their races by wide margins. In Kentucky, Republican incumbent Jim Bunning appeared to be in trouble as he made numerous strange statements (Bunning said his opponent looked like Saddam Hussein's sons) and missteps in his reelection campaign. Some of Bunning's supporters questioned the sexual orientation of Daniel Mongiardo, Bunning's opponent, by claiming he was a "limp wristed switch hitter."[82] Bunning won reelection by a 51–49 percent margin.

CONCLUSION

The Democrats' failure in the South in 2000 and 2004 was different from some of their other debacles in the region. Candidates George McGovern in 1972 and Walter Mondale in 1984 lost every southern state, but each also only carried one state outside the South. In 1988, Michael Dukakis lost all thirteen southern states, and while he did carry ten states, he also lost a majority of the electoral vote outside the South to George H. W. Bush. In 2000 and 2004 Al Gore and John Kerry lost all of the southern electoral votes to George W. Bush, but won the majority of the electoral votes cast outside the South. The nation was divided into conservative and liberal regions. The South was not the only conservative region, but it provided the majority of the Republican electoral votes in each election.

Since 1960, no northern Democrat has been elected president of the United States. No Democrat has ever won a presidential election without carrying at least five southern states. All of the strategies of the Democrats to win various southern states in 2004 came to naught. A Democrat could conceivably win the presidency without carrying a single southern state. However, to pull off such a feat the Democratic candidate needs to win 74 percent of the electoral votes outside the South. Given the rock solid Republican nature of several Rocky Mountain and Great

Plains states, a Democrat who cannot win electoral votes in the South has little room for error and must win virtually every closely contested state outside the South. Al Gore, with 267 electoral votes, and John Kerry with 252, came close to accomplishing this feat, but both fell short because George W. Bush was able to win non-southern states such as Ohio, Missouri, and Nevada.

On the face of it, Democrats face a difficult dilemma as they contemplate the 2008 presidential election. They must either find a way to win some southern electoral votes or win more states outside the region. On the other hand, a Democrat like Bill Clinton who was able to win southern electoral votes also captured states like Ohio and Missouri that were won by George W. Bush in 2000 and 2004. In any event, winning electoral votes in the South will be a stiff challenge for future Democratic presidential candidates.

NOTES

1. Senator Jim Jeffords of Vermont is an independent who caucuses with the Democrats and has been counted as a Democrat.
2. Independent Bernie Sanders of Vermont, who calls himself a democratic socialist, caucuses with the Democrats and is counted as a Democrat here.
3. The major historical work on Reconstruction is Eric Foner, *Reconstruction: America's Unfinished Revolution, 1863–1877* (New York: Harper and Row Publishers, 1988).
4. Jack Bloom, *Class, Race, and the Civil Rights Movement* (Bloomington: Indiana University Press, 1987). Also see, Neil R. McMillen, *Dark Journey: Black Mississippians in the Age of Jim Crow* (Champaign-Urbana: University of Illinois Press, 1990).
5. The legal and political mechanisms of black disfranchisement are discussed in a classic work by V. O. Key first published in 1949, *Southern Politics in State and Nation* (New York: Random House, 2000).
6. Dewey Grantham, *The Life and Death of the Solid South: A Political History* (Lexington: University of Kentucky Press, 1992).
7. Key, *Southern Politics in State and Nation.*
8. Grantham, *The Life and Death of the Solid South*. Also, Earl Black and Merle Black, *Politics and Society in the South* (Cambridge, MA: Harvard University Press, 1987).
9. Ibid.
10. Harvard Sitkoff, *A New Deal For Blacks: The Emergence of Civil Rights As a Political Issue in the Depression Decade* (New York: Oxford University Press, 1981).
11. Kevin J. McMahon, *Reconsidering Roosevelt on Race: How the Presidency Paved the Road to Brown* (Chicago: The University of Chicago Press, 2004).
12. Alan Brinkley, "The New Deal and Southern Politics," in James C. Cobb and Michael Namorato, eds., *The New Deal and the South* (Jackson: University of Mississippi Press, 1984).
13. Earl Black and Merle Black, *The Vital South: How Presidents Are Elected* (Cambridge, MA: Harvard University Press, 1992).
14. Ibid., 144.

15. Robert A. Caro, *The Years of Lyndon Johnson: Master of the Senate* (New York: Vintage Books, 2002), 194.

16. Taylor Branch, *Parting the Waters: America in the King Years* (New York: Simon and Schuster, 1988).

17. Earl Black and Merle Black, *The Vital South*.

18. Earl Black and Merle Black, *Politics and Society in the South*.

19. Theodore White, *Making of the President, 1964* (New York: New American Library, 1964).

20. Dan T. Carter, *The Politics of Rage: George Wallace, the Origins of the New Conservatism, and the Transformation of American Politics* (Baton Rouge: Louisiana State University Press, 2000).

21. Ibid.

22. Theodore White, *The Making of the President, 1968* (New York: Atheneum, 1969).

23. Black and Black, *The Vital South*.

24. Ibid.

25. Nelson W. Polsby, *The Consequences of Party Reform* (New York: Oxford University Press, 1983). Nicol C. Rae, "The Democrats' Southern Problem in Presidential Politics," *Presidential Studies Quarterly* 22 (1992), 135–152.

26. Donald W. Beachler, "The South and the Democratic Presidential Nomination, 1972–1992," *Presidential Studies Quarterly* 26 (1996), 402–414.

27. Earl Black and Merle Black, *The Rise of the Southern Republicans* (Cambridge, MA: Harvard University Press, 2002), 213.

28. Ibid., and Dan T. Carter, *From George Wallace to Newt Gingrich: Race in the Conservative Counterrevolution, 1963–1994* (Baton Rouge: Louisiana State University Press, 1999).

29. Jim Rutenberg, "Kerry, in Show of Confidence Plans $18 Million Ad Push," *The New York Times*, May 29, 2004, A11.

30. Zell Miller, *A National Party No More: The Conscience of a Conservative Democrat* (Atlanta: Stroud and Hall, 2003).

31. Thomas Byrne Edsall and Mary D. Edsall, *Chain Reaction: The Impact of Race, Rights, and Taxes on American Politics* (New York: W.W. Norton, 1992).

32. Dan Carter, *From George Wallace to Newt Gingrich: Race in the Conservative Counterrevolution, 1963–1994* (Baton Rouge: Louisiana State University Press, 1999).

33. Alexander P. Lamis, *The Two Party South* (New York: Oxford University Press, 1997).

34. Richard Skinner and Philip A. Klinkner, "Black, White, Brown, and Cajun: The Racial Dynamics of the 2003 Louisiana Gubernatorial Election," *The Forum* 2: 1 (2004), available at http://bepress.com/forum

35. Clyde Wilson, *Onward Christian Soldiers: The Religious Right in American Politics* (Boulder, CO: Westview Press, 2000).

36. For a provocative, though polemical, look at the Christian Conservatives and the Republican Party in a single state, see Thomas Frank, *What's The Matter With Kansas? How Conservatives Won the Heart of America* (New York: Metropolitan Books, 2004).

37. John Kenneth White, *Values Divide: American Politics and Culture in Transition* (New York: Chatham House, 2002).

38. Bill Clinton, *My Life* (New York: Alfred A. Knopf, 2004).

39. Taylor Dark, *The Unions and the Democrats: An Enduring Alliance* (Ithaca, NY: Cornell University Press, 1999).

40. Donald W. Beachler, "Labors Triumphs and Frustrations," *Working USA: The Journal of Labor and Society* 5 (2001), 103–123.

41. Barbara S. Griffith, *The Crisis of American Labor: Operation Dixie and the Defeat of the CIO* (Philadelphia: Temple University Press, 1988). Michael Goldfield, *The Decline of Organized Labor in the United States* (Chicago: The University of Chicago Press, 1989).

42. The 2000 presidential election in Florida is analyzed in Steven C. Stauber and William C. Hulbarry, "Florida: Too Close to Call." In Robert P. Steed and Laurence Moreland, eds., *The 2000 Presidential Election in the South: Partisanship and Southern Party Systems in the Twenty-first Century* (Westport, CT: Praeger, 2002).

43. Jeffrey Toobin, *Too Close to Call: The 36 Day Battle That Decided the 2000 Election* (New York: Random House, 2002).

44. Abby Goodnough, "Election Troubles Already Descending On Florida," *The New York Times*, July 15, 2004.

45. Chris Davis and Matthew Doig, "Voter-Purge Decision Could Haunt Jeb Bush," *Sarasota Herald Tribune*, July 15, 2004.

46. Ibid.

47. Mark Stern, "Florida" in Laurence W. Moreland, Robert P. Steed, and Tod A. Baker, eds., *The 1984 Presidential Election in the South: Patterns of Southern Party Politics* (New York: Praeger, 1986). Also, William Hulbarry, Anne Kelly, Lewis Bowman, "Florida: The Republican Surge Continues," in Robert P. Steed, Laurence W. Moreland, and Tod A. Baker, eds., *The 1988 Presidential Elections in the South: Continuity Amidst Party Change* (New York: Praeger, 1991).

48. The 1996 election in Florida is analyzed in Kathryn Dunn Tenpas, William E. Hulbary, and Lewis Bowman, "Florida: An Election With Something For Everyone," in Laurence W. Moreland and Robert P. Steed, eds., *The 1996 Presidential Election in the South: Southern Party Politics in the 1990s* (Westport, CT: Praeger, 1997).

49. The evolution of presidential politics in Florida from the 1970s through the 1990s is discussed in Donald W. Beachler, "The Clinton Breakthrough? Presidential Politics in Florida," *Political Chronicle* 11 (Spring, 1999), 1–12.

50. Michael Barone and Grant Ujifusa, *The Almanac of American Politics, 2004* (Washington: The National Journal, 2004).

51. Susan Milligan, "New U.S. Travel Restrictions Irk Some Anti-Castro Cubans," *Boston Globe*, July 4, 2004.

52. Dan Balz, "Kerry Learns Lesson of Gore in Florida," *The Washington Post*, June 3, 2004.

53. Abby Goodnough, "Reassurance for the Florida Voters Made Wary by the Electoral Chaos of 2000," *The New York Times*, May 24, 2004.

54. Adam C. Smith, "Democrats Forge Edge With Registration Drives," *St. Petersburg Times*, June 19, 2004.

55. Ibid.

56. Abby Goodnough, "For Florida, the Campaigning Just has to Wait," *The New York Times*, September 25, 2004.

57. Information on Florida job gains posted on www.jobwatch.org on November 19, 2004.

58. Christopher Drew and Abby Goodnough, "It Was Our Turnout Governor Bush Says," *The New York Times*, November 4, 2004.

59. Jennifer Senior, "The Life of the Party?," *The New York Times Magazine*, May 9, 2004, 50.

60. Adam Nagourney, "Candidates Face Sprawling and Complex Electoral Map," *The New York Times*, May 12, 2004, A18.

61. David Halbfinger, "Senators Press Kerry to Pick Edwards as V.P.," *The New York Times*, June 14, 2004, A1.

62. James C. Cobb, *The Selling of the South: The Southern Crusade for Industrial Development, 1936–1990*, Second edition (Urbana-Champaign: The University of Illinois Press, 1993).

63. Jim Du Plessis, "State's Unemployment Rate Drops to 6.3 Percent in May," *The State*, June 19, 2004.

64. North Carolina Rural Development Center, www.ncrural.org

65. www.Rasmussenreports.com

66. Adam Nagourney, "Kerry Camp Sees Edwards Helping With Rural Vote," *The New York Times*, July 9, 2004, A1.

67. Nick Anderson, "Kerry, Edwards Face Uphill Battle in Republican-Leaning North Carolina," *The Los Angeles Times*, July 9, 2004.

68. Jack Bass, "Open Season in the South," *The New York Times*, July 8, 2004.

69. Shaila K. Dawan, "Old or New, The South Remains a Place Apart," *The New York Times*, July 11, 2004.

70. Nagourney, July 9, 2004.

71. James Rainey, "It's Just the Ticket for North Carolina," *The Los Angles Times*, July 11, 2004.

72. Janet Hook, "Initiatives to Ban Gay Marriage Could help Bush in Several Key States," *The Los Angeles Times*, July 12, 2004.

73. Glen Justice and Eric Lichtblau, "Bush's Backers Donate Heavily to Veterans Ads," *The New York Times*, September 11, 2004.

74. Dan Balz, "Size of Battleground May Be Smaller than Expected," *The Washington Post*, September 12, 2004.

75. Exit Polls are available at www.us.cnn.com/ELECTION/2004

76. Gary Jacobson, *The Politics of Congressional Elections*, Sixth edition (New York: Longman, 2004).

77. Barone and Ujifusa, *The Almanac of American Politics, 2004*.

78. John Nichols, "Will the Senate Tip?," *The Nation*, July 12, 2004, 15–17.

79. Ibid.

80. Abby Goodnough, "For Florida, the Campaigning Just has to Wait," *The New York Times*, September 25, 2004.

81. Henry Eichel, "Senate Candidates Avoid Hot Topics in Debate," *Charlotte Observer*, October 26, 2004.

82. Al Cross, "Anti-Gay Vote Saved Bunning," *Louisville Courier Journal*, November 7, 2004.

7

THE MIDWEST
The Arching Divide

David M. Rankin

The regional electoral divide across America made closely contested midwestern states like Ohio, with its twenty-one electoral votes, all the more important in the 2004 election. Both presidential campaigns focused much of their regional travel in close proximity to the Great Lakes and the northern reaches of the Mississippi River.[1] In 2004, the upper Midwest had five of the most competitive states nationwide. When they were not in Ohio, candidates Kerry and Bush crisscrossed nearby states such as Michigan, Wisconsin, Minnesota, and Iowa.[2] Neither candidate, on the other hand, spent much time traversing the central Midwest Plains states of the Dakotas, Nebraska, and Kansas, states that have solidly voted for Republican presidential candidates without exception since 1968.

In what makes the upper Midwest both unique *and* similar in recent elections, *The Economist* explains, "A number of common threads connect the Great Lake states. The region remains the country's industrial heartland. One-fifth of the country's manufacturing base is there, and even if the 'Rust Belt' tag is hardly fair for the home of Motorola, Medtronic and Abbott Laboratories, much of the commercial base is old: cars, steel, shipping, agriculture. This heartland—whether heavy manufacturing in Detroit, Cleveland and Green Bay or farming in Minnesota and Wisconsin—has seen wrenching changes in recent decades. Factory jobs have moved offshore or to lower-wage states further south, unions have seen their membership decline, family farmers have sold out to big agribusinesses and moved to the suburbs."[3] Historically within the Midwest region, it has been the states experiencing the greatest social, economic, and demographic transition that have caused the most compelling electoral upheaval.

THE GRAND OLD PARTY, THE
NEW DEAL COALITION, AND THE MIDWEST

Illinois' Abraham Lincoln presided over the electoral emergence of the Republican Party during the critical election of 1860.[4] The presidential election of Lincoln, a candidate sympathetic to the abolition of slavery, would be one of the final breaking points in the increasing strain between the northern and southern states leading to the Civil War, from 1861 to 1865. For the ensuing 100 years, the Republican Party would continue to be associated with the more urban industrial interests of the rapidly developing upper Midwest and Northeast while the opposition Democratic Party would become the party of the South and more agrarian-based states.

After the impeachment and near removal of Lincoln's successor, the Unionist Andrew Johnson of Tennessee, the United States elected three straight Republican presidents from Ohio: Ulysses S. Grant for two terms (1869–1877), Rutherford B. Hayes (1877–1881), and James Garfield (elected in 1881 and assassinated shortly thereafter). Republican Benjamin Harrison of the neighboring Great Lakes state of Indiana was elected in 1888, and three more Republican candidates from Ohio, William McKinley (1897–1901), William Taft (1909–1913), and Warren Harding (1921–1923) were also elected. With the exception of Chester Arthur, who took over for Garfield and served out the term until 1885, Theodore Roosevelt of New York (1901–1909) was the only Republican from outside the upper Midwest elected president until Calvin Coolidge from Massachusetts (1923–1929).

The only successful Democratic candidates elected president during the period 1860–1928 were Grover Cleveland of New York (1884 and 1892) and Woodrow Wilson from New Jersey (1912 and 1916). Still, it was the upper Midwest that would become a significant piece of New York native Franklin Delano Roosevelt's Democratic New Deal Coalition and that in the critical election of 1932 shattered the long-running Republican advantage in the Electoral College.[5] Under Roosevelt's leadership, the Democrats became strongly associated with the labor union movement increasing in conjunction with the rapidly growing industrial base of the Great Lakes and midwestern river-ways.[6] After FDR's death following four straight electoral victories (1932–1944), a Democrat won from the central region of the Midwest for the first time, when FDR's successor Harry Truman of Missouri secured a narrow electoral victory. However, President Truman's 1948 decision to integrate the armed forces set off permanent fissures in the southern base of the Democratic Party, leading to the Dixiecrat challenge of former South Carolina Democrat Strom Thurmond in the 1948 election.

The Democratic Party still relied on Midwest working-class whites, Catholics, urban liberals, and African Americans moving from the South to work in industrial cities from Detroit to Cleveland.[7] The local party machine under Democratic Chicago mayor Richard Daley peaked during the presidential elections of the 1960s. In the close 1960 election between Richard Nixon and John Kennedy, many Republican loyalists believed that Daley had somehow improperly helped deliver the critical votes in Illinois in favor of Kennedy, not unlike the accusations to be later leveled by embittered Democratic activists in Florida in 2000 and Ohio in 2004.

Civil Rights, Conflict, and Chicago

After taking the oath of the presidency after John F. Kennedy's assassination in November 1963, Texas native Lyndon B. Johnson (LBJ) would win by a landslide, garnering 61 percent of the popular vote over Arizona Republican senator Barry Goldwater in the 1964 election. An immediate objective for President Johnson was to press for the congressional passage of the 1964 Civil Rights Act and the 1965 Voting Rights Act that were initiated in the final stages of the Kennedy administration and were an outgrowth of the civil rights movement. These actions succeeded in putting the black vote firmly into the Democratic column as the African American population became an increasingly larger component of the urban population throughout the Great Lakes states and Missouri. On the other hand, these Democratic administration federal directives not only alienated the formerly Democratic and states rights–oriented southern white base, it fractured the once solidly Democratic blue-collar white vote throughout the Midwest region.

In the 1964 election, LBJ swept the Midwest, including all of the region's states that had helped Nixon run such a close race in the 1960 election. Johnson won not just in the industrial upper Midwest but also across all of the midwestern Plains states. But he would be the last Democratic presidential candidate to win in Indiana, Kansas, Nebraska, and the Dakotas. And it would be his administration's handling of the Vietnam War and his personal decision to not seek the presidency again in 1968 that would fracture his own Democratic Party gains in the Great Lakes states. The Democratic Party had split over policy in Vietnam, and primary challengers New York senator Robert Kennedy (before his assassination upon winning the 1968 California primary) and Minnesota senator Eugene McCarthy were roundly criticizing the Johnson administration and gaining significant support among the antiwar movement. Thus when former Minnesota senator and LBJ's vice president Hubert

Humphrey accepted the nomination at the 1968 Democratic Party convention in Chicago, an already tense standoff between the police and antiwar protesters outside the convention hall exploded on national television.

The 1968 Republican Party candidate, Richard Nixon, capitalized on broadcast images of Mayor Daley's police scuffling with protesters. Nixon seized the moment to call upon America's "silent majority" fed up with the nation's violent division, presumably a failing of the incumbent Democratic administration, to elect him for a return to traditional midwestern-style values, law and order. Nixon's electoral strategy relied extensively on winning in the Midwest region.[8]

Humphrey lost narrowly, largely because of voter backlash to the Chicago convention riots. In 1972, Senator George McGovern, who was a vocal critic of the ongoing Vietnam War, lost in a landslide to Nixon. Nixon swept the entire Midwest region in 1972, including McGovern's home state of South Dakota. Despite the fact that Humphrey was the vice president during the military escalation of the war in Vietnam, and McGovern was a decorated World War II veteran, the Democrats were increasingly labeled as the weaker party on defense. Whether or not this was a fair accusation, it began to resonate particularly among white working-class men in the Midwest who increasingly perceived Republicans as the "tougher" party when it came to military matters and national security. Many of these white working-class voters also increasingly viewed the Democratic Party as less a party of their Midwest values and interests and a party more concerned with civil rights, minorities, and the liberal elite.[9]

Ironically, it was the overzealous actions of the Committee to Re-elect the President (CREEP) that led to Nixon's resignation in 1974 as a result of the 1972 Watergate break-in at the offices of the Democratic National Committee, ensuing cover-up, and crisis, which reopened an opportunity for Democrats in the Midwest. For a region that birthed the Republican Party and was home to so many of its presidents, it took nearly fifty years and the resignation of a president until the next and only other Republican president was to come from the upper industrial Midwest, Gerald Ford of Michigan.

Former House leader Ford presided over a Republican congressional delegation consisting heavily of midwesterners before he replaced Nixon's vice president, Spiro Agnew, in 1973. And Ford may have won back the White House in 1976 had he not pardoned Nixon for the Watergate crimes, thereby losing narrowly to Georgia upstart Jimmy Carter. Ford was unable to capture the presidency but did win many of the states Nixon charted out as part of a Midwest-centered strategy. Carter captured Wisconsin, Missouri, and Ohio, states won by Nixon in 1968 and 1972, as well as Minnesota, which Nixon won in 1972 but not in 1968. Ford held Illinois, Iowa, and his home state of Michigan, and also won the Midwest Plains states that Nixon won every time he ran for president in 1960, 1968, and 1972.

Carter managed to convey a relatively populist image on the 1976 campaign trail, with a focus on born-again Christian faith and his peanut farm, despite the fact that he was trained as a nuclear engineer at Annapolis. A "down home" campaigning style, faith-based and genuine persona appeared to resonate with midwestern voters, particularly the increasingly volatile voting bloc of white working-class voters, once firmly in the New Deal coalition, now up for grabs.[10] These voters were faced with multiple challenges and concerns as the once secure jobs of the industrial base were dwindling based on domestic economic transition and foreign competition. Whole towns and cities were threatened throughout a Midwest region that relied extensively on particular industries that simply could no longer compete and exist, or had to dramatically scale back the local production and workforce.

Collaring the Reagan Democrat: Class, Race, and Gender in the Industrial Midwest

A feeling of helplessness throughout the once proud industrial heartland of America was amplified by the energy shortage, Iranian hostage crisis, and the Soviet invasion of Afghanistan all occurring under President Carter's watch. Thus, when one-time New Deal Democrat, former movie actor, and California Republican governor Ronald Reagan rode in from the mythical Wild West, his symbolic message to "restore American pride" and take down the Soviet "Evil Empire" resonated with this new bloc of swing voters.

The Democratic New Deal coalition had been successful because of the significant inroads among the working-class population in the upper Midwest into the 1960s, but Nixon had a strategy to bring the industrial Midwest back into the Republican fold.[11] This strategy would be mastered in 1980 and 1984 with the emergence of swing voters who came to be known as "Reagan Democrats," including white working-class midwesterners who had since abandoned the dwindling New Deal coalition to help Reagan secure the White House for two terms.[12]

Whether intentional or not, race was a defining feature that split critical elements of the white vote from the New Deal coalition, leading midwestern white voters to align themselves increasingly with the Republican ticket and midwestern black voters to almost uniformly vote for the Democratic candidate.[13] Class, long the mainstay of division between voting Republican or Democratic in the Midwest, became less relevant for voters than did race.[14] Working-class whites in the Midwest became increasingly likely to support Republican presidential candidates, with white males emerging as the most dependable Republican bloc.[15]

The emerging gender gap, on the other hand, opened up a new opportunity for Democrats to win back upper Midwest states. While Democrats were only able to win Carter Vice President Walter Mondale's home state of Minnesota during Reagan's sweep of the Midwest in 1980 and 1984, the 1988 Democratic candidate Michael Dukakis won Iowa and Wisconsin. It marked the first time that a Democratic candidate had won Iowa since 1964 and only the second time a Democrat won Wisconsin since the LBJ landslide, and Iowa and Wisconsin had supported Nixon in 1960. The 1988 victory in Iowa and Wisconsin would mark a turning point in favor of Democratic success within the two formerly solid Republican states, by relying increasingly on women, the college educated, the unmarried, and urban residents.[16]

Many college-educated, single, and urban women, in particular, were increasingly drawn to the Democratic presidential candidacies in part because of a more vocal Republican Party stance on the pro-life side of the divisive abortion issue. Conversely, noncollege graduates, those with lower incomes, and rural residents focused less on economic issues while considering more of the social implications of their vote for president and party. Values from morality to patriotism competed with economic platforms, and at times "values trumped issues" in midwestern minds.[17]

The values debate became intertwined with religious belief and practice when it came to electoral politics.[18] With Reagan's strategic embrace of Jerry Falwell's "Moral Majority," the Republican Party was becoming a party for the religious conservative, and many such newly engaged voters resided in the rural Midwest. In 1988, the Bush–Quayle campaign continued Republican domination of the Great Plains states while holding Illinois, Michigan, Missouri, and Ohio, despite the fact that these states had been hit hard during the 1980s with job loss and economic downturn.[19]

In 1980, candidate Reagan had focused on what he considered the failings of the Democratic incumbent administration when he asked voters, "Are you better off now than you were four years ago?" In 1992, Democratic candidate Bill Clinton would use similar tactics when he sought to win back the very voters Reagan had successfully moved from the traditional midwestern Democratic base, reminding "Reagan Democrats" of the job loss and economic hardship of the region during the Reagan/Bush years. While 1992 Clinton campaign lore focuses on the "war room" in Little Rock, Arkansas, a centerpiece of Clinton's electoral strategy hinged on Stanley Greenberg's polling and focus groups in Macomb County, Michigan.[20]

Macomb County resembled many counties across the industrial Midwest and helped the Clinton campaign to win back many blue-collar "Reagan Democrats" through campaign appeals to the economic and health care needs of the working and middle class. According to Greenberg, these voters were feeling squeezed by the conservative economic policies of the Republican Party and neglected by the liberal social policies of Democrats. Clinton turned electoral attention to the domestic and economic concerns of the white working class while also relying on groups that were a firm new part of the Democratic base, including college-educated women, minorities, singles, and urban residents.

The Clinton Democratic midwestern strategy was successful, winning back Missouri and Ohio for the first time since 1976, Michigan for the first time since 1968, Iowa and Illinois for the first time since 1964. Clinton effectively swept the Great Lakes states with the exception of Indiana, an electoral feat he would duplicate in 1996 over Kansas senator Bob Dole. Thus, it was perfectly symbolic for the 1996 Democratic national party convention to return to the city of Chicago for the first time since the 1968 party implosion in order to celebrate Clinton's impending reelection, the first Democrat to be reelected since FDR. Illinois, the launching pad of the Republican Party under the leadership of Abraham Lincoln, had been solidly Republican from the 1968 through the 1988 presidential elections. However, starting with the 1992 presidential election, Illinois would become the most dependable Democratic state in the entire Midwest region.

ACROSS URBAN AND
RURAL TERRAIN IN THE MIDWEST

Illinois has become a reliable "blue" state, not so much because the entire state is suddenly Democratic terrain or because another Mayor Daley presides over Chicago, but primarily because of the expanding metropolitan area along Lake Michigan and other vibrant and increasingly diverse metropolitan areas across the state. In fact, neighboring Gary, Indiana, a predominantly industrial city with a sizable African American population, voted solidly for the Democratic candidate Al Gore in 2000 despite the fact that Gore lost the state of Indiana by 15 points to George W. Bush. Political geography is critical to understanding this electoral dynamic. As the Indiana *and* Illinois state maps shift south and become decidedly more rural toward the Kentucky border, the electoral terrain also becomes decidedly more Republican.

It is largely an electoral game of rural vs. urban population math when it comes to winning in the upper Midwest. For example, Bush lost the state of Illinois to Gore by 10 points in 2000 despite winning by solid margins in central and southern Illinois. Across the Mississippi River from southwestern Illinois is the city of St. Louis from which rises the unmistakable Gateway Arch. The arch, at one time the symbolic division of the American East and West, could today serve to signify the arching divide between urban and rural America, between the industrial heartland and the Great Plains. Missouri was a state that Clinton won in 1992 and 1996, but Gore lost narrowly in 2000. Gore didn't lose based on the urban area surrounding the arch but lost based on the vote outside of St. Louis as well as Kansas City. By the time the map extends to the western borders of Missouri, it is approaching the geographic center of the United States and the epicenter of Republican strength in the Electoral College.

Certain Great Lakes states remain competitive for Republicans and Democrats because they consist of significant metropolitan areas and rural communities, college communities and farming towns, industry and agriculture, educated professionals and the working class, single and married persons, career women and stay-at-home moms, churchgoers and non-churchgoers, significant white and nonwhite populations, all of which fuel a division over government policies, and social and economic viewpoints.[21] However, there are certain rural states in which few of these distinctions are prominent, in which the state populations are predominantly rural, religious, older, married, and white, and these states have voted Republican for president without exception since 1964.

Despite Clinton's success in winning back the industrial heartland in both 1992 and 1996, he made no inroads in the most Republican swatches of the Midwest. Including the staunchly Republican Great Lakes state of Indiana, the more rural and western Great Plains states of North and South Dakota, Nebraska, and Kansas have voted Republican in every presidential election since the LBJ landslide of 1964. And Gore fared even worse in 2000, losing by 23 points on average across the same states.

Table 7.1. Electoral College Partisan Trends in the Midwest Region, 1960–2004

	60	64	68	72	76	80	84	88	92	96	00	04	04+	00+
Rural Red													+26	+23
Indiana	R	*D*	R	R	R	R	R	R	R	R	R	R	21	15
Kansas	R	*D*	R	R	R	R	R	R	R	R	R	R	26	21
Nebraska	R	*D*	R	R	R	R	R	R	R	R	R	R	35	29
North Dakota	R	*D*	R	R	R	R	R	R	R	R	R	R	27	28
South Dakota	R	*D*	R	R	R	R	R	R	R	R	R	R	22	23
Lake Blue													+10	+12
Illinois	*D*	*D*	R	R	R	R	R	R	*D*	*D*	*D*	*D*	10	12
Battleground													+3	+2
Iowa	R	*D*	R	R	R	R	R	*D*	*D*	*D*	*D*	R	1	0.3
Michigan	*D*	*D*	*D*	R	R	R	R	R	*D*	*D*	*D*	*D*	3	5
Minnesota	*D*	*D*	*D*	R	*D*	*D*	*D*	*D*	*D*	*D*	*D*	*D*	4	2
Missouri	*D*	*D*	R	R	*D*	R	R	R	*D*	*D*	R	R	7	3
Ohio	R	*D*	R	R	*D*	R	R	R	*D*	*D*	R	R	2	4
Wisconsin	R	*D*	R	R	*D*	R	R	*D*	*D*	*D*	*D*	*D*	0.4	0.2

Note: Table compiled by the author based on electoral data from the office of the Federal Register. The 04+ and 00+ columns calculate the popular vote margin for each state and the average popular vote margin for solid red, solid blue, and the closer battleground states. For example, the Republican candidate, George W. Bush, won Indiana by a 21-point popular vote margin in 2004 and a 15-point popular vote margin in 2000. The average red state popular vote margin was 26 points in 2004 and 23 points in the 2000 election. Additional percentage points ≤ 0.4 are rounded down (e.g., 2.4% = 2%) and additional percentage points ≥ 0.5 are rounded up (e.g., 15.6% = 16%) unless the overall percentage of the state popular vote is less than 1 (e.g., 0.1% 0.9%).

The unbending support of Republican presidential candidates among these states despite the perceived economic hardships on the Great Plains and small-town America during the 1980s has led most Democratic presidential candidates to simply abandon the campaign trail through the middle of America, while it has led others to question why the Republican Party has locked up its support among these states. For one, there is longstanding Republican identity throughout many of these states, not unlike the southern embrace of the Democratic Party during the long period following Lincoln until the 1960s civil rights era. In Great Plains states like Kansas, the state's very identity was forged in the Lincoln Republican tradition as "free soiler" Jayhawks battled across the border with slave-holding Missourians.[22]

Dwight "Ike" Eisenhower was the only Kansan, or native of the Great Plains for that matter, to be elected to the White House, in 1952 and 1956. While Ike made his military career and political residence largely outside Kansas, his election success signified the fortunes ahead for the Republican Party throughout the breadbasket of America. Still, it was unclear whether Ike was a Democrat or Republican, and he did not offer his partisanship until he declared his candidacy. Eisenhower would attempt a similarly "hidden" hand while presiding over a contentious period of Court-determined and executive-enforced desegregation of public schools, with Topeka, Kansas, at the epicenter of the 1954 decision, *Brown v. Board of Education*.[23]

When the longtime U.S. Senate leader from Kansas, Bob Dole, received the 1996 Republican nomination, Kansas remained solidly "red" as did its neighboring Plains states. However, Kansas had changed dramatically in the past forty years in a way that makes it an even more solid lock for Republicans heading into the twenty-first century. Kansans like Alf Landon, Dwight Eisenhower, and Bob Dole have since disappeared from political life and a new breed of midwesterners have jockeyed for partisan control even in solidly Republican states. The electoral divisions have extended beyond rural and urban to the splintering suburban areas, increasingly divided into an inner and outer suburban ring throughout the Plains states and into the upper Midwest.

Ain't that America? From Small Town to Suburban Main Street, USA

John Mellencamp sang of the "little pink houses" of small-town America reminiscent of his native rural Indiana before he turned his attention to the plight of the American farmer during the 1980s and 1990s. But rural Indiana is less pink than a solid shade of Republican red, resembling the colors of a basketball home game for the University of Indiana Hoosiers. Rural Indiana also resembles the rural Midwest, in which smaller, predominantly rural Midwest states overwhelmingly vote

Republican, and a solid devotion to Republican presidential candidates on the Great Plains stretches increasingly into every corner.

Thomas Frank makes this point, in which he describes Kansas as "the heart of the heartland . . . the reddest of the red states" and explains that "one thing unites all different groups of Kansans, millionaires and trailer-park dwellers, farmers and thrift-store managers and slaughterhouse workers and utility executives, they are almost all Republicans."[24] While the fellow Plains states of the Dakotas and Nebraska share this deep red shade, Kansas' eastern neighbor, Missouri, paints a more complicated picture, in which the candidate who carries it has won the presidency in every election, except 1956, since 1900. Dave Robertson, a political scientist at the University of Missouri–St. Louis, describes his state as a combination of the mid-South and the upper Midwest, and Missouri's political evolution has closely mirrored broader national trends, particularly a sharp divide between rural and urban voters. The state's two biggest cities, St. Louis and Kansas City, are staunch, pro-union Democratic strongholds with sizeable black minorities but declining populations. Otherwise, Missouri is "a socially conservative state: pro-guns, pro-life and firmly against gay marriage, and the Republicans have been working hard to push issues that fire up their conservative base."[25]

An urban–rural divide still reflects racial divisions that have a strong geographic component throughout the Midwest.[26] Voters in St. Charles County, across the Missouri River from a predominantly African American section of St. Louis, used to be Democrats. But these suburban voters identify Democrats with St. Louis' black community, and vote heavily for Republicans.[27]

From at least the 1960s, the suburbs have been a critical swing vote. But the suburbs as well are now split, quite appropriately, into subdivisions. In Missouri, the inner suburbs are trending Democratic as more blue-collar voters move out of the inner cities. The sprawling outer suburbs, in contrast, trend Republican. *The Economist* notes how in "St. Charles County, a fast-growing mass of new houses, trimmed lawns and good schools, residents cast more votes than St. Louis city in 2000, and they were largely for Bush."[28]

Stanley Greenberg describes "Exurbia," composed in large part of displaced voters from the older cities, older inner suburbs, and rural areas within the Midwest, as "Republican loyalist territory."[29] Moreover, he contends that conservative views in this growing area offset some of the rural decline. One such example is Scott County, Minnesota, which increased rapidly in population, by more than 50 percent during the 1990s. In 1996, Dole lost the county by six points, but Bush won the county in 2000 by 15 points.[30]

Even within Kansas it is a more complicated political geography than what simply appears to be red to the electoral eye. Frank explains that "there is a geographic divide separating the older, inner suburbs of Johnson County, where more Moderate Republicans tend to live, from the newer, outer suburbs, where everyone seems to be pro-life, pro-gun, and anti-evolution. . . . From the elections of the last ten years, those parts in Johnson County with the lowest per capita income and lowest median housing values consistently generated the strongest support for the conservative faction. . . . The more working class an area is, the more likely it is to be conservative. . . . The situation is the opposite of what it was thirty years ago. . . . In Kansas, the political geography of social class has been turned upside down."[31]

However, Democrats also claim to be making gains based on emerging demographic trends and rapid population growth throughout the Midwest. In *The Emerging Democratic Majority*, John Judis and Ruy Texeira argue that Democrats are countering Republicans through the emergence of the "ideopolis," described as metropolitan, postindustrial regions growing at more than twice the rate as the rest of the country. Ideopolises develop around information technology, entertainment and media, major universities or research centers, concentrations of professionals and technicians, immigrant and ethnic diversity, and artistic and gay communities, such as Chicago's Cook County.[32]

In 1972, Nixon won Chicago and Cook County. But between 1970 and 1997, Chicago lost 60 percent of its manufacturing jobs, and in the nineties Chicago became one of the leading areas for high technology and information technology. The metropolitan area now has twice as many professionals and technicians as production workers. Judis and Texeira thus describe what was "once a larger version of Kansas City, Chicago became a much larger version of San Francisco, with its theater and music, its artists, and its visibly gay population on the North Side. In Cook County, working-class whites also backed Gore 78–11 percent, and college educated white voters backed Gore 69–20 percent. Hispanics also increased from 14 to 20 percent of Cook County, and neighborhoods once demarcated by ethnic loyalty now became integrated. With Cook County tallying about 40 percent of the votes in Illinois, Bush would have had to win 65 percent outside of Cook County and such voting patterns resemble other advanced ideopolises."[33]

Most postindustrial metropolises also include a major university or several major universities. For example, Dane County, which houses the capitol and the University of Wisconsin, Madison, is the fastest growing county in the state, relies heavily on biomedical research, and went for Gore in 2000 by nearly 30 points.[34] Other emerging Democratic strongholds include postindustrial areas with major universities around Detroit, such as Ann Arbor and Lansing. Upscale Oakland County, recording the largest Michigan county growth in the 1990s, is home to the high-tech sector of the auto industry, and voted overwhelmingly Republican in the 1980s, but turned Democratic in 1996 narrowly.[35]

Judis and Texeira claim, "The New Deal coalition of the Upper Midwest, once dominated by blue-collar workers and small farmers, now includes a large contingent of professionals, and Democratic success in these counties signaled the diminution of race as a divisive factor and the re-identification of the Democrats as the party of prosperity among these voters."[36] However, the Republican Party counters with a persistent program of tax cuts, gun rights, targeted farm aid,[37] strong defense, and social conservatism that reaches rural and suburban, upper- and lower-income whites. For example, *Washington Post* writer Mike Allen, notes, "Minnesota and Wisconsin have been trending Republican for at least eight years and Republican strategists believe that they can turn them by targeting suburbs, along with rural areas that used to be solidly Democratic, with promises of a muscular foreign policy, preservation of traditional values and lower taxes."[38]

THE 2004 MIDWEST:
GREAT LAKES INDUSTRIAL
BLUE AND MIDDLE-AMERICA RURAL RED

Based on recent and emerging electoral trends, it was clear that the upper industrial Midwest would be a central focus of the 2004 presidential campaign. The second presidential debate was scheduled for Washington University in St. Louis, Missouri, and the only vice presidential debate was to be held at Case Western Reserve University in Cleveland, Ohio. After record amounts of money raised throughout the 2004 election by both candidates, there was a saturation of ad buys in critical Midwest markets.[39] In the final days of a hotly contested region, there were record levels of ground mobilization of critical voting blocs.[40]

In the end, the Midwest region exit poll shows that Bush won the Midwest by the same margin with which he won the nationwide popular vote, 51–48 percent. No other region came close to mirroring the outcome of the nation more than the battle for the Midwest. Unlike the Northeast exit polls that found Kerry winning by 13 points or South region exit polls giving a 16-point victory to President Bush, the Midwest ended up every bit of the hard-fought region it has become in recent presidential election after election. Quite fittingly, the bellwether region consisted of the bellwether state of the 2004 election, in which Ohio also produced a similar margin of victory for the president-elect.

The real Midwest battle of recent presidential elections comes down primarily to the Great Lakes states, with the exception of now solidly blue Illinois and dependably red Indiana. In 2004, four of the states, Michigan, Wisconsin, Minnesota, and Ohio, made up 57 electoral votes. Securing the increasingly red state of Missouri and picking up the hotly contested state of Iowa just up the Mississippi River, Bush garnered 66 electoral votes compared with Kerry's 58 electoral votes in the Midwest. Still, Bush needed to double up Kerry's state total, winning eight of the twelve Midwest states for an eight electoral-vote margin of victory in the region.

Despite the fact the Kerry–Edwards challenge came up short against the incumbent Bush ticket in the electoral vote count in the Midwest and across the nation, the exit poll findings show that both parties effectively mobilized their social groups around the issues they had highlighted during the long and costly campaign. The election was so close in many of the Midwest states because the electorate was simply very divided, by race, by religion, by community, and by region. In cases in which Midwest states had more homogeneity within the demographic composition of the electorate, there was a definite Republican partisan advantage.

Table 7.2 shows how social forces influenced the breakdown in voting across the Midwest region. Bush did particularly well among white voters while Kerry dominated the nonwhite voting bloc by an even larger margin. Although white men and women supported Bush while nonwhite men and women overwhelmingly supported Kerry, there was a 15-point gender gap among whites and a 21-point gender gap among nonwhites. White males clearly favored Bush, with nonwhite females very strong Kerry backers. Bush benefited from a higher percentage of white voters, particularly in the red states in which white voters were nearly universal in some of the more rural Midwest farm states. Kerry picked up states in which there was a relatively higher voter turnout among nonwhite voters.

Midwest white union members, a mainstay of the Democratic New Deal Coalition later carved off by Nixon and Reagan, have returned to Democrats in recent presidential voting, including 2004. However, despite Kerry's hunting rifle displays in the great outdoors of the Midwest and a campaign focus on his Vietnam War heroics, his "manly" exploits were either offset by the NRA, 527 ads like the "Vietnam Swift Boat Veterans for Truth," or Bush campaign attack ads discrediting, if not ridiculing, Kerry's record and character. Bush easily won the vote of Midwest gun owners and voters with military service, many of whom are white males in rural areas and staunch Republicans.

Social class was of little consequence in the red state voting, with Bush winning by substantial margins among lower- and higher-income groups. Yet class did make a difference in the blue states, with Kerry doing substantially better among the lower income group and actually losing higher-income voters. College-educated voters were more likely to support Bush in red states, but narrowly backed Kerry in blue states. Overall, Kerry did better among the younger and unmarried voters throughout the Midwest, but had his biggest advantage in the blue states, where these voters helped him with several narrow victories in the region.

166

Table 7.2. Social Forces in Voting Across the Midwest, Red and Blue States, 2004, in %

	Total Mid Vote	Bush Mid Vote	Kerry Mid Vote	Mid Bush + −	Red State Avg.	Bush Red +	Blue State Avg.	Bush Blue + −
Race and gender								
White	85	56	43	+13	93	+45	86	+4
Black	8	10	90	−80	3	NA	8	−76
Latino	5	32	64	−32	3	NA	3	−31
White men	41	60	39	+21	45	+35	41	+8
White women	44	53	46	+7	49	+29	45	+1
Nonwhite men	7	27	72	−45	NA	NA	NA	NA
Nonwhite women	8	16	82	−66	NA	NA	NA	NA
Demographic profile								
< $50,000 income	47	44	56	−12	46	+19	45	−16
> $50,000 income	53	57	43	+14	54	+33	55	+5
No college degree	63	49	50	−1	NA	NA	60	−1
College graduate	37	53	46	+7	NA	NA	40	−3
Married	65	57	42	+15	69	+35	62	+12
Not married	35	40	59	−19	31	−11	37	−22
18–29 years old	19	47	52	−5	17	+19	21	−18
60 years old+	23	55	45	+10	23	+17	21	−2
First time voter	11	47	51	−4	NA	NA	10	−25
Union member	18	35	64	−29	NA	NA	18	−32
Gun owner	47	58	41	+17	NA	NA	NA	NA
Military service	16	61	39	+22	NA	NA	18	+2
Religion and religiosity								
White Evangelical	25	76	23	+53	32	+57	24	+42
Not White Evangelical	75	43	56	−13	68	+13	76	−17
White Cons. Protestant	NA	NA	NA	NA	25	+82	16	+83
Not White Cons. Protest.	NA	NA	NA	NA	75	+9	84	−21
Attend church weekly	41	60	39	+21	NA	NA	38	+20
Occasional attend church	42	46	53	−7	NA	NA	43	−10
Never attend church	12	37	61	−26	NA	NA	14	−43
Catholic	29	50	49	+1	22	+24	31	−5
Party identification								
Democrat	37	9	91	−82	28		38	−86
Republican	38	94	6	+88	48	+91	35	
Independent	25	47	51	−4	26	+6	27	−10
Community size								
Suburban	43	55	45	+10	25	+30	44	+6
Rural	31	60	39	+21	47	+34	28	+8
Urban	26	35	64	−29	28	+5	28	−34

Note: Table 7.2 column figures include percentages from the Midwest region results of the National Election Pool exit poll. Total vote is the percentage polled for each group, "+" indicates the point margin advantage for Bush, "−" indicates the point margin advantage for Kerry. The red state average includes the states of Nebraska, North Dakota, Kansas, and Indiana. Red state married status relies only on the Indiana exit poll. The blue state average includes the states of Illinois, Minnesota, Michigan, and Wisconsin. Blue state military service relies only on the Wisconsin exit poll. The blue state category of white evangelicals relies only on the Michigan exit poll. Italicized figures refer to categories in which George W. Bush held an advantage.

College-age voters or recent college graduates were a particular boon for the Kerry campaign in the upper industrial Great Lakes states, with eighteen- to twenty-nine-year-old voters and first-time voters giving Kerry a substantial margin despite the fact that Bush won all age groups by a large margin across the red states. Despite losing the election, Kerry can credit these groups with helping him win tight races in states with substantial college towns such as Minnesota, Michigan, and Wisconsin. While the 2004 "Concert for Change" tour may have alienated rural conservative voters, it likely encouraged younger suburban and urban groups to vote and it likely helped Kerry. When Kerry descended on the state capitol and university town of Madison, Wisconsin, during the final stages of the campaign with Bruce Springsteen in tow, approximately 80,000 people filled the streets.

Bush, on the other hand, can credit other groups for keeping him close in all of these Great Lakes states, taking him over the top in tight races in Iowa and Ohio, and coasting to victory in the other Midwest states. Married and older voters favored Bush across the Midwest, while Bush received his biggest lift from devoutly religious churchgoers, particularly white evangelicals and white conservative Protestants, whether in red or blue states. Furthermore, such religious groups made up about a third of the electorate in many of the most rural red states and even a quarter in the more industrial blue states. Not only did Bush receive nearly universal support from deeply religious voters, the margin dwarfed the amount Kerry received from voters who are not white evangelicals or white conservative Protestants.

Much was made of the fact that Kerry, a self-described former altar boy, lost the Catholic vote narrowly to Bush. Not only had Kerry lost the vote of his own religious affiliation, he lost a vote that had been a staple of the Democratic Party. And in the Midwest, there is the highest regional concentration of Catholics outside of the Northeast. However, Kerry did win the Catholic vote in the more industrial Great Lakes states and among all but the most devout churchgoing Catholics.

The fact is that Kerry and Bush won in the Midwest states in which they had a demographic advantage in voting characteristics among particular social groups. Kerry did best, as did Gore in 2000, in the states with more urban and diverse populations while Bush locked up the more rural and socially homogeneous states. Bush carried the rural areas by a solid margin across the Midwest, and consequently crushed Kerry in Plains states in which rural voters outnumbered urban voters nearly 2–1. Bush, moreover, did particularly well in the suburban battleground of the Midwest, winning by similar margins as in rural areas across red states. It was Kerry's substantial urban voter support that offset the rural and suburban advantages Bush had throughout the Great Lakes states, enough for Kerry to win substantially in Illinois and just enough in other states. In the states in which demographic and geographic advantages were most balanced it was a battle to the end, most notably in the upper Midwest.

PEACE, PROSPERITY, PRAYER, AND PEORIA

Peoria, Illinois, has long served as a symbolic reference to middle America, in which American dreams led to secure jobs and homes with white picket fences. It is also a place that evokes notions of American sacrifice throughout the heartland in devoted service to God and country. Thus, it is not surprising that during times of war, Peoria has supported both incumbent Democratic and Republican administrations. In 2004, Peoria split 50–50, delivering Kerry a narrow victory margin of fewer than 100 votes out of 81,000 votes cast.

The upper Midwest was a focal point of the Kerry strategy to unseat an incumbent administration that had lost more jobs than it had created for the first time since Herbert Hoover. The Kerry–Edwards ticket felt that an economic message would resonate particularly in states like Michigan and Ohio that were hit hard with job loss during recent years.[41] And table 7.3 shows that the 55 percent of Midwest voters who felt that the national economy was in bad shape overwhelmingly voted for Kerry. Kerry also received the strong backing of the 48 percent of Midwest voters who felt the job situation in the area had gotten worse and the 36 percent who had a household member lose a job.

However, the Bush campaign countered Kerry's criticism of the "jobless economy" and John Edwards's critical theme of Bush's "two Americas" of disparate wealth and poverty, by claiming that the economic climate was rebounding throughout America and in the Midwest.[42] It appeared to work with Bush supporters, in which voters with more positive assessments of the economy and job situation in their area backed Bush in even higher numbers than the economically pessimistic backed Kerry. Bush's tax cuts, a target of much Democratic criticism during the primary and general election campaign, were thought to help rather than hurt the economy by a plurality of Midwest voters, which strongly backed Bush. With Midwest voters literally split in half on whether they trusted Bush or Kerry to better handle the economy, Bush benefited by neutralizing domestic economic concerns in a region that had cost his father reelection in 1992.[43]

By countering Democratic economic criticism in a way his father was unable, Bush could turn attention to what the campaign felt was one of their strongest cards, particularly throughout the Midwest: the war on terrorism. Despite Kerry's criticism of what he called the administration's misguided military expansion of the war on terror into Iraq at the expense of U.S. global relations and domestic security, a majority of Midwest voters felt the United States was now safer from terrorism and trusted Bush by 16 points over Kerry in handling terrorism, which also translated into a solid advantage for Bush in the voting booth.

Table 7.3. Midwest Voter Evaluation of Issues, Performance and Leadership, 2004, in percent

	Total Midwest Vote	Bush % of Total	Kerry % of Total	Bush + −
Economic evaluation				
Natl. economy excellent/good	*43*	90	9	+81
Natl. economy not good/poor	55	20	79	−59
Financial situation better	*28*	81	19	+62
Financial situation worse	32	21	78	−57
Job situation in area better	*20*	89	11	+78
Job situation in area worse	48	18	80	−62
A household member lost job	36	32	67	−35
Bush tax cuts help economy	*41*	93	6	+87
Bush tax cuts hurt economy	34	7	93	−86
Trust Bush handling economy	*46*	94	6	+86
Trust Kerry handling economy	47	13	87	−74
War on terrorism and Iraq				
U.S. safer from terrorism	*54*	80	20	+60
U.S. less safe from terrorism	42	14	85	−71
Trust Bush handling terrorism	*57*	85	15	+70
Trust Kerry handling terrorism	41	7	93	−86
Approve of Iraq decision	*52*	83	17	+66
Iraq part of war on terrorism	*54*	80	20	+60
Things going well in Iraq	*44*	91	9	+82
Things going badly in Iraq	52	17	82	−65
Policy preferences				
Abortion mostly illegal	*29*	69	31	+68
Abortion always illegal	*19*	79	21	+58
No legal recognition of gay couple	*40*	68	31	+37
Govt. do more solve problems	46	29	70	−41
Most important issue				
Moral values	*24*	84	15	+69
Economy/jobs	21	17	82	−65
Terrorism	*16*	87	13	+74
Iraq	13	28	72	−44
Taxes	6	53	46	+7
Education	5	32	67	−35
Health care	8	27	72	−45
Most important quality				
Will bring change	24	4	96	−92
Strong leader	*17*	86	13	+73
Clear stand on issue	*17*	81	17	+64
Cares about people	10	25	74	−49
Religious faith	*9*	92	7	+85

Source: Column percentages from the Midwest region exit poll of the National Election Pool. Italicized figures refer to categories in which George W. Bush held an advantage.

With the "antiwar" tradition of states like Minnesota, Wisconsin, and even parts of Iowa, the Kerry campaign felt that their criticism of the administration's handling of the war in Iraq would help to close these tightly contested states.[44] Yet while this tact may have helped in more urban areas and college communities, a slight majority of midwesterners approved of the decision to go to war in Iraq and viewed Iraq as part of the war on terrorism despite the fact that a majority also felt that things were now going badly there. Furthermore, the Bush campaign sought to make inroads in these very same recent Democratic voting states by heavily targeting rural and suburban communities that have been trending Republican.[45]

Lawrence Jacobs, director of the 2004 election project at the University of Minnesota's Hubert Humphrey Institute of Public Affairs, explained that Minnesota "has become more suburban, and the New Deal generation is dying out." Jacobs observes, "It no longer looks like Little Sweden, with support for higher taxes and more government services, and the state is like everywhere else in that national security is eclipsing traditional Democratic issues such as health care."[46] Alan Greenblatt of *The New York Times* notes how in "Wisconsin, suburban residents between Green Bay and the Illinois border were relatively pleased with the low unemployment rate and leaned Republican."[47]

The Bush campaign's mobilization of socially conservative rural and suburban voters was assisted by the same-sex marriage ban on the 2004 ballot in North Dakota and Ohio, two states Kerry lost, and in Michigan, a state that he won by less than expected.[48] The first state in 2004 to vote to ban gay marriage was Missouri, a closely contested state in 2000 that had been trending solidly to Bush in 2004.[49] Overall, the 40 percent of midwesterners who felt that gay couples should have no legal right to marry voted by 37 points more for Bush than Kerry.

Voter concern with the war on terrorism and domestic cultural issues affected the relative voter salience of one of the Kerry campaign's central points, turning around the poor economy and creating jobs. While the economy and jobs were still considered the second most important issue by 21 percent of Midwest voters, the most important issue was moral values, likely affected by the gay marriage ban on many state ballots. Furthermore, Bush's significant advantage among Midwest voters concerned with moral values and terrorism outweighed Kerry's advantages with voters more concerned with the economy and the situation in Iraq.

Midwest voters displeased with the current state of domestic and foreign affairs overwhelmingly voted for Kerry. And despite his portrayal as an "aloof and distant patrician," Kerry benefited among midwesterners who felt he cares about people, a connection Clinton had successfully forged with a struggling Midwest region in 1992 when he claimed to "feel their pain." Nevertheless, these attributes did not translate into what Midwest voters considered to be a strong leader with a clear stand on issues, in which Bush, a self-described man of deep Christian faith, apparently resonated with voters who considered moral values the most important issue, and faith as a critical quality in a presidential candidate.

IN THE BUCKEYE OF THE HURRICANE: THE 2004 CONFLUENCE OF ELECTORAL FORCES IN OHIO

While other states have been important bellwethers throughout the history of presidential elections, Ohio remains one of the most consistent barometers of electoral success. And Ohio, like Florida in 2000, was at the eye of the storm during the 2004 electoral campaign and late finale.[50] The importance of Ohio was nothing new to presidential elections. No Republican presidential candidate has won the Electoral College without winning Ohio. Only two Democratic presidential candidates since 1892 have won the Electoral College without winning Ohio, the last in 1960.[51]

Ohio is a measure of a candidate's ability to appeal across the electoral spectrum.[52] Ohio is in many ways a microcosm of America with historical and demographic components that make many of the Great Lakes states competitive for both Democrats and Republicans.[53] Not only is Ohio a confluence of significant waterways, it is a confluence of regions, with Pennsylvania on the eastern side, Kentucky to the south, and the Indiana heartland on its western border. The north of Ohio resembles the more urban/industrial and Democratic centers of Detroit and Chicago, while the southern reaches are more similar to the states it borders. Indeed, many people live in northern Kentucky and commute across the river to work in Cincinnati, Ohio. Its southern tier, including Cincinnati, is traditionally Republican. Democrats have done exceedingly well in Cleveland and have gained ground in Columbus's Franklin County, which includes Ohio State University. Democrats lost Franklin County in 1988 by 60–39 percent, but Gore won it 49–48 percent in 2000.[54]

Although Clinton won Ohio in 1992 and 1996 largely on an economic platform, Gore lost the state in part because of Clinton's success in making the economy a less concerning issue and his personal conduct, making values and personal character a more important concern. Judis and Texeira surmise, "Gore suffered in Ohio from the same disabilities that sank him in Missouri: rural and small-town voters' concerns about guns, abortion, and the Clinton scandals, and Gore's difficulty in communicating with them."[55] According to exit polls in 2000, 61 percent of Ohioans had an unfavorable view of Clinton as a person, of whom 70 percent voted for Bush, leading Judis and Texeira to conclude, "a Democrat who evoked a reasonable level of trust could have won Ohio in 2000 and could in future elections."[56] Thus, both Kerry and

Bush visited Ohio more times than any other state and the Buckeye state was a focus of national media attention.[57]

Jobs and the economy received prominent electoral attention in a state in which Cleveland had recently been labeled the most impoverished big city in America.[58] And table 7.4 demonstrates that 57 percent of Ohio voters viewed the state economy as "not

Table 7.4. Voter Evaluation of Issues and Performance in Ohio, Michigan, and S. Dakota

	Ohio Bush	Ohio Kerry	Bush + −	Ohio Total	MI Total	SD Total
Economic evaluation						
State economy good	86	13	+73	38	35	62
State economy not so good	36	63	−27	38	40	24
State economy poor	10	90	−80	19	19	6
Financial situation better	87	13	+74	29	27	36
Financial situation same	55	45	+10	32	38	43
Financial situation worse	15	85	−70	37	34	20
Job situation in area better	93	6	+87	17	14	NA
Job situation in area same	77	23	+54	28	31	NA
Job situation in area worse	25	75	−50	55	55	NA
Trust Bush to handle economy	92	8	+84	51	45	61
Trust Kerry to handle economy	91	9	−82	44	49	41
War on terrorism/war in Iraq						
U.S. safer from terrorism	78	22	+56	58	54	66
U.S. less safe from terrorism	14	85	−71	39	42	32
Trust Bush to handle terrorism	81	19	+62	58	53	61
Trust Kerry to handle terrorism	6	94	−88	40	44	38
Approve of Iraq war decision	83	17	+66	54	49	57
Disapprove of Iraq war decision	10	90	−80	40	47	39
Things going well for U.S. in Iraq	90	9	+81	45	42	50
Things going badly for U.S. in Iraq	16	84	−68	49	54	45
Most important issue						
Economy/jobs	17	83	−66	24	25	17
Moral values	85	14	+71	23	19	24
Terrorism	90	10	+80	17	18	19
Iraq	28	72	−44	13	17	15
Taxes	62	38	+24	6	5	6
Education	32	66	−34	5	4	3
Health care	25	75	−50	5	6	4
Most important quality						
Will bring change	6	93	−87	24	24	20
Strong leader	87	13	+74	19	19	23
Clear stand on issue	79	20	+59	13	14	14
Cares about people	32	68	−36	12	13	8
Religious faith	95	5	+90	10	9	11

Source: Column percentages from the Ohio, Michigan, and South Dakota exit polls of the National Election Pool, 2004.

so good" or "poor" when casting ballots for president. Fifty-five percent of Ohio voters felt that the job situation in the area had gotten worse, compared with 14 percent who felt it was better. These figures mirrored Michigan exit polls, another Great Lakes state suffering disproportionate job loss during recent years, in which Lansing pollster Ed Sarplous noted, "There's never been a day where the positive economic message nationally was not answered the next day by bad news in the state."[59]

However, Michigan and Ohio voter similarities end with economic evaluation. Fifty-one percent of Ohioans trusted Bush over the 44 percent who trusted Kerry to handle the economy, while in Michigan the numbers were reversed, with Kerry holding a 5-point advantage. The state electoral results were also reversed, with Kerry winning Michigan by 3 percentage points, and losing by a similar margin in Ohio. Instead, Ohio voted for Bush, just like the state of South Dakota, in which 62 percent of that state's voters viewed the economy as good, more voters felt that their own financial situation was better than worse, and trusted Bush to handle the economy by 20 points over Kerry. Indeed, Ohio joined the Dakotas, Nebraska, and Kansas in voting Republican despite the fact that Plains states had a far more favorable evaluation of the economy, jobs, and their financial situation.

What Ohioans did have in common with states like South Dakota was approval of the war in Iraq, the belief that the United States was now safer from terrorism, and trust in Bush by significant margins over Kerry in handling terrorism. While Michigan voters also gave Bush an advantage in handling terrorism, they were more evenly divided over the Iraq War decision, and a majority of Michigan voters felt that things were going badly in Iraq, the reverse of South Dakota.

Jobs and economic concern resonated with a quarter of Ohio voters at a level similar to Michigan, but moral values were an issue for just as many Ohioans, more in line with the issue priorities of South Dakotans. With terrorism and Iraq serving as a counterbalance, in which Iraq concern led to overwhelming support for Kerry and terrorism concern leading to nearly universal support for Bush, the Ohio division on values vs. the economy split the difference. Here again, Kerry benefited from more disgruntled voters seeking a candidate who cared about their pressing needs and sought to chart a new course. But Bush carried Ohio's voters who yearned for strong leadership with a clear stand on issues and the importance of religious faith.

With such an equally divided Ohio, the ground war of voter mobilization was critical to victory in 2004. Before the election it was clear that Democrats held an advantage among lower-income voters, blacks and urban voters, and the region of northern industrial Ohio. Republicans had the advantage among higher-income voters, whites and rural voters, and the regions of central and southern Ohio. In the end, both parties secured their base, with white voters supporting Bush by a similar margin as 2000, while black voters once again overwhelmingly voted for the Democratic

Table 7.5. Social Forces and Presidential Choices in Ohio and Michigan, in percent

	OH 00 Bush + −	OH 04 Bush + −	OH 04 Bush	OH 04 Kerry	OH 04 Total	MI 04 Total	MI 04 Bush + −
Race and gender							
White	+14	+12	56	44	86	82	+10
Black	−80	−68	16	84	10	13	−79
Latino	NA	−30	35	65	3	2	−26
White men	+27	+13	56	43	40	40	+16
White women	+3	+10	55	45	46	40	+5
Nonwhite men	NA	−46	27	73	7	9	−62
Nonwhite women	NA	−64	18	82	8	9	−64
Demographic profile							
<$50,000 income	−6	−16	42	58	48	46	−19
>$50,000 income	+11	+16	58	42	52	54	+11
No college	−2	0	50	50	62	62	−10
College graduate	+13	+7	53	46	38	38	+8
Union member	−37	−21	39	60	17	19	+12
Married	+9	+18	59	41	62	61	+12
Not married	−13	−24	38	62	38	39	−24
18–29 years old	+4	−14	42	56	21	21	−12
60 years old+	−5	+14	57	43	20	24	−5
First-time voter	NA	−8	46	54	15	12	−34
Religion and religiosity							
White Evangelical	NA	+52	76	24	25	24	+42
Not White Evangelical	NA	−13	56	43	75	76	−17
White Cons. Protestant*	+47	+82	91	9	17	17	+84
Not White Cons. Protestant	−6	−14	43	57	83	83	−20
Catholic	+7	+11	55	44	26	29	−1
Attend church weekly	+19	+30	65	35	38	42	+13
Occasional attend church	−9	−14	43	57	41	40	−12
Never attend church	−21	−28	35	63	13	13	−32
Party identification							
Democrat	−79	−81	9	90	35	39	−86
Republican	+80	+88	94	6	40	34	+88
Independent	+16	−19	40	59	25	27	−2
Community size and region							
Suburban	+9	+2	51	49	49	49	+7
Rural	+25	+20	60	40	25	28	+8
Urban	−22	−17	41	58	25	23	−43

continued

Table 7.5. continued

	OH 00 Bush + −	OH 04 Bush + −	OH 04 Bush	OH 04 Kerry	OH 04 Total	MI 04 Total	MI 04 Bush + −
Cuyahoga OH & Wayne MI	NA	−30	35	65	12	17	−39
N. West OH & Uni. Belt MI	NA	−5	47	52	15	24	−6
N. East OH & Macomb MI	NA	0	50	50	*27*	*22*	*+4*
Central OH & S. West MI	NA	*+18*	58	40	*20*	*21*	*+19*

Note: Column percentages from the Ohio and Michigan exit polls of the 2004 National Election Pool, and the Ohio exit poll of the 2000 Voter News Service. *White religious right in the 2000 exit poll. Italicized figures refer to categories in which George W. Bush held an advantage.

candidate. However, both parties were able to carve into 2,000 numbers, with black Democratic support in Ohio declining by 12 points and white male Republican support dropping 14 points. Any decline in Democratic allegiance from African Americans was particularly harmful to Democratic chances in Ohio, with support 11 points lower among this group than in Michigan. A rise in white female support behind Bush helped to offset the drop in Ohio's white male support.

Scammon and Wattenberg described a "forty-seven-year-old housewife from the outskirts of Dayton, Ohio, whose husband is a machinist" as the prototypical Democratic defector of the 1970s who became the Reagan Democrat of the 1980s.[60] With crosscutting target voters that ranged from NASCAR Dads to Security Moms in 2004, Democrats and Republicans both sought to close the gender gap in Ohio. Democrats sought to appeal to working-class male interests, including jobs and health care.[61] Republicans aimed for protective suburban mothers in the post-9/11 environment on issues of national security and the war on terrorism.[62] Both strategies appeared to narrow the gender gap among white voters in Ohio, from 20 points in 2000 to 3 points in 2004.

Class differences, a theme of John Edwards's "two Americas," did affect Ohio voting, with a 16-point advantage for Kerry among lower-income voters and a 16-point advantage for Bush among higher-income voters, a partisan increase among both groups from 2000. Bush again had an advantage with Ohio college graduates, while Kerry had no advantage among Ohioans without a college degree, despite receiving a 10-point advantage among this group in Michigan. Kerry's support from Ohio union members, while still substantial, dropped 16 points from 2000, and like noncollege graduates was likely affected by concerns over national security and social issues that originally led many union members and noncollege graduates to first support Republican candidates in the industrial Midwest.

Voter Turnout and
Mobilization, County by County in Ohio

The Democrats had a record mobilization on the ground in Ohio to register and turn out younger and first-time voters,[63] and eighteen- to twenty-nine-year-olds turned their support away from Bush in 2000 to Kerry in 2004, swinging by 18 points. Ohio's first-time voters, many of whom were the youngest voters, also supported Kerry, but by not nearly as much as in Michigan. Moreover, the Ohio turnout for Kerry from younger, single, and first-time voters was offset by the larger turnout among married voters and the elderly, which increased their margin for Bush in 2004.

A key to countering the historic Democratic push in Ohio voter mobilization was an even more historic Republican strategy to get out the vote, assisted by the gay marriage ban on the ballot, which further mobilized an already energized white conservative, rural and suburban religious base almost universally committed to voting for George W. Bush.[64] In Ohio, white evangelicals and weekly churchgoers gave Bush a much stronger margin than in Michigan, with Bush also increasing his advantage among Ohio Catholics in 2004. While Kerry's close victory in Michigan was assisted by an electorate with slightly more Democratic than Republican voters, Bush's Ohio advantage was compounded by an electorate with more Republican voters who were also more committed to voting the party line than were Democrats.

Efficient and effective voter mobilization was made possible by the heavy concentration of target groups in rural, urban, and suburban counties.[65] Rural Ohio voted solidly for Bush in 2000 and was a target for turnout in 2004, while Democrats similarly targeted urban areas. However, Bush had a slight advantage from rural voters compared with Kerry's showing among urban voters in 2004, a population for which Kerry won by 43 points in Michigan. Thus, the remaining votes shifted to the suburban battleground, with Kerry narrowing Bush's advantage there from 2000, but by not enough to pull out a victory in the state.

The electoral map in figure 7.1 also reveals a regional county-by-county divide across Ohio in which Kerry solidly carried Cuyahoga County (65–35 percent), home to the city of Cleveland, with similar margins as Wayne County, Michigan, both Midwest urban areas with more racially diverse, younger, and single populations. Kerry also carried university-dominated areas like Franklin County in Ohio and the University Belt in Michigan by similar margins. Kerry and Bush drew even in Northeast Ohio, a region with university towns, small cities, and rural areas, playing

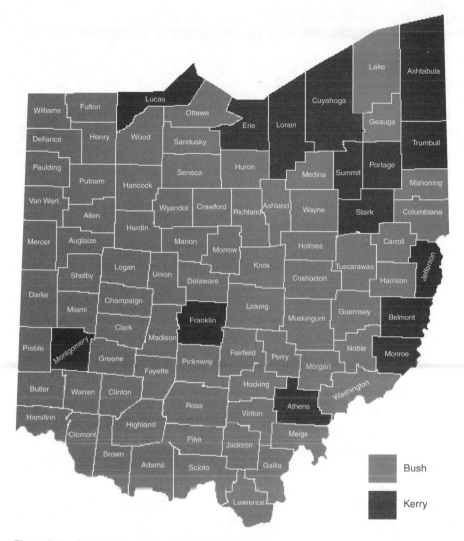

Figure 7.1. Ohio Electoral Map of the 2004 Election

to each party's recent strengths and gains, but Kerry narrowly lost Macomb County, Michigan, the epicenter according to pollster Stan Greenberg of both Republican and Democratic success at winning the white vote in the industrial upper Midwest. But Bush successfully won throughout rural counties and suburban areas in Central Ohio (58–40 percent) and around Cincinnati in southwestern Ohio (55-45 percent), enough to take him over the top in the statewide vote total.[66]

THE MIDWEST AND CONGRESSIONAL
ELECTIONS: THE TIMES THEY ARE A-CHANGIN'

Ohio voted Republican in five out of six presidential elections from 1968 to 1988, before going Democratic in 1992 and 1996, and returning narrowly to the Republican fold in the past two elections. Less secure in the statewide presidential vote, Ohio has become a solid Republican state when it comes to congressional elections. Republican House members currently outnumber Democrats twelve to six, and both U.S. Senators are Republicans serving second terms. Overall, the Midwest region has a solid Republican delegation to the House with a twenty-member advantage following the 2004 elections (see table 7.6).

In recent elections, a rural, conservative constituency has become a backbone of Republican success in Midwest congressional elections, evident in the substantial advantage in House delegations from Indiana, Iowa, Nebraska, and Kansas. While Democratic representatives may win the most urban or large university communities within such states, Republicans carry the rest, and conservative Republican success is often intertwined with a religious values platform. For example, Thomas Frank explains how a representative from central Kansas, "the track star Jim Ryun, says he ran for office because God wanted him to," a beneficiary Frank claims of a "populist conservative movement that conquered the Kansas Republican Party from the ground up."[67] More moderate Republican figures like Senator Nancy Kassebaum, daughter of Alf Landon, and Senator Bob Dole, are long gone from the Kansas congressional delegation. In fact, Frank notes, "when Dole resigned his Senate seat in order to pursue the presidency, it would be won by the pious Sam Brownback who had become a celebrity of the conservative movement nationwide for his humble but uncompromising style."[68] U.S. Senator Brownback and Representative Ryun were both reelected by wide margins in 2004.

Neighboring Nebraska has an all-Republican House delegation, including former University of Nebraska football coaching legend Tom Osborne, who won with 93 percent of the vote in his first attempt at the House, his first run at any elected office. But unlike Kansas, Nebraska has a Democratic and Republican senator, although Democrat Ben Nelson squeaked by with 51 percent for his first term in 2000 while Republican Chuck Hagel won a second term with 83 percent in 2002. And Nelson is likely to face a tough reelection challenge in 2006.

Democrats hold a two-seat advantage in the Midwest delegation to the U.S. Senate, but their seats are concentrated in blue states. Democrats hold both seats in Illinois, Michigan, and Wisconsin, states that all voted Democratic for president in the past four elections. In the industrial upper Midwest, Democratic candidates benefit from a heavier concentration of urban and metropolitan areas that offset rural, if not

Table 7.6. Congressional Elections and Party Delegation in the Midwest Region

State	House #GOP	House #DEM	Senate 2000	Senate 2002	Senate 2004	Senate #GOP	Senate #DEM
Bush States 2004	*+18*					*+4*	
Indiana	7	2	R*		D*	1	1
Iowa	4	1		D+	R*	1	1
Kansas	3	1		R*	R*	2	0
Missouri	5	4		R+	R+	2	0
Nebraska	3	0	D+	R*		1	1
North Dakota	0	1	D*		D*	0	2
Ohio	12	6	R*		R*	2	0
South Dakota	0	1		D+	R+	1	1
Red States Total	34	16				10	6
Kerry States 2004	*+2*						*+6*
Illinois	9	10		D*	D*	0	2
Michigan	9	6	D+	D*		0	2
Minnesota	4	4	D+	R+		1	1
Wisconsin	4	4	D*		D+	0	2
Blue States Total	26	24				1	7
Midwest Total	60	40				11	13

Note: Table compiled by the author from data at congress.org. # = Congressional delegation following 2004 election. * ≥ 60% of vote. + ≤ 60% of vote. Italicized D or R includes party pickup of seat as a result of the 2000, 2002, or 2004 elections.

many suburban, voting trends, the reverse of what is happening in deeply red states. Thus, while the Illinois delegation includes Republican House speaker Dennis Hastert, in 2002 the state elected Democrat Barack Obama, a rising star in the party and only the third African American elected to the U.S. Senate since Reconstruction.

Party success in congressional elections increasingly mirrors presidential outcomes in which voters appear less willing to split votes in the Midwest. Popular and dutiful incumbents are still reelected despite partisan trends, such as Democratic senator Evan Bayh, son of Indiana political icon Birch Bayh, and the incumbent all-Democratic North Dakota delegation in a state that voted for Bush by over 27 points in both 2000 and 2004. But there are signs of stricter party-line voting in other Midwest states. The most notable Senate defeat was incumbent Democratic Senate leader Tom Daschle, elected with 62 percent of the vote in 1998, but losing narrowly with 49 percent of the vote in 2004. Daschle was in many ways the victim of a concerted effort by the Republican White House to help knock out the opposition party leader from a state that has been voting for Republican presidents for forty straight years. The newly elected Republican senator, John Thune, had come close to defeating the other Democratic senator, Timothy Johnson, before winning in a second consecutive try with substantial national party backing.

Congressional victories in the Midwest have helped the Republicans to hold and expand their majority in Congress. As Midwest states trend Republican for the presidency, they are bringing along congressional partisans. Missouri, a state represented for over two decades by Democratic House leader Richard Gephardt before his recent retirement, now has two Republican Senators and a slight Republican advantage in House delegation.

Bob Dylan's "The Times They Are A-Changin" still seems particularly appropriate in the upper Midwest, including Dylan's home state of Minnesota. After all, Hubert Humphrey III lost in a three-way race for Minnesota governor in 1998 to former professional wrestler and Reform Party candidate Jesse "The Body" Ventura. In 2002, Governor Ventura and Republican congressional leaders were raucously booed during an emotion-laden memorial for the late Minnesota Democratic senator Paul Wellstone. Ventura's outspoken disgust at such treatment may have helped swing the narrow election from Wellstone's replacement and Democratic icon Walter Mondale to Republican candidate Norm Coleman, a Minnesotan "The Body" had defeated in 1998. Minnesota is no longer a Democratic bastion and the upper Midwest is a fertile battleground for the presidency and Congress. An increasingly central region in recent elections, it is quite possible that one of the next presidential or vice presidential candidates, man or woman, white or nonwhite, as part of the Republican or Democratic ticket, will come from one of these Midwest states.

NOTES

1. Charlie Cook, "Great Lakes States Will See Plenty of Bush, Kerry," *National Journal*, February 14, 2004, 482.
2. Jim Vandehei, "Candidates Stake Claim to Great Lakes: Campaigns Speak to Midwest Values of Minnesota, Wisconsin Voters," *Washington Post*, August 29, 2004.
3. "The Battle for the Great Lakes," *The Economist*, October 23, 2004, 25–26.
4. V. O. Key, Jr., "A Theory of Critical Elections," in *Electoral Change and Stability in American Political History*, edited by Jerome Chubb and Howard Allen (New York: Free Press, 1971).
5. Kristi Anderson, *The Creation of a Democratic Majority, 1928–1936* (Chicago: University of Chicago Press, 1979).
6. Taylor Dark, *The Unions and the Democrats* (Ithaca, NY: Cornell University Press, 1999).
7. Everett Carll Ladd, Jr. with Charles D. Hadley, *Transformations of the American Party System: Party Coalitions from the New Deal to the 1970s* (New York: Norton, 1975).
8. Kevin Phillips, *The Emerging Republican Majority* (Garden City, NY: Anchor Books, 1970).
9. Edward G. Carmines and James A. Stimson, *Issue Evolution: Race and the Transformation of American Politics* (Princeton, NJ: Princeton University Press, 1989).

10. John Petrocik, *Party Coalitions: Realignment and the Decline of the New Deal Party System* (Chicago: University of Chicago Press, 1981).

11. Theodore White, *America in Search of Itself: The Making of the President, 1956–1980* (New York: Harper and Row, 1982).

12. Ruy Texeira and Joel Rogers, *America's Forgotten Majority: Why the White Working Class Matters* (New York: Basic Books, 2000).

13. Katherine Tate, *From Politics to Protest: The New Black Voter in American Elections* (Cambridge, MA: Harvard University Press, 1994).

14. Jeffrey Stonecash, *Class and Party in American Politics* (Boulder, CO: Westview Press, 2000).

15. Robert Huckfeldt and Carol Weitzel Kohfeld, *Race and the Decline of Class in American Politics* (Urbana: University of Illinois Press, 1989).

16. Francis E. Rourke and John T. Tierney, "The Setting: Changing Patterns of Presidential Politics, 1960 and 1988," in *Elections of 1988*, edited by Michael Nelson (Washington, DC: CQ Press, 1989), 1–24.

17. John Kenneth White, *The New Politics of Old Values*, 2nd ed. (Hanover, NH: University Press of New England, 1990).

18. David Keege and Lyman Kellstedt, *Rediscovering the Religious Factor in American Politics* (Armonk, NY: Sharpe, 1993).

19. Peter Goldman and Tom Mathews, *The Quest for the Presidency: The 1988 Campaign* (New York: Simon and Schuster, 1989).

20. Stanley Greenberg, *Middle Class Dreams: The Politics and Power of the New American Majority* (New Haven, CT: Yale University Press, 1995).

21. John Sperling, *The Great Divide: Retro vs. Metro America* (Sausalito, CA: Polipoint Press, 2004).

22. Thomas Frank, *What's the Matter with Kansas? How Conservatives Won the Heart of America* (New York: Metropolitan Books, 2004).

23. Fred I. Greenstein, *The Hidden-Hand Presidency: Eisenhower as Leader* (New York: Basic Books, 1982).

24. Frank, 28.

25. "Swing States: Missouri," *The Economist*, June 5, 2004.

26. Daniel Wirls, "Voting Behavior: The Balance of Power in American Politics" in *The Elections of 2000*, edited by Michael Nelson (Washington, DC: CQ Press, 2001), 104.

27. John B. Judis and Ruy Teixeira, *The Emerging Democratic Majority* (New York: Scribner, 2002), 74.

28. *The Economist*, June 5, 2004.

29. Stanley Greenberg, *The Two Americas: Our Current Political Deadlock and How to Break It* (New York: St. Martin's Press, 2004), 108.

30. Ibid.

31. Frank, 104.

32. Judis and Texeira, 72–76.

33. Ibid., 98–99.

34. Ibid., 103.

35. Ibid., 105.

36. Ibid., 108.

37. Dan Balz and Amy Goldstein, "Iowans Hear Two Views of Economy," *Washington Post*, August 4, 2004, A1.

38. Allen, A5.
39. Paul Farhi, "Toledo Tube War: Ohio City Bombarded With More Political Spots Than Any Other U.S. Market," *Washington Post*, October 11, 2004, A1.
40. Ford Fessenden, "A Big Increase of New Voters in Swing States," *New York Times*, September 26, 2004, A1.
41. Jim Vanderhei, "Kerry Woos a Divided Street in a Very Divided Ohio," *Washington Post*, July 26, 2004, A10.
42. Amy Goldstein, "Bush Talks Job Issues in Swing States: In Ohio and Michigan, He Touches on Themes for a Second Term," *Washington Post*, August 6, 2004, A6.
43. Jonathan Weisman, "Is it the Economy? Predictive Models Are Breaking Down in Face of Mixed Messages, Foreign Affairs," *Washington Post*, October 29, 2004, E1.
44. Dana Milbank and Jim VanderHei, "Rivals Stick to Issue of Security: Bush, Kerry Trawl Midwest for Votes of Uncommitted," *Washington Post*, October 29, 2004, A1.
45. Mike Allen, "President Ventures to Democratic Territory: Bush is Working to Win Minnesota and Wisconsin," *Washington Post*, September 17, 2004, A5.
46. Quoted in Allen.
47. Alan Greenblatt, "Neck and Neck Around the Country," *New York Times*, October 26, 2004, G1.
48. James Dao, "Same-Sex Marriage Issue Key to Some GOP Races," *New York Times*, November 3, 2004, P4.
49. Alan Cooperman, "Gay Marriage Ban in Mo. May Resonate Nationwide," *Washington Post*, August 5, 2004, A2.
50. Howard Fineman, "The Next Florida," *Newsweek*, November 1, 2004, 20; Ford Feesenden and James Dao, "Ohio Remains a Battleground as Late Voting Delays Count," *New York Times*, November 3, 2004, P1.
51. Elissa Gootman with others, "Some Important Victories for Kerry, But a Death Blow in Ohio," *New York Times*, November 4, 2004, P15.
52. Gary Langer, "Poll: Ohio Reflects Divisions Across the Nation," *ABC News.com*, November 3, 2004.
53. John C. Green, "Ohio: The Heart of it All," *The Forum* 2: 3 (2004), 1–5.
54. Judis and Texeira, 107.
55. Ibid., 108.
56. Ibid.
57. Green, 1.
58. James Barnes, "Swing States: Ohio," *National Journal*, August 28, 2004, 2585; James Dao, "Swaying Unhappy Ohio Voters Could Be a Key to the Presidency," *New York Times*, July 4, 2004, A17.
59. Quoted in Greenblatt.
60. Richard Scammon and Ben Wattenberg, *The Real Majority* (New York: Coward-McCann, 1970), 30.
61. Nicholas Kristof, "Kerry's Blue-Collar Bet," *New York Times*, July 7, 2004, A21.
62. Mike Allen, "Bush Makes Pitch to 'Security Moms': President Hopes to Narrow Gender Gap at Expense of Democratic Issues," *Washington Post*, September 18, 2004, A14; Mark Niquette, "First Lady Stumps for Women's Votes in Ohio: Republican Hoping to Narrow Gender Gap," *Columbus Dispatch*, June 19, 2004, D7.
63. James Dao, "To Get Ohio Voters to the Polls, Volunteers Knock, Talk and Cajole," October 31, 2004, A1.

64. David Finkel, "Bush Emphasis on Values Drew Ohio Evangelicals," *Washington Post*, November 5, 2004, A3.

65. Laurie Goodstein and William Yardley, "President Benefits From Efforts to Build a Coalition of Religious Voters," *New York Times*, November 5, 2004, A22; Rick Lyman, "In Crunch Time, Racing Door to Door," *Washington Post*, November 2, 2004, P1.

66. Matt Bai, "Who Lost Ohio," *New York Times Magazine*, November 21, 2004, 6:67.

67. Frank, 95.

68. Ibid., 98.

8

THE WEST

The Electoral Gateway

David M. Rankin

The transformation of the American West has opened a dynamic gateway to victory in the Electoral College. As a monument to the early western gateway, the St. Louis Arch now leads across a Republican heartland through the Great Plains to the Rockies. Unlike the steel frame of the manmade arch on the western banks of the Mississippi River, the natural monuments of the West continue to change their shape over time albeit not as quickly as demographic trends reshape the western electoral landscape.

Rustic red Republican states stretch across the Mountain West while coastal states have become a more Democratic shade of Pacific blue. Beneath the Big Sky states and between the left coast and right-leaning bulwark of the central Plains are emerging battleground states. These states, which include Nevada, New Mexico, Arizona, and Colorado, provide the ingredients for Democratic *and* Republican victories.

HOW THE WEST WAS WON, TIME AND AGAIN

The American West of the nineteenth century was a place to make your mark and fortune, to develop untamed land, to explore and conquer new terrain, yet the West region meant little for about the first 100 years of the Electoral College. As western territories became states, they developed partisan ties and at times a unique brand of presidential voting. The first western states, California and Oregon, voted with the North for Republican candidate Abraham Lincoln in the critical election of 1860, even though California supported the Democrat Buchanan in 1856.[1] By 1864, Nevada had joined the Union and voted with the West for Lincoln's reelection.

All the western states continued to support victorious Republican presidents, with the exception of 1880, and in 1884 all three states went Republican even as Democrat Grover Cleveland won the presidency. By 1892, the addition of four new states altered the electoral balance in the expanding West. While Oregon, Washington, Montana, and Wyoming all voted Republican, California supported Cleveland in his second successful presidential bid, while Idaho and Nevada voted for the People's Populist Party candidate, James Weaver. The "Wild West" embrace of a reform candidacy was a harbinger for the next two elections. Ohio's William McKinley won the critical election of 1896 with the support of the upper Midwest, Northeast, California, and Oregon,[2] but Nebraskan William Jennings Bryan on the Democratic and Populist Party ticket won the other western states, which now included Colorado. The West split 5–4 in 1900's McKinley and Bryan rematch.

Assuming the presidency after the 1901 assassination of President McKinley, Theodore Roosevelt swept the West in 1904. Bryan was again the 1908 nominee when Democrats held the first national convention out west, in Denver. Bryan won Colorado and Nevada, gaining West voters who viewed Washington, D.C., as a corrupt, distant influence on their lives. In 1912 California and Oregon supported Teddy Roosevelt's Progressive candidacy. Roosevelt, known by then as a reformer, had as a Republican president and conservationist established federal protection of western natural sites, parks, and monuments, which would at times continue to be a source of local and national debate. But Roosevelt lost his Progressive candidacy as Utah voted for the Republican Taft, and the rest of the western states for the Democrat Woodrow Wilson. In 1916, Wilson recaptured the entire West except Oregon. Besides Wilson, Republican domination included the West from 1908 to 1928, and from 1920 to 1928 the entire West supported three straight Republican presidential candidacies.

Between 1908 and 1960, the Democratic Convention did not again convene west of St. Louis with the exception of 1928 in Houston to nominate Alfred E. Smith to face the Republican Herbert Hoover. The Stanford-educated Hoover served from 1929 to 1933, the only California native to be president until 1968. From 1933 to 1968 there was only one Republican president, the Kansan Dwight "Ike" Eisenhower (1953–1961), until Ike's vice president Richard Nixon returned California residents and Republican control to the White House.

Franklin Delano Roosevelt had tremendous western success winning all states in 1932 and 1936, losing only Colorado in 1940, and Colorado and Wyoming in 1944. The far west states, particularly California, grew in part because of economic displacement from the Great Depression, also affecting the central Plains from which many displaced had left. In a saga of American migration featured in California resident John Steinbeck's *The Grapes of Wrath*, families from the Depression-era Dust Bowl packed everything onto jalopies to find work in a largely agrarian California. The FDR administration simultaneously fueled the West's economy with governmental assistance, with World War II demanding military equipment and aircraft. Aerospace companies grew, propelled by military contracts, including Lockheed Martin in southern California and Boeing in Seattle. These industry giants also employed a large unionized workforce with solid wages, a critical western piece of the Democratic New Deal coalition.[3] However, early western cracks in the Democratic juggernaut were exposed as Colorado joined neighboring Plains states voting Republican.

The government also utilized states like Nevada and Arizona for extensive military testing. Strategic placement and space made San Diego a major naval base and the military a focus in many western states. Economic and social transition also transformed partisan affiliation. After FDR's successor Harry Truman narrowly won the presidency in 1948 relying heavily on support out West, Eisenhower swept the West for Republicans in the next two elections. Like the Midwest, the unionized workforce supported Democrats, while the military culture and industry was increasingly Republican. As the former World War II allied commander, Eisenhower himself warned of a military-industrial complex, yet his administration presided over its escalation. Individualism and government dependence were developing as strange bedfellows in the West as Republicans became the party of opposition to federal government authority associated with Democrats, while fueling the West's growth through government contracts and spending.

Until 1956, no Republican national convention was held west of Kansas City. But California was increasing in importance. When Hoover was elected president in 1928, California had thirteen electoral votes. California was up to 32 votes by 1956. Thus, Eisenhower became the first presidential candidate to accept his party's nomination west of the Rockies by accepting his bid for reelection in San Francisco.

With California's increasing importance, the Democrats followed the Republicans by holding their 1960 convention in Los Angeles. Massachusetts Senator John F. Kennedy liked spending time out on the California coast, honeymooning in Santa Barbara, and carousing with Hollywood pals in the southern California scene of the rich and famous. Thus, it was fitting that Kennedy was the first candidate to accept his party's nomination at the Sports Arena, the new home for the Los Angeles Lakers, who had left Minneapolis the same year.

Kennedy faced Vice President Richard Nixon, a hard-nosed, cunning campaigner, and with relatively humble southern California roots that contrasted sharply with Kennedy's privileged East Coast pedigree. Nixon's personal story and a fighter instinct alienated many voters and East Coast elite, but he resonated with the individualistic "pull yourself up by your own bootstraps" mentality of many western voters. In 1960, Nixon won every mainland western state except Nevada and New Mexico, winning the new state of Alaska while losing the other new state of Hawaii (see table 8.1). Still, Nixon lost the Electoral College narrowly to Kennedy, following up that tough defeat by losing to Democratic candidate Edmund "Pat" Brown in California's 1962 guber-natorial election. After losing in two straight attempts for political office a dour Nixon pined before reporters, "You won't have Nixon to kick around anymore." But Nixon would be back, having laid the groundwork in the West for a successful Republican run.

Electoral focus was moving west for Republicans, with the 1964 convention in San Francisco for the second time in three elections. With the prospect of facing a president who took office following Kennedy's 1963 assassination, Nixon avoided another futile electoral attempt. Arizona senator Barry Goldwater secured the Republican Party nomination and lost to Lyndon Johnson in a historic landslide.

In Goldwater's acceptance speech he uttered the defining statement, "extremism in the defense of liberty is no vice and . . . moderation in the pursuit of justice is no virtue," and the Johnson campaign portrayed the senator as too conservative, if not radical, for the average American voter. Goldwater was swept in the West with the exception of Arizona. However, Goldwater appealed to states-rights white voters alienated by what they felt were intrusive policies of the Democratic Kennedy and Johnson administrations. In his critique of government largess and the Democratic Party that he argued promoted such policy, Goldwater laid the ideological foundation for Republican electoral success for decades in the West.[4]

In 1968, California was again a focus of the race for the presidency. Democratic primary challenger Robert Kennedy had just finished his acceptance speech in Los Angeles after winning the California primary when he was assassinated. Yet Kennedy's earlier assault on the Vietnam War policies of the Johnson administration, exacerbated by fractious Chicago Democratic Convention riots, opened the door for two-time electoral loser, Richard Nixon.

Nixon was a strategic politician and his campaign built upon much of Goldwater's strategy to win not only in the South but also the West.[5] He advocated that more power and decision-making should return to the states and played to the small-town values of a rustic West alienated by urban-centered protest and conflict. In 1968, Nixon carried the West except Hawaii and Washington, adding Nevada and New Mexico, two states he lost in 1960. In 1972, Nixon won the entire West in a landslide reelection while locking the region in as a Republican stronghold in presidential elections.[6] In 1976, President Gerald Ford swept the mainland West despite losing the election to Jimmy Carter, after pardoning Nixon following his 1974 resignation over the Watergate crisis.

In 1980 Republican candidate Ronald Reagan carried the West just like Ford *and* Reagan won the presidency. On his path to the White House, Reagan had accomplished what Nixon could not. He defeated Pat Brown, and was elected California governor in 1966 and 1970. Reagan had graduated from Eureka College in Illinois and started his career in broadcasting in his native Midwest. But Reagan made his name in Hollywood as a movie actor predominantly in the 1940s and 1950s. However, Reagan's last role before elected office was perhaps most fitting. From 1965 to 1966, Reagan hosted the popular television series entitled *Death Valley Days*, also known as *Call of the West*.

FROM THE DEMOCRAT
REAGAN TO REAGAN DEMOCRATS

By 1960, the Democrat Reagan was increasingly enamored with Republican presidential candidates out West. Unlike much of Hollywood supporting Kennedy for president, Reagan gave more than 200 speeches as a "Democrat for Nixon," and in 1962 he officially changed his party affiliation to Republican. In 1964, Reagan became the cochair of California Republicans for Goldwater, and in one of his many speeches on behalf of Goldwater, Reagan delivered an attack on big government and Johnson's "Great Society" programs. Reagan soon succeeded to the leadership of the conservative movement within the Republican Party.

Whether it was his movies, his personality, or his policies, Reagan struck a nerve in California and throughout the West with Nixon- and Goldwater-inspired attacks on government and in defense of states rights and lower taxes, which resonated from the suburbs to rustic western terrain. Reagan also promoted defense spending and American military superiority, which helped him in military-reliant communities across the West and with former white blue-collar union workers who once staunchly supported the Democrats.[7] Reagan, a former FDR Democrat himself, successfully converted many former members of a crumbling New Deal Coalition.[8] Reagan reinforced the growing perception of the Republican Party as an advocate of smaller government symbolized by his famous statement, "Government is not the solution to the problem, government is the problem."

Reagan utilized and solidified electoral forces that Nixon had set in motion, sweeping the West in his bid for reelection in 1984 mirroring Nixon's own landslide reelection.[9] The Reagan persona symbolized the "rugged individualism" of the Wild West, which lent itself to the philosophy of the "free market" and slashing government programs.[10] President Reagan reinforced the western myth of the cowboy, riding his horses, chopping wood, and entertaining dignitaries on his rustic California ranch.

Electoral success had a future electoral price in the West as the Reagan coalition attracted western working-class whites through social conservatism.[11] This strategy included allying with conservative religious organizations necessitating, among other social debates, an increasingly partisan pro-life position on the fractious abortion issue.[12] The 1988 Bush–Quayle ticket swept the Mountain West and Southwest, but the Democratic Dukakis-Bentsen campaign made inroads on the Pacific Coast, aided by expanding metropolitan areas, an increasingly diverse population, and more socially moderate viewpoints.[13]

Furthermore, President Bush's decision to raise taxes to contend with the federal deficit despite asking voters to read his lips to the contrary did not play well in many western states. Western voters again threw support behind a reform-minded third-party candidacy, the independent Ross Perot, and the 1992 Clinton–Gore ticket could build upon the urban-based Pacific Coast success of the Dukakis 1988 campaign to gather western states rebelling over the economic policies of the incumbent administration.[14] In 1992, Democrats regained California, the largest electoral prize with 54 electoral votes, and won the long-time Republican states Nevada, New Mexico, Colorado, and Montana.

The Clinton administration, in turn, alienated voters in states like Montana with support for gays in the military, gun control, and environmental laws that

Table 8.1. Electoral College Partisan Trends in the West Region, 1960–2004

	60	64	68	72	76	80	84	88	92	96	00	04	04+	00+
Rustic Red													+34	+36
Alaska	R	D	R	R	R	R	R	R	R	R	R	R	26	31
Idaho	R	D	R	R	R	R	R	R	R	R	R	R	38	40
Montana	R	D	R	R	R	R	R	R	D	R	R	R	20	25
Utah	R	D	R	R	R	R	R	R	R	R	R	R	45	41
Wyoming	R	D	R	R	R	R	R	R	R	R	R	R	40	41
Pacific Blue													+9	+15
California	R	D	R	R	R	R	R	R	D	D	D	D	10	12
Hawaii	D	D	D	R	D	D	R	D	D	D	D	D	9	18
Battleground													+5	+5
Arizona	R	R	R	R	R	R	R	R	R	D	R	R	10	6
Colorado	R	D	R	R	R	R	R	R	D	R	R	R	5	8
Nevada	D	D	R	R	R	R	R	R	D	D	R	R	3	4
New Mexico	D	D	R	R	R	R	R	R	D	D	D	R	1	1
Oregon	R	D	R	R	R	R	R	D	D	D	D	D	4	5
Washington	R	D	D	R	R	R	R	D	D	D	D	D	7	6

Note: Table compiled by the author based on electoral data from the office of the Federal Register. The 04+ and 00+ columns calculate the popular vote margin for each state and the average popular vote margin for solid red, solid blue, and the closer battleground states. For example, the Republican candidate, George W. Bush, won Alaska by a 26-point popular vote margin in 2004 and a 31-point popular vote margin in 2000. The average red state popular vote margin was 34 points in 2004 and 36 points in the 2000 election. Additional percentage points ≤ 0.5 are rounded down (e.g., 2.4% = 2%) and additional percentage points ≥ 0.6 are rounded up (e.g., 15.6% = 16%) unless the overall percentage of the state popular vote is less than 1 (e.g., 0.1%, 0.9%).

butted heads with many local views and interests. In his 1996 reelection over Kansas senator Bob Dole, Clinton lost Montana and Colorado back into the Republican column.[15] Clinton did hold Nevada and picked up Arizona for Democrats for the first time since 1948, but both returned to Republicans in 2000.

The electoral lines have been carved into the western landscape. In 2000 and 2004, Republican candidate George W. Bush won the rustic Mountain West by an average margin of at least 34 points. Democratic strength rests on the coast, where California's 55 electoral votes have become as blue as the Pacific surrounding Democratic Hawaii. Thus, there are six remaining competitive states in the West. Democrats won by single digits in each of the past two elections in Oregon and Washington. New Mexico went narrowly to Gore in 2000 and narrowly to Bush in 2004. Nevada, Arizona, and Colorado went Republican in the past two elections, but by single-digit margins and with demographic trends that make Democrats hopeful.

THE WESTERN LANDSCAPE, FROM CHANGING PACIFIC TIDES ACROSS AN ELECTORAL GRAND CANYON

States lining the Pacific have always attracted new residents and migrants, and California was already a relatively diverse state when Republicans were racking up victory after victory on the West Coast. Besides Hawaii, these states were solidly Republican from 1972 to 1984, yet Reagan was the last Republican to sweep the Pacific Coast. More recently, Democratic presidential candidates have gained the electoral advantage within the coastal states because the population has changed dramatically from even the 1970s and 1980s, with even more diversity in race and lifestyle alongside rapid population growth and concentration in metropolitan areas. Republican presidential candidates, on the other hand, continue to rule throughout the Mountain West states where the population hasn't changed nearly as much and remains predominantly white, rural, and older. The biggest challenge for both parties are states exhibiting both trends, rural throughout large swaths of the state but rapidly expanding in metropolitan areas with the sort of younger, diverse residents flooding into coastal cities.

The 2004 exit poll reveals the West as where future presidential elections may be won. With the Northeast voting for Kerry by 13 points and the South for Bush by 16 points, the West region was divided with a single percentage point, with the Independent Ralph Nader stealing off the missing point. Urban rich areas helped tilt the exit poll to Kerry 50–49, but the rural-dominated mountain, desert, and plains helped Bush run up incredible electoral margins of victory across multiple states. The urban–rural divide is starkly apparent in a region in which Bush won 9 out of 13 states but Kerry received 77 of the 124 electoral votes.

Bush had a solid advantage among western white voters with the bulk of his white vote concentrated in the states he won (see table 8.2). Bush won the white vote by 33 points in red states while narrowly losing white voters in states that went to Kerry. Bush's advantage was strengthened by the higher percentage of white voters residing in more rural red states, in some states pushing 100 percent. The gender gap played a more significant role in blue states, with white women giving Kerry a 12-point advantage and white men giving Bush a 7-point margin. Democrats have an advantage in urban-dominated blue western states more populated by women who are nonwhite, unmarried, college-educated, and professionals, and who vote increasingly for Democrats on economic and social policy.[16] Red western states consist of fewer professional and college-educated women, and more women who are married and living in rural areas. In these states, Bush won convincingly among white men and women.

Stanley Greenberg interviewed what he called "Super-Educated Women" in Seattle's King County, describing such voters as "the most committed to the regulatory state" in which "they reject aggressive individualism, whether in personal behavior or for the country."[17] Such women, residing in urban and suburban areas, contrast with what Greenberg calls the "F-U Boys" who he finds are "anti-government, pro-NRA, military values, blue collar, without college degrees, under fifty, mainly with young families, like the Republican view on taxes, that American security depends on its own strength, not alliances."[18]

Table 8.2. Social Forces in Voting Across the West, Red and Blue States, 2004, in %

	Total West Vote	Bush West Vote	Kerry West Vote	West Bush + −	Red State Avg.	Bush Red +	Blue State Avg.	Bush Blue + −
Race and gender								
White	77	54	45	+9	91	+33	72	−3
Black	5	18	80	−62	2	NA	4	−56
Latino	13	39	58	−29	4	NA	10	−27
White men	33	60	39	+21	44	+39	33	+7
White women	49	49	50	−1	46	+28	40	−12
Nonwhite men	10	38	57	−19	NA	NA	NA	NA
Nonwhite women	13	31	69	−38	NA	NA	NA	NA
Demographic profile								
<$50,000 income	44	47	52	−5	53	+25	41	−14
>$50,000 income	56	51	47	+4	47	+37	60	−4
No college degree	56	55	44	+11	56	+19	54	−3

continued

Table 8.2. continued

	Total West Vote	Bush West Vote	Kerry West Vote	West Bush + −	Red State Avg.	Bush Red +	Blue State Avg.	Bush Blue + −
College graduate	44	43	55	−12	50	0	46	−20
Married	60	55	43	+12	59	+13	NA	NA
Not married	40	39	59	−20	NA	NA	33	−25
18–29 years old	15	47	51	−4	22	+27	16	−16
60 years old+	28	51	48	+3	19	+25	25	+2
First time voter	10	43	53	−10	13	+8	10	−23
Union member	15	40	57	−17	NA	NA	18	−19
Gun owner	41	59	40	+19	NA	NA	NA	NA
Military service	20	59	37	+22	23	+35	NA	NA
Religion and religiosity								
White Evangelical	19	79	20	+59	28	+67	32	+52
Not White Evangelical	81	40	58	−18	72	+13	68	−31
White Cons. Protestant	NA	NA	NA	NA	19	+87	18	+83
Not White Cons. Protest.	NA	NA	NA	NA	81	+17	85	−23
Attend church weekly	34	62	36	+26	41	+22	32	+18
Occasional attend church	39	43	56	−13	NA	NA	41	−14
Never attend church	23	36	62	−26	NA	NA	24	−38
Catholic	22	39	60	−21	18	+20	18	−21
Party identification								
Democrat	34	8	91	−83	24		37	−78
Republican	36	92	7	+85	46	+91	31	
Independent	30	44	52	−8	30	+11	32	−11
Community size								
Suburban	42	50	48	+2	6	+27	49	−6
Urban	37	45	54	−9	24	+17	36	−33
Rural	21	69	30	+39	30	+39	22	+10

Note: Table 8.2 column figures include percentages from the West region results of the National Election Pool exit poll. Total vote is the percentage polled for each group. "+" indicates the point margin advantage for Bush, "−" indicates the point margin advantage for Kerry. The red state average includes the states of Alaska, Idaho, Montana, and Wyoming. The red state average of white evangelicals only includes the states of Idaho and Montana. Military service includes combined totals for Alaska and Arizona. First time voters, voters with no college, and college graduates are based only on the Arizona exit poll. Married people are based only on the Nevada exit poll. Attend church weekly relied solely on the New Mexico exit poll. The blue state average includes the states of California, Hawaii, Oregon, and Washington. Unmarried voters and white evangelicals in blue states are based only on the Oregon exit poll. The blue state of Hawaii and the red state of Alaska both distinguished the majority of their population as living in suburban communities, with no real urban population. Italicized figures refer to categories in which George W. Bush held an advantage.

Democratic candidates have also increased their success in states like California because of the increasing Latino population, and the party benefited from the Latino backlash to California's Proposition 187.[19] Passed in 1994 but later ruled unconstitutional, Proposition 187 denied public service to illegal immigrants including their children, and had the visible backing of then Republican governor Pete Wilson. In

1996, President Clinton won nearly three quarters of California's Latino vote over Bob Dole, who visibly supported an English-only language requirement for Americans.

As a candidate who regularly addressed Latino audiences in Spanish, George W. Bush won 35 percent of Latinos nationwide in 2000 according to the exit poll. Still, Gore beat Bush by 27 points nationwide among Latinos and by similar margins in critical western states. In New Mexico, Gore won by 366 votes where 43 percent of the population is Latino.[20] Recognizing the increasing importance of this group, particularly out West, the Bush campaign aimed to increase its Latino vote.

Ronald Brownstein and Kathleen Hennessey of the *Los Angeles Times* point out "more than any single factor, it has been the Latino community's steady growth that has moved these states from reliably Republican toward the tossup category. From 1990 through 2002, the Latino population soared by 272 percent in Nevada, 115 percent in Arizona, 93 percent in Colorado, and 38 percent from a large base in New Mexico, according to census figures. Latinos now constitute about a fifth of the population in Nevada and Colorado, more than a fourth in Arizona and more than two-fifths in New Mexico."[21]

In the 2004 exit poll, Bush won a record 44 percent of the Latino vote for a Republican candidate, surpassing Reagan's 37 percent in 1984. Bush claimed more secure victories in Arizona and Colorado with the relatively strong showing among Latinos, which also helped him over the top in Nevada and New Mexico. In New Mexico Latinos made up 32 percent of exit poll respondents yet Latinos supported Kerry by a relatively narrow 12-point margin in a state with a Democratic Latino governor. Kerry still carried the West's Latino vote by 29 points, but the margin among Latinos for the Democratic candidate was lower than in 2000.

Republicans view courting Latino voters as a necessity but also see an opportunity.[22] Many Latinos have conservative social values and serve in the military, both advantages for Republican candidates.[23] Roberto de Posada, president of the business-oriented Latino Coalition, claims Latino opposition to "the gay marriage issue is a concept that worked very, very well for Bush."[24] Democrats, on the other hand, retain an advantage among Latinos for what are viewed as Democratic commitment to civil rights and economic policies addressing the needs of a group with disproportionately lower income and education levels.

Overall in the West, there was a slight income difference, with lower-income voters supporting the Democrat and higher-income voters supporting the Republican for president. However, such differences have as much to do with regional as with class distinction. In red states Bush received the overwhelming support of higher- *and* lower-income voters. In blue states Kerry carried both groups, and lower-income voters with a larger spread. Voters without college degrees were more likely to support Bush in red states, while college graduates gave Kerry a much more significant advantage in blue states.

Abramson, Aldrich, and Rohde note, "Democrats may be appealing to disadvantaged Americans because of the party's economic policies and better educated Americans—especially better-educated women—may reject the interpretation of traditional values emphasized by Republicans in recent elections."[25] This appears to be the trend in solid blue states, while in red states the Republican emphasis on traditional values apparently has the *opposite* effect. Democrats are gaining among higher income, skilled professionals in places like what Greenberg calls "Eastside Tech," which includes the rapidly growing and high-tech area of Bellevue and Redmond, Washington.[26] Judis and Texeira refer to the "ideopolis" of Seattle's King County and Portland's Mutnomah County in terms similar to California's Silicon Valley, areas with highly skilled professional voters who "back regulatory capitalism, but are wary of social engineering," which in their minds includes the electoral rejection of the Republican brand of social conservatism.[27]

Bush had a substantial advantage across nearly each social group in red states, while Kerry had the advantage among key demographics for the most part only in blue states. For example, Kerry benefited from the eighteen- to twenty-nine-year-old turnout and first-time voters in states where he was victorious, but these groups turned out to support Bush in solidly Republican western states. The Vietnam War veteran Kerry could not reverse a consistent Republican advantage among voters with military service. And with 41 percent in the West exit poll claiming to be a gun owner, Kerry lost their vote by a solid margin among a group that apparently didn't view Kerry's heavily publicized hunting experience in the same light as that of Wyoming native and hunting enthusiast Vice President Dick Cheney. Forty years earlier, Goldwater's presidential campaign was based on his statement to "go hunting where the ducks are,"[28] which Kerry did with some success. Kerry won West union members, but these were unlikely the same white blue-collar workers that once earned high wages in the aerospace industry on the West Coast. Many of those very companies have downsized, if not closed up shop or moved offshore in recent decades.

IN GOD'S COUNTRY

The rock band U2 recorded "In God's Country" for their 1987 album *The Joshua Tree*, named for the southern California desert site, a musical commentary on the intersection of American politics, God, and the West. Like the Second Great Awakening in which evangelism spread along with the American frontier in the nineteenth century, the West has turned to religion at times of economic and social upheaval. Indeed, the American prairie evokes images of revivals and traveling preachers, with the church serving as a place of social gathering in a sparsely populated rustic region. The wide-open land of the West is often referred to as God's country, with its seemingly endless big sky and awe-inspiring mountain backdrops, desert expanses, and spectacular natural monuments. And for many towns dotting this landscape, Christianity is central to beliefs and community.

As a candidate and president, Ronald Reagan often evoked imagery from an extensive show-biz career. Reagan's 1943 portrayal of Father Michael O' Keefe in *For God and Country* fittingly symbolized a later policy vision that rejected the government programs of the New Deal and Great Society for greater reliance on the charitable deeds of the church and churchgoers. Reagan had done what Goldwater would not. He made conservative religious groups a critical component of the Republican strategy to win the West, and the synergy of Christian faith and the philosophy of limited government translated into Republican domination in the Mountain West.[29] George W. Bush's own outspoken Christian faith, support of extensive tax cuts, and faith-based programs solidified nearly universal support of white conservative Protestants and gained overwhelming support from white evangelical voters throughout the West. By contrast, Kerry had a much smaller advantage among voters who were not white conservative Protestants in blue states and lost the same group in red states. With the solid support of weekly churchgoers, Bush built upon the advantage Reagan established between the Religious Right and the Republican Party.[30] The Catholic Kerry did carry the Catholic vote in states he won but he lost by 20 points in states that went to Bush, including the vote of pro-life Catholic Latinos.

Democratic voters are also outnumbered by Republicans in the states that voted for Bush, with Republicans holding a 22-point advantage. Democrats had a 6-point advantage in states that voted for Kerry. In red states, Bush benefited from the higher percentage of rural areas that gave him a 39-point average margin. In blue states, Kerry benefited from a higher concentration of urban areas that gave him a 33-point average margin. Kerry had a slight 6-point advantage in blue state suburbs, while Bush easily won the suburbs in red states.

STRIP MINING AND STRIP MALLS,
COWBOYS AND CONSERVATIONISTS

Democrats stand the best odds at winning in states growing rapidly around metropolitan areas with diverse inner suburbs. Republicans' best bets include states with predominantly rural areas with fast-growing smaller communities and outer suburbs. Therefore, Nevada is the kind of place for both parties to roll the dice.

Nevada, once known for remote nuclear testing and brief visits to "Sin City," has become the fastest-growing state because people are not just visiting Las Vegas but moving into its surrounding community to set up permanent residence. Nevada also consists of communities that trend Democratic *and* Republican, trends also occurring in Arizona and Colorado.[31] Twenty percent of Nevada's voters claimed to have moved to Nevada since 2000, and they narrowly supported Kerry, while only 14 percent claimed to be Nevada natives and they supported Bush. The Nevada exit poll showed Kerry winning the 51 percent of voters classified as urban residents while Bush won 71 percent from the 14 percent now considered rural voters. Latinos also made up 10 percent of Nevada voters and 60 percent went for Kerry.[32]

Nevada is an accelerated version of trends across the region, in which urban areas are solidly Democratic, rural areas Republican, with suburban sprawl becoming battlegrounds. New communities extending beyond Phoenix and Portland are electoral targets in closely divided states as metropolitan areas extend into once remote rural communities. There is a synthesis and collision of voting interests at the periphery of urban and rural areas where growth now connects once disparate geographic terrain. It is here that the policy demands of the urban/inner suburbs meet outer suburb/rural resistance, and vice versa.

As metropolitan life extends into once sparsely populated lands there is greater concern for the environment, solid public schools, clean air and water, public access to environmentally friendly recreational activities, valued in university communities like Eugene, Oregon, and Tucson, Arizona. With high percentages of undergraduates and postgraduates in the changing population of Colorado and Washington, these states are considered top "New Economy" states. As John Kenneth White explains, "the environment is an important issue to well educated New Economy voters who desire its preservation and see it as a values issue."[33] These are values and policies many of these voters associate with Democratic presidents, and a reason they now consistently vote Democratic.

There is also rural conservative backlash to 80s-style economic wealth and 60s-influenced social values embodied by what David Brooks calls these "bourgeois bohemians."[34] Their expansion encroaches upon local interests of the agrarian and rustic West, long accustomed to unhindered access to logging, mining, fishing, hunting, and land. When the federal government imposes environmental protections and gun restrictions, it infringes upon traditional ways of life in rural communities. At least that is how voters in states like Alaska and Idaho tend to view federal directives they associate with Democratic presidents, and thus vote Republican.

Of the 40 percent of western voters who felt government should do more to solve problems, they solidly supported Kerry (see table 8.3). For voters who felt the government should not get involved, they heavily supported Bush. In tightly contested Oregon, 57 percent of voters felt jobs were more important than the environment, and they voted for Bush. Of the 34 percent who sided with the environment, 81 percent voted for Kerry. In neighboring Washington, there was a nearly identical breakdown. Thus, Kerry won Oregon and Washington by winning substantial margins in the metropolitan coastal areas of Portland and Seattle, while Bush kept the race close with heavy margins in the Pacific Northwest's smaller towns. In Nevada, 40 percent of voters believed the Yucca Mountain Waste site to be a very important concern, and 73 percent of those voters supported Kerry. Of the 32 percent who claimed it was not important, over three quarters voted for Bush. The challenge for both parties is to appeal to vital blocs without alienating other critical groups with policy positions. Clinton managed both sides of this electoral coin, picking up Montana for Democrats in 1992 and losing back the state in 1996.

Kerry tried to walk this fine line but his economic critique of this President Bush carried less weight than Clinton's did in 1992. In 2004, the West was split down the middle between those who viewed the national economy in relatively good or bad shape. Moreover, in critical western states there was a relatively favorable economic evaluation, which made it harder for Kerry to gain certain voters out West based on an economic criticism of the Bush administration that resonated more strongly in the industrial Midwest.[35] Nearly twice as many voters in Nevada (74 percent) as in Ohio (38 percent) rated the state economy as excellent or good, and those voters solidly backed the incumbent. Furthermore, more western voters believed Bush's tax cuts helped rather than hurt the economy, neutralizing Kerry's economic attack, and more voters trusted Bush than Kerry to handle the economy. Bush's economy, for the most part, resonated in a region that had embraced similar policies under Reagan.

In fact, Bush's persona is more reminiscent of Reagan's western styling than of the president's own father. The forty-first president liked to vacation at the family compound in Kennebunkport, Maine, while "43" prefers to spend his free time, like Reagan, on a sprawling and rustic Western ranch, dressed in cowboy attire, chopping wood and clearing brush. With Reaganesque western movie lingo, President Bush spoke of bringing in Osama bin Laden "Dead or Alive," evoking Wild West imagery with Bush in the protective role as both town sheriff and gunslinger. Such imagery appears to play well in a West region with its share of cowboys as well as dependence on the military and defense industry.

Bush received a 21-point western advantage over Kerry in trust in handling terrorism in which more voters than not thought the United States was safer from terrorism. However, the West was split over the war in Iraq, and a significant majority felt that things were now going badly there. More than the economy, Iraq demonstrated a deep divide between red and blue states. Even in Hawaii, the site of the 1941 Pearl Harbor attack, 53 percent were opposed to the war in Iraq, while in Utah, site of the 2002 Winter Olympics, 70 percent were in favor of the war in Iraq. With debate raging over Iraq policy in a nation divided over the Bush administration, approval for the war in Iraq and president Bush was no less than 65 percent in every

Table 8.3. West Voter Evaluation of Issues, Performance, and Leadership, 2004

	Total West Vote	Bush West Vote	Kerry West Vote	West Bush + −
Economic evaluation				
Natl. economy excellent/good	49	84	16	+68
Natl. economy not good/poor	50	20	77	−57
Financial situation better	33	78	20	+58
Financial situation worse	23	20	77	−57
Job situation in area better	27	90	10	+80
Job situation in area worse	37	16	82	−66
A household member lost job	29	38	61	−23
Bush tax cuts help economy	43	91	8	+83
Bush tax cuts hurt economy	31	5	92	−87
Trust Bush handling economy	52	88	12	+76
Trust Kerry handling economy	42	9	90	−81
War on terrorism and Iraq				
U.S. safer from terrorism	53	79	20	+59
U.S. less safe from terrorism	41	12	87	−75
Trust Bush handling terrorism	60	82	17	+65
Trust Kerry handling terrorism	39	5	94	−89
Approve of Iraq decision	50	86	12	+74
Iraq part of war on terrorism	52	81	18	+63
Things going well in Iraq	41	88	9	+79
Things going badly in Iraq	56	19	90	−71
Policy preferences				
Abortion mostly illegal	24	70	27	+43
Abortion always illegal	9	67	30	+37
No legal recognition of gay couple	31	72	26	+46
Govt. do more solve problems	40	32	66	−34
Most important issue				
Moral values	22	71	26	+45
Terrorism	19	83	17	+66
Iraq	20	24	76	−52
Economy/jobs	17	22	74	−52
Taxes	5	63	34	+29
Education	4	22	78	−56
Health care	7	23	77	−54
Most important quality				
Will bring change	24	4	94	−90
Strong leader	18	86	11	+75
Clear stand on issue	15	76	23	+53
Religious faith	7	86	14	+72
Cares about people	7	23	75	−52

Source: Column percentages from the West region exit poll of the National Election Pool. Italicized figures refer to categories in which George W. Bush held an advantage.

red western state. In Cheney's home state of Wyoming, at the intersection of the Mountain West in the northwest and the central plains on its southwest borders, the oft-controversial vice president had a 71 percent favorable rating and there was 72 percent approval for President Bush.

Social forces and policy preferences create nearly unbeatable combinations in certain western states. In Utah, Bush won by 40 points in 2000 and 45 points in 2004 in a state that is deeply religious, almost all white, and Republicans outnumbered Democrats by nearly 40 points in the 2004 exit poll. By contrast, Hawaii voted for Gore by 18 points and Kerry by a 9-point margin in a state that was 42 percent white, and Democrats outnumbered Republicans by 16 points in the 2004 exit poll.

Social divisions have been entrenched, if not growing for some time, and do not hinge on any particular issue. Nevertheless, many credit or blame the anti-gay marriage amendment on the 2004 ballot in many states for turning out religious conservative voters and swinging the election. The gay marriage issue had particular salience and divisiveness in a region after a highly visible discussion following the 1998 Wyoming murder of gay student Matthew Shepard as well as the high-profile decision by San Francisco mayor Gavin Newsom to recognize gay marriage. Whatever the effect on turnout, the nearly one-third of voters who felt there should be no legal recognition of gay couples voted by a 46-point margin in the West for President Bush. With the amendment on the Oregon ballot, the race was significantly closer than anticipated, with 32 percent of voters classified as white evangelicals. The gay marriage debate made moral issues a more important issue for certain West voters, providing Bush with a significant advantage.

John Kerry appeared to appeal to the populist streak in western voters who wanted change and a candidate who cares for the people. For West voters supporting Bush, he exhibited the qualities many now associate with Reagan during the Cold War, that of strong leadership and a clear stand on issues. In a region that has transformed dramatically over the past century, candidate Bush was able to merge an economic agenda reminiscent of the Republican McKinley with the common-man religious persuasion of McKinley's Democratic challenger Bryan, a mix that seems to have a timeless quality in any electoral showdown out West.[36]

COLORADO'S ROCKY MOUNTAIN DIVIDE

When William Jennings Bryan accepted the 1908 Democratic nomination at the national convention in Denver, the Democrats were at an electoral disadvantage that had translated into an era of Republican domination. It was also the last, and only time, either party selected a western locale north of Texas and east of California to nominate their candidate. Nearly 100 years later, the state of Colorado is the centerpiece of a westward electoral strategy.

Colorado has voted Republican for president in three straight elections, and in nine out of the past ten elections, but the state did swing Democratic in 1992. More important, Colorado's rapid population growth and nine electoral votes make it the most desirable competitive state between the Pacific Coast states and the eastern borders of the Great Plains. Colorado represents the Democrats' best chance to win in the central region of the country and Republicans' to hold the middle.

The centrality of Colorado reflects an electoral map divided by just a few votes in 2000, which contributed to the campaign for Amendment 36 on the 2004 ballot. If passed, the amendment would have immediately changed Colorado's procedure for awarding electoral votes from "winner takes all" to proportional allocation utilized by only two states, Maine and Nebraska. Colorado's amendment reflected a desire by some to represent electoral divisions across the state. If Colorado had a proportional mechanism in 2000, Gore not Bush would have been elected president. As late as September 2004 a slim majority of potential voters supported Amendment 36, but upon defeating the amendment on Election Day, Colorado voters apparently viewed the state's nine electoral votes as a more tantalizing prospect to presidential candidates than fewer electoral votes divided into blue and red pieces.[37]

Colorado is the new western gateway to the Electoral College. Colorado shares two of the "four corners" border points with New Mexico and Arizona. Arizona's neighbor Nevada borders Oregon, which shares its northern boundary with Washington. These five states and Colorado were the most closely contested in the West region in 2000 and 2004, and should remain close in upcoming elections.[38] Colorado, like Arizona, has been experiencing a boom in recent years with residents streaming into the state for economic and lifestyle opportunities. And in the 2004 exit poll (see table 8.4), Colorado and Arizona had almost identically positive evaluations of the state economy, a boon for the incumbent president. This contrasts with the more negative evaluations of the California state economy leading to the voter recall of the California Democratic incumbent governor and translating into a big defeat for the president. However, Coloradoans weren't entirely optimistic about their financial and job situation perhaps competing within a saturated job market in what Kerry referred to as the "jobless economy." Negative Colorado evaluations of the job situation helped Kerry, but more Colorado voters still trusted Bush on the economy.

With the Colorado economy having little of the impact that hurt Bush's father when he lost the state, other policy concerns became of greater importance. In a state with the United States Air Force Academy and a substantial defense industry, a majority of Coloradoans believed the country was now safer from terrorism, and by a 22-point margin trusted Bush over Kerry to handle terrorism. In another boost for

Table 8.4. Voter Evaluation of Issues and Performance in Colorado, Arizona, and California

	CO Bush	CO Kerry	Bush + −	CO Total	AZ Total	CA Total
Economic evaluation						
State economy good	74	25	+49	53	55	37
State economy not so good	29	69	−40	35	28	45
State economy poor	16	80	−64	9	7	13
Financial situation better	90	8	+82	30	34	32
Financial situation same	71	28	+43	28	42	40
Financial situation worse	22	77	−55	41	23	26
Job situation in area better	90	8	+82	18	NA	NA
Job situation in area same	71	28	+43	38	NA	NA
Job situation in area worse	22	77	−55	44	NA	NA
Trust Bush to handle economy	92	7	+85	52	55	46
Trust Kerry to handle economy	12	88	−76	43	41	46
War on terrorism/war in Iraq						
U.S. safer from terrorism	84	15	+69	53	56	48
U.S. less safe from terrorism	15	84	−69	41	39	46
Trust Bush to handle terrorism	85	14	+71	60	61	53
Trust Kerry to handle terrorism	94	6	−88	37	38	42
Approve of Iraq war decision	90	9	+81	54	55	42
Disapprove of Iraq war decision	9	90	−81	44	42	50
Things going well for U.S. in Iraq	93	6	+87	46	50	37
Things going badly for U.S. in Iraq	17	82	−65	51	48	59
Most important issue						
Moral values	83	16	+67	24	22	17
Iraq	26	72	−46	23	21	23
Terrorism	89	11	+78	19	22	20
Economy/jobs	18	80	−62	18	13	16
Health care	22	77	−55	5	7	5
Taxes	74	23	+51	4	4	6
Education	23	77	−54	3	5	5
Most important quality						
Will bring change	4	95	−91	25	22	26
Strong leader	86	13	+73	22	22	19
Clear stand on issue	87	13	+74	13	13	13
Cares about people	34	66	−32	7	8	8
Religious faith	94	5	+89	7	9	6

Source: Column percentages from the Colorado, Arizona, and California exit polls of the National Election Pool, 2004. Italicized figures refer to categories in which George W. Bush held an advantage.

Bush, a majority of Colorado voters, like in Arizona, approved of the decision to go to war in Iraq, which differed from California, where a majority disapproved. A slight majority of Coloradoans did share Californian views that things were now going badly in Iraq, but it was not enough for Kerry to overcome Bush's relatively positive support on the economy, war on terrorism, and Iraq decision. Colorado, like Arizona, was fractured over Iraq, but in a way that slightly helped Bush. Whereas California voters viewed Iraq as the most important issue of the election, which helped Kerry to win the Golden State, voters in Colorado viewed moral values as a slightly more important concern, which helped Bush's candidacy there.

The values debate exploded across America in 1999 in the wake of the horrifying massacre of twelve high school students and a teacher by fellow students at Columbine High in suburban Littleton, Colorado.[39] While many Coloradoans and Americans questioned the state of our families and children, the role of religion, and the influence of entertainment media, the debate also raged over the responsibility of gun sellers, gun owners, and the NRA amid calls for more stringent background checks and gun control. A part of the cultural backlash involved Trey Parker and Matt Stone, Colorado natives and creators of *South Park*, the controversial yet popular cartoon series, particularly among young adults. Parker and Stone developed many of the outrageous plots in fictional *South Park* from divisions alive in America, on issues like gay rights, stem cell research, and the war in Iraq. Their all-puppet feature film *Team America: World Police*, released during the 2004 campaign, apparently offended, if not entertained, both supporters and opponents of the Bush administration's war on terrorism. Yet for voters in Colorado, Arizona, and California, the importance attached to the terrorism issue translated into nearly universal support for President Bush.

During his 2004 nomination acceptance speech, President Bush joked that his "swagger," often a subject of derision by detractors, is "what they call walking in Texas," much to the whooping delight of the cowboy-hat-waving Texas Republican delegates. But Bush was also addressing his supporters in states like Colorado and Arizona who valued what they perceived as strong leadership and a clear stand on issues. While more Coloradoans resembled Californians than Arizonans in a desire for a candidate who will bring change, benefiting Kerry, Colorado voters were slightly closer to Arizona voters in the value they associate with religious faith in a president, a connection that helped Bush.

Bush's western "swagger" likely appealed to many white male voters in Colorado and across the West buoyed by visible endorsements from the likes of Denver Bronco legend John Elway, who also played high school football in Granada Hills, California, and college ball at Stanford. In 2004, Bush carried the white male vote in both Colorado and California by double-digit margins, although Bush's 27-point margin in 2000 among white males in Colorado dropped by 8 points (see table 8.5). Bush's margin among white Colorado female voters was halved from 2000 to 2004, but he still managed to carry their vote by double-digits again. This was not the case in California, where the gender gap left Kerry with a 5-point advantage among white women and a huge advantage among nonwhite women and men in both states. The increasingly important Latino vote went by over 30 points for Kerry in both

Table 8.5. Social Forces and Presidential Choices in Colorado and California

	CO 00 Bush + −	CO 04 Bush + −	CO 04 Bush	CO 04 Kerry	CO 04 Total	CA 04 Total	CA 04 Bush + −
Race and gender							
White	+19	+15	57	42	86	65	+4
Black	−100	−74	13	87	4	6	−63
Latino	−33	−38	30	68	8	21	−31
White men	+27	+19	58	39	37	32	+14
White women	+22	+11	55	44	49	34	−5
Nonwhite men	NA	−45	27	72	7	17	−35
Nonwhite women	NA	−44	28	72	7	18	−38
Demographic profile							
< $50,000 income	0	+1	50	49	42	41	−18
> $50,000 income	+31	+7	53	46	58	59	−3
No college degree	+7	+17	58	41	49	55	−17
College graduate	+14	−2	48	50	51	45	−22
Married	NA	+17	58	41	62	NA	NA
Not married	NA	−13	43	56	38	NA	NA
18–29 years old	+20	−4	47	51	15	22	−19
60 years old+	0	+13	56	43	24	23	−6
First time voter	NA	−6	47	53	10	13	−29
Religion and religiosity							
White Evangelical	NA	+73	86	13	26	NA	NA
Not White Evangelical	NA	−73	41	58	74	NA	NA
White Cons. Protestant*	+80	+87	93	6	20	11	+87
Not White Cons. Protestant	−4	−14	42	56	80	89	−22
Catholic	+10	+6	52	46	19	28	−33
None	−26	−39	30	69	18	15	−33
Other	−34	−50	24	74	7	8	−48
Party identification							
Democrat	−52	−86	7	93	29	39	−75
Republican	+68	+87	93	6	38	33	+80
Independent	+6	−7	45	52	33	27	−23
Community size and region							
Urban (big & small cities)	NA	−7	46	53	47	47	−23
Suburban (surrounding area)	NA	+8	53	45	33	40	−5
Rural (small towns)	NA	+27	63	36	20	13	+19
Arapahoe/Jefferson & LA	NA	−1	49	50	27	23	−28
Denver/Boulder & Bay Area	NA	−23	38	61	24	18	−43
Western CO & Ctrl. Val. Cal	NA	+36	62	36	23	20	+24
Eastern CO & So. Cal	NA	+29	64	35	18	28	+7
Central CO & Coastal Cal	NA	+6	52	46	8	11	−22

Note: Column percentages from the Colorado and California exit polls of the 2004 National Election Pool, and the Colorado exit poll of the 2000 Voter News Service. *White religious right in the 2000 exit poll. Italicized figures refer to categories in which George W. Bush held an advantage.

California and Colorado in 2004. And in Colorado, a state in which 30 percent of exit poll respondents claimed to be of Latino descent in 2004, Bush lost by a slightly larger margin among this group than in 2000.

Bush stayed about even in his standing with lower-income groups in 2000 and 2004 in Colorado while losing the same group by 14 points to Kerry in California. However, Bush dropped substantially in his bid for reelection among higher-income voters in Colorado, winning the group but by a much narrower margin in 2004 while losing higher-income voters by double-digits to Kerry in California. This pattern was also apparent in Bush's improvement with Colorado voters with no college degree, but loss of college graduates in 2004 after winning this more educated group comfortably in 2000. Kerry, on the other hand, carried both groups by double-digits in California, but with college graduates by a higher margin.

The similarities developing between higher-income and college-educated voters in Colorado and California likely have to do with the similar preferences and communities in which these groups are increasingly concentrated. Higher-educated and diverse residents are moving into metropolitan areas and university communities, where the highest-paying jobs demand the highest levels of education. The less educated, less skilled, and consequently lower income voters remain in rural communities with some brushing up against the outer suburbs. Since California has more densely populated urban areas than Colorado, lower-income and less-educated groups are more concentrated among higher-educated professionals in sprawling metropolitan areas. Like voting coalitions of the past, these metropolitan groups tend to share common concerns related to the economic vitality of the broader area while demonstrating more socially tolerant viewpoints due to living with so many diverse residents.[40] In areas like Denver that increasingly resemble larger California metropolitan growth, there are similar voting patterns taking shape.

Among the younger age group most likely to move out of rural and suburban communities to opportunities in larger metropolitan areas, Bush's support dropped substantially from 2000 to 2004 in Colorado, and Bush lost California's eighteen- to twenty-nine-year-olds by 19 points. Nevertheless, Bush had solid Colorado support from two of the most dependable groups in sheer numbers of voting turnout, older and married voters. White evangelicals in Colorado, like every state across the country, were a key voting bloc for Bush in turnout and nearly universal support for the president, already energized by a cultural divide raging across Colorado since Columbine. White conservative Protestants, a fixture of western Republican support since Reagan, made up nearly two times the percentage of voters in Colorado as they did in California. The intersection of social conservatism and religion was more evident in Colorado than California, with Bush winning the Colorado Catholic vote by 19 points but losing California Catholics by 33 points.

The changing composition of California has led to a Democratic voter advantage over Republicans as shown by the 2004 exit poll, while Republicans still hold an advantage over Democrats in Colorado. However, the historical independent streak in Colorado is still evident in the one-third of Independent voters, outnumbering Colorado Democrats and California Republicans as a percentage of the respective voting population. Independents voted narrowly for Bush in 2000 but flipped by an almost identical percentage against the president in 2004, making independents a critical and uncertain voting bloc in the race to win Colorado.

Colorado's partisan landscape reflects Democratic and Republican strengths across red and blue America. Kerry carried urban-dominated counties with big and small cities (see figure 8.1). Bush handily won rural counties consisting of smaller towns. If Colorado were a predominantly rural state like its neighboring Mountain West and Plains states, the entire middle of the country would be colored red on Election Day for the foreseeable future. However, in 2004 urban voters outnumbered rural voters by more than 2-to-1 in Colorado. And in the Denver/Boulder area, Kerry won by margins (61–38 percent) more like his total in Los Angeles than elsewhere in Colorado.

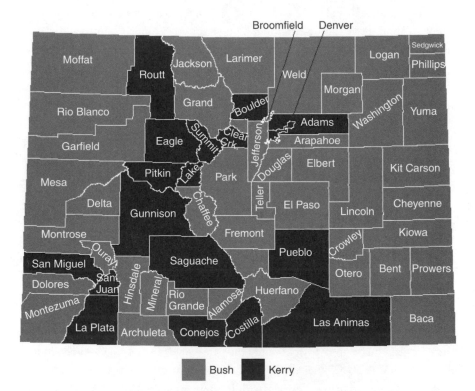

Figure 8.1. Colorado Electoral Map of the 2004 Election

Kerry, like Gore, carried the Denver/Boulder area by at least 20 points, and both Democratic candidates won Portland's Multnomah County and Seattle's King County by similar margins. More agrarian and rural counties of Colorado, like those in California, Washington, and Oregon, went heavily for Bush in both elections. In western and eastern Colorado, Bush won by 62–36 percent and 64–35 percent over Kerry, respectively.

Across central Colorado, there is tension and convergence in suburban communities like Littleton, Colorado. As the Denver/Boulder area stretches into previously remote rural communities mixed with a military and defense industry presence, it resembles a dynamic not unlike southern California. And central Colorado and southern California gave Bush an almost identical slight majority in 2004. Such geographic space is in play for Democrats and Republicans, in between urban and rural, astride inner and outer suburbs, where cultural diversity clashes with social conservatism, and economic individualists meet environmental activists.

GO WEST, YOUNG CONGRESS MAN *AND* WOMAN!

The call of the West led Americans across the country in search of fortune and opportunity, with Colorado a centerpiece of westward movement and the technological transformation necessary to traverse the rugged heights of Pike's Peak and exploit the resources of Durango. Colorado also witnessed firsthand the upheaval of westward expansion and the delicate balance necessary to preserve its communities. Yet Colorado had not been the focus of national electoral attention since the JFK-styled Colorado senator Gary Hart was a frontrunner for the 1988 Democratic presidential nomination. Before scandalous media coverage of an extramarital affair ruined Hart's presidential chances, many pundits felt that he was the best candidate to end the Republican reign, particularly across the West region.

In 2004 Colorado was again a focus of national attention with the senatorial victory of Democrat Ken Salazar over a Republican candidate whose name is synonymous with Colorado, Pete Coors of the "Rocky Mountain" Coors brewing company.[41] Ironically, the self-identified "traditional values" candidate Coors was derailed by moral outrage, not for what Coors personally did, but because of the sexually tinged television ads associated with Coors beer.[42] A relatively conservative Salazar benefited by gaining what would have been Republican rural and suburban votes while holding the metropolitan area and university communities trending Democratic.[43] Salazar also appealed to populist roots across the state, as he often dressed in cowboy attire on the campaign trail as a "man of the people," in contrast to the wealthy Coors.

The rugged individualistic spirit of the West that embodied much of Reagan's persona and policy so appealed to Colorado senator Ben "Nighthorse" Campbell that he switched from Democrat to Republican in 1994. Campbell, the only Native American U.S. senator, has been replaced by Salazar, the only Latino in the West delegation and one of two Hispanics in the entire Senate. Salazar's brother, John, also won a first term to the House in Colorado's Third District. Democratic Latino sibling success was reminiscent of the Sanchez sisters' 2002 House victories in southern California. Latinos have become not only a significant electoral presence but also serious candidates in western states. New Mexico's Latino Democratic governor Bill Richardson, first elected in 2002, is considered a 2008 presidential contender.

Loretta Sanchez's initial 1996 victory over long-time conservative Republican House incumbent Robert Dornan indicates how demographic changes have altered the electoral map, as well as the role of women in Democratic gains out West. Since 1992, California has had two Democratic female senators, Barbara Boxer and Dianne Feinstein. In 2000 Washington Democratic U.S. Senate candidate Maria Cantwell, by the narrowest of electoral margins, joined Senate incumbent Patty Murray. After a contentious recount in 2004, Washington added a first-term female Democratic

Table 8.6. Congressional Elections and Party Delegation in the West Region

State	House #GOP	House #DEM	Senate 2000	Senate 2002	Senate 2004	Senate #GOP	Senate #DEM
Bush States 2004	*+13*					*+10*	
Alaska	1			R*	R*	2	
Arizona	6	2	R*		R*	2	
Colorado	4	3		R+	*D+*	1	1
Idaho	2			R*	R uc	2	
Montana	1		R+	D*		1	1
Nevada	2	1	*R+*		D*	1	1
New Mexico	2	1	D*	R*		1	1
Utah	2	1	R*		R*	2	
Wyoming	1		R*	R*		2	
Red States Total	21	8				14	4
Kerry States 2004		*+21*					*+6*
California	20	33	D+		D+		2
Hawaii		2	D*		D*		2
Oregon	1	4		R+	D*	1	1
Washington	3	6	*D+*		D+		2
Blue States Total	24	45				1	7
West Total	45	53				15	11

Note: Table compiled by the author from data at congress.org. # = Congressional delegation following 2004 election. * ≥60% of vote, + ≤60% of vote, uc = uncontested incumbent. Italicized D or R includes party pickup of seat as a result of the 2000, 2002, or 2004 elections.

governor, Christine Gregoire. In a contest between two women for Hawaii governor, first-term Republican Linda Lingle was elected in 2002. Democrat Janet Napolitano also won her bid for Arizona governor in 2002, a state represented by two popular incumbent Republican U.S. senators (see table 8.6).

Arizona was a Democratic state before Goldwater narrowly won a Senate seat in 1952, but it has only voted for a Democratic president once since, in 1996. In his own bid for the 2000 Republican nomination, Arizona Senator John McCain lost in part because of the religious conservative wing that Goldwater had been openly critical of until his dying days.[44] McCain lost handily to George W. Bush when the primary shifted to southern states in which religious groups and social conservatives attacked McCain's social stances and worked to undermine his credibility. Still, McCain was a hot commodity for both parties in 2004, when rumors abounded that Kerry even courted McCain for the vice presidency. Bush instead benefited from McCain's appeal to Independents, socially moderate Republicans, old-style Reagan Democrats, and West voters. John McCain won his own reelection to the Senate with 76 percent of the vote and is considered a potential presidential candidate for 2008, if only he can survive the Republican primary this time.

On the other hand, it may take a Republican candidate like McCain to regain the Pacific Coast, with Reagan in 1984 the last Republican to do so. But the man most closely following Reagan's career path, a former actor occupying California's governor's mansion, has a slight constitutional obstacle. Thus, there is a movement afoot to amend the U.S. Constitution for the Austrian-born former Mr. Olympus and star of *Conan the Barbarian* to duel with the Electoral College beast. Stanford political scientist Morris Fiorina contends, "Arnold Schwarzenegger is the kind of socially moderate Republican who can win elections in California," in which "the unusual nature of the recall election saved the Republican Party from itself."[45] Whether or not the "Governator" will be given an opportunity to terminate the Democratic hold on California and the Pacific Coast is uncertain. Even with a constitutional amendment in place, the action star's main obstacle would be clearing the Republican primary in which his support of stem cell research and a woman's right to choose abortion could stop him in a way that a movie villain never could.

Democrats may consider an amendment to the Constitutional requirement of two U.S. senators per state, a Republican advantage based on sparsely populated but numerous Mountain West and Central Plains states. Nevertheless, Democrats are winning House seats and even statewide positions in what have been solid Republican states. Colorado set the tone for Democrats with the Salazars' congressional success,[46] but also by reversing state House and Senate majorities to take Democratic control of both chambers for the first time in forty-four years.[47] Moreover, in a state that went by 21 points for President Bush in 2004, Democrat

Brian Schweitzer narrowly won a first term as Montana governor while Democrats won control of most statewide offices, including in the state legislature.[48] Even in rock-solid Republican states like Wyoming, a Democrat won the race for governor in 2002, and in Utah, a Democrat has been reelected three times to the Second District representing the Salt Lake City area including the University of Utah.

Democrats are winning such communities across western states, forging majorities in Oregon and Washington, challenging in Arizona and Colorado, and even gaining ground in Republican strongholds like Montana. Republicans, on the other hand, are replacing a declining rural population by winning in the outer suburbs surrounding many of the metropolitan areas that are Democratic bases. At the same time, the electoral vote count of western states, namely California, Washington, Arizona, Nevada, and Colorado should continue to rise based on recent trends, making winning the West critical to both the presidency and Congress.

LOOKING FOR THE ELECTORAL PROMISED LAND

Midway through the twentieth century, Marjorie Randon Hershey sums up how "Republican strength could be seen in congressional delegations all across the northern tier of the United States. The Pacific Coast, the Plains states, the rest of the Midwest, and the Northeast were all Republican dominated. The South was the most dependably Democratic region of the country; to be openly Republican was a form of deviance."[49] By the end of a tumultuous century, Hershey explains, "there had been an almost complete reversal of regional party strength. The Northeast, the Upper Midwest, and most of the Pacific Coast were now dependably Democratic. . . . The backbone of the Republican Party has become the South, as well as the states of the mountain West and much of the Plains. It has been an issue-driven switch, as cultural issues have come to rival the economy in public concern, the parties' coalitions have changed in significant ways."[50]

Republican Party leadership now resides largely in the rapidly growing southern Sun Belt states, with U.S. Senate majority leader Bill Frist of Tennessee considering a bid for the 2008 presidential nomination. President George W. Bush and House majority leader Tom DeLay are both from Texas, the centerpiece of a Republican electoral grip across the South, Central Plains, and Mountain West. Democrats have concentrated their strength in the Northeast and are battling Republicans to hold the upper Midwest. But the future electoral struggle has turned westward.

After the 2004 defeat of former Democratic Senate leader Tom Daschle in South Dakota, there is a Democratic concern of getting "Daschled" in similar states that almost uniformly vote Republican for president. The Democratic Senate leadership is now represented by the relatively conservative Harry Reid, reelected in 2004 with a solid margin in a rapidly changing Nevada, reflecting Republican and Democratic opportunities emerging out West. The soft-spoken yet determined personality of the teetotaller Reid will seek to steady his party after consecutive narrow defeats, beginning with a West region in electoral transformation. At the same time, Democratic House leadership reflects the party's recognition of its regional strengths across a geographic cultural divide. When Missouri representative Dick Gephardt stepped down from his House leadership position before retiring in 2004, he was replaced with California representative Nancy Pelosi of San Francisco, the highest position ever for a congresswoman.

Social forces continue to transform the parties, electoral success, and opportunities across a red and blue spectrum of ongoing and evolving debates facing America. Gender, racial, and religious differences are only a few of the distinctions that will continue to reshape the regional dimensions of the electoral map as emerging events and groups transform the nation.[51] After all, the Jacksonian Democratic Party was born with the emerging electoral importance of rural and agrarian states as America began its expansion westward, and the rise of the Republican Party was met with civil war as the nation divided firmly and violently for 100 years into a Republican North and a Democratic South. The Wild West was just that for much of its early electoral history, shifting support across both parties as well as to third-party reform candidacies, until the region fell under the electoral force of the New Deal coalition. However, a tradition of "rugged individualism" and rejection of distant federal directives led the West into the Republican fold with the Midwest and Northeast, leaving the South as the only Democratic bastion until civil rights flipped the regional divide upside down. Led by Nixon and Reagan, the West turned Republican along with the South, but a conservative push that secured the central and mountain region through the reelection of George W. Bush also moved the increasingly metropolitan Pacific coastal states to the Democrats, from Clinton to Kerry.

The ongoing competition to win the Electoral College and control of the U.S. Congress is largely a story of issue, social, and regional transformation. The most competitive states now include those in the rapidly expanding West, an industrial Midwest in the midst of tumultuous change, and increasingly populated Sun Belt states in the southern reaches of the United States. The current regional electoral focus is likely to change as societal trends and patterns eventually shift across America, but new competitive states and, consequently, regions will reemerge as geographic centers of the electoral map.

NOTES

1. V. O. Key, Jr., "A Theory of Critical Elections," in *Electoral Change and Stability in American Political History*, edited by Jerome Chubb and Howard Allen (New York: Free Press, 1971), 43.
2. See Walter Dean Burnham, *Critical Elections and the Mainsprings of American Politics* (New York: Norton, 1970).
3. Kristi Anderson, *The Creation of a Democratic Majority, 1928–1936* (Chicago: University of Chicago Press, 1979).
4. Rick Perlstein, *Before the Storm: Barry Goldwater and the Unmaking of the American Consensus* (New York: Hill and Wang, 2001).
5. Kevin Phillips, *The Emerging Republican Majority* (Garden City, NY: Anchor Books, 1970).
6. Everett Carll Ladd, Jr. with Charles D. Hadley, *Transformations of the American Party System: Party Coalitions from the New Deal to the 1970s* (New York: Norton, 1975).
7. Ruy Texeira and Joel Rogers, *America's Forgotten Majority: Why the White Working Class Matters* (New York: Basic Books, 2000).
8. John Petrocik, *Party Coalitions: Realignment and the Decline of the New Deal Party System* (Chicago: University of Chicago Press, 1981).
9. Paul Light and Celinda Lake, "The Election: Candidates, Strategies, and Decisions," in *The Elections of 1984*, edited by Michael Nelson (Washington, DC: CQ Press, 1985), 83–110.
10. See Robert Dallek, *Ronald Reagan: The Politics of Symbolism* (Cambridge, MA: Harvard University Press, 1999).
11. Stanley Greenberg, *Middle Class Dreams: The Politics and Power of the New American Majority* (New Haven, CT: Yale University Press, 1995).
12. See Mark Rozell and Clyde Wilcox, *God at the Grass Roots* (Lanham, MD: Rowman & Littlefield, 1995).
13. Francis E. Rourke and John T. Tierney, "The Setting: Changing Patterns of Presidential Politics, 1960 and 1988," in *Elections of 1988*, edited by Michael Nelson (Washington, DC: CQ Press, 1989), 1–24.
14. See Gerald Pomper, ed., *The Election of 1992* (New York: Chatham House, 1993).
15. See Gerald Pomper, "The Presidential Election," in *The Election of 1996*, edited by Gerald Pomper (New York: Chatham House, 1997), 173–204.
16. Mary Barabak, "Women May Call Election: The Gender Gap May be Reemerging, With More Female Voters Leaning Toward Kerry, Bush Has the Advantage with Men," *Los Angeles Times*, October 23, 2004, A20.
17. Stanley Greenberg, *The Two Americas: Our Current Political Deadlock and How to Break It* (New York: St. Martin's Press, 2004), 127.
18. Ibid., 110.
19. Rudolfo de la Garza and Louis DeSipio, eds., *Awash in the Mainstream: Latino Politics in the 1996 Election* (Boulder, CO: Westview Press, 1999).
20. "Every Four Years, the Anglos Return: Latinos and the Election," *The Economist*, July 3, 2004.
21. Ronald Brownstein and Kathleen Hennessey, "The Race for the White House: Latino Vote Still Lags Its Potential," *Los Angeles Times*, September 25, 2004, A1.
22. Kirk Johnson, "Hispanic Voters Declared Their Independence," *New York Times*, November 8, 2004, A1.

23. Richard Alonso-Zaldivar, "Election 2004: Bush Snags Much More of the Latino Vote, Exit Polls Show," *Los Angeles Times*, November 4, 2004, A30.

24. Quoted in Alonso-Zalvidar, A30.

25. Paul R. Abramson, John H. Aldrich, and David W. Rohde, *Change and Continuity in the 2000 and 2002 Elections* (Washington, DC: CQ Press, 2003), 104.

26. Greenberg, *The Two Americas*, 154–159.

27. John B. Judis and Ruy Teixeira, *The Emerging Democratic Majority* (New York: Scribner, 2002), 85.

28. Karl A. Lamb and Paul A. Smith, *Campaign Decision-Making: The Presidential Election of 1964* (Belmont, CA: Wadsworth, 1968), 59.

29. John C. Green, Mark J. Rozell, and Clyde Wilcox, eds., *Prayers in the Precincts: The Christian Right in the 1998 Elections* (Washington, DC: Georgetown University Press, 2000).

30. Dennis Farney, "Religious Right," *Wall Street Journal*, April 10, 1995.

31. Carla Marinucci, "Watching the West: Polls Show Nevada, Colorado, Arizona, New Mexico as Toss-Ups," *San Francisco Chronicle*, October 18, 2004, A1.

32. R. Drummond Ayres, "The Expanding Hispanic Vote Shakes Republican Strongholds," *New York Times*, November 10, 1996, A1.

33. John Kenneth White, *The Values Divide: American Politics and Culture in Transition* (New York: Chatham House Publishers, 2003), 167.

34. David Brooks, *Bobos in Paradise: The New Upper Class and How They Got There* (New York: Simon and Schuster, 2000), 43.

35. Dana Milbank, "Bush, Cheney Tout Job Growth in Ohio, Nevada," *Washington Post*, June 21, 2004, A5.

36. See Thomas Frank, *What's the Matter with Kansas? How Conservatives Won the Heart of America* (New York: Metropolitan Books, 2004), 16.

37. Kirk Johnson, "Colorado: As the Race Tightens, Enthusiasm for a Ballot Proposal Wanes," *New York Times*, October 28, 2004, A14.

38. Timothy Egan, "An Evolving Identity Helps to Leave Five States in Search of a President," *New York Times*, October 30, 2004, A15.

39. White, 105.

40. See Judis and Texeira, 81.

41. Kirk Johnson, "Politics Are Both Local and National in Colorado Race," *New York Times*, October 15, 2004, A10.

42. "Beer Today, Gone Tomorrow?" *The Economist*, August 13, 2004, 28.

43. Susan Greene, "Election Reshaped Colorado Politics," *Denver Post*, November 7, 2004, A1.

44. Barry Goldwater with Jack Casserly, *Goldwater* (New York: Doubleday, 1988).

45. Morris Fiorina, *Culture War? The Myth of a Polarized America* (New York: Pearson, 2005), 106.

46. T. R. Reid, "Democrats May Use Results in Colorado as Political Primer," *Washington Post*, November 21, 2004, A18.

47. John Nichols, "Democrats Score in the Rockies," *The Nation*, December 6, 2004.

48. Ibid.

49. Marjorie Randon Hershey, "The Congressional Elections," in Pomper, ed., 228–229.

50. Ibid.

51. See, for example, Arian Campo-Flores, "The Swing Vote: Coming of Age," *Newsweek*, November 1, 2004, 24.

INDEX